American Pragmatism and Organization

For Csabi, Michael and Amily for being here and to my mother,
Rodica, for who I am.
Mihaela

For Peter, Susan and Lady Buckley.
Nick

American Pragmatism and Organization

Issues and Controversies

Edited by

MIHAELA KELEMEN
Keele University, UK

and

NICK RUMENS
University of Bristol, UK

LONDON AND NEW YORK

First published 2013 by Gower Publishing

2 Park Square, Milton Park, Abingdon, Oxon OX14 4RN
711 Third Avenue, New York, NY 10017, USA

Routledge is an imprint of the Taylor & Francis Group, an informa business

First issued in paperback 2016

Gower Applied Business Research
Our programme provides leaders, practitioners, scholars and researchers with thought
provoking, cutting edge books that combine conceptual insights, interdisciplinary rigour and
practical relevance in key areas of business and management.

British Library Cataloguing in Publication Data
A catalogue record for this book is available from the British Library.

The Library of Congress has cataloged the printed edition as follows:
American pragmatism and organization studies : issues and controversies / [edited] by
Mihaela Kelemen and Nick Rumens.
    pages cm
Includes bibliographical references and index.
ISBN 978-1-4094-2786-5 (hbk) 1. Organizational sociology. 2. Pragmatism.
3. Management--Research--United States. I. Rumens, Nick. II. Kelemen, Mihaela, 1968-
HM786.A49 2013
302.3'5--dc23

2012047427

ISBN 978-1-4094-2786-5 (hbk)
ISBN 978-1-138-25007-9 (pbk)

Contents

PART 1   THEORY AND CONTEXT

PART 2   AMERICAN PRAGMATISM APPLIED

List of Figures and Tables

Figures

Tables

About the Editors

Mihaela Kelemen is Professor of Management at Keele Management School, Keele University, UK. She holds a DPhil in Management Studies from Oxford University and a PhD in Applied Economics from the Academy of Economic Studies, Bucharest. Her current research focuses on community leadership, volunteering and theatre experiments in management. This research is underpinned by an American pragmatist paradigm. She has published articles in journals such as *Journal of Management Studies*, *Human Relations* and *Organization* as well as five books.

Email: m.l.kelemen@keele.ac.uk

Nick Rumens is Reader in Management and Organisation at the University of Bristol, UK. After completing his PhD at Keele University on the role and meaning of friendship in the work lives of gay men in the UK, he has written widely on this subject in journals such as *Human Relations*, *Gender, Work & Organization* and *The Sociological Review* and, at length, in a research monograph titled *Queer Company* (Ashgate 2011). His research interests also extend to American Pragmatism, especially its intersections with feminism and its influence on shaping research methodologies. Research in this area, co-authored with Mihaela Kelemen, has been published in the journal *Contemporary Pragmatism* and in a research methods text titled *An Introduction to Critical Management Research* (Sage 2008).

Email: nicholas.rumens@bristol.ac.uk

About the Contributors

Diane-Laure Arjaliès is Assistant Professor at the Accounting and Control Department of HEC Paris, France. She received her PhD in Management from ESSEC Business School and the University Paris West Nanterre la Défense. She teaches Management Accounting, Business Ethics and Responsible Investing on postgraduate, MBA and PhD programs. Before joining the HEC Paris faculty, she was an SRI analyst in a French asset management company and a research fellow at Ecole Polytechnique in France and Manchester Business School in the UK.

Patrick Baert is Reader in Social Theory at the University of Cambridge, UK, and Fellow and Director of Studies at Selwyn College, Cambridge. He studied at the Universities of Brussels and Oxford where he completed the DPhil under supervision of Rom Harré. He has taught at Cambridge for two decades and has held visiting posts in Aix-en-Provence, Amiens, Berlin, Cape Town, Concepcion, London, Paris, Providence (RI, US), Rome and Vancouver. Amongst his publications are *Philosophy of the Social Sciences: Towards Pragmatism* (2005) and (with Filipe Carreira da Silva) *Social Theory in the Twentieth Century and Beyond* (2010) and the co-edited collections *Conflict, Citizenship and Civil Society* (2010) and *The Politics of Knowledge* (2012). More recently, he has written on the sociology and history of intellectuals in *Theory and Society*, the *European Journal of Social Theory*, the *Journal of Classical Sociology* and the *Journal for the Theory of Social Behaviour*.

John R. Bartle is Acting Dean of the College of Public Affairs and Community Service and the David Scott Diamond Alumni Professor of Public Affairs at the University of Nebraska at Omaha, US. He is a Fellow of the National Academy of Public Administration. He is the co-author of *Sustainable Development for Public Administration*, editor of *Evolving Theories of Public Budgeting*, and is currently co-editing *Management Policies in Local Government Finance*. He previously was a Visiting Professor, Center for Public Administration, Sun Yat-Sen University, Guangzhou, China. His teaching and research interests are in the areas of public financial management, public budgeting and sustainable development. He holds a BA (honours) from Swarthmore College, an MPA from The University of Texas and a PhD in public policy and management from Ohio State University. He worked in city and state government in Minnesota, and for state and national non-profit research organizations on tax policy issues.

Emma Bell is Professor of Management and Organisation Studies at Keele University, UK. She is interested in the critical study of management and organizational behavior in a range of contexts, including her own. Her research is informed by a commitment to understanding cultures and the role of belief systems in management and organization. She also teaches and writes about methods of management research. Her research has been published in journals such as *Organization* and *Human Relations*, and she is the author of two books: *Business Research Methods* (2011), with Alan Bryman; and *Reading Management and Organisation in Film* (2008).

Ulrik Brandi is Associate Professor in Organisational Learning at Aarhus University's Department of Education in Denmark. His PhD in organizational learning and change is from Learning Lab Denmark, Aarhus University. Ulrik Brandi teaches workplace and organizational learning, research methodologies and organizational change on graduate programs. Ulrik's research interests include workplace and organizational learning and change, knowledge sharing, and mixed research methodologies. He examines how organizations and their members learn new practices and share knowledge, and studies factors that facilitate or impede these learning processes. His research is founded in both public and private organizations. His research is theoretically inspired by concepts originating in classical pragmatism, primarily by John Dewey and neo-pragmatists such as Richard Rorty and Hilary Putnam. Ulrik is currently part of the research program 'Organization and Learning' at Aarhus University's Department of Education.

Bente Elkjaer holds a Chair in Organisational and Workplace Learning at Aarhus University's Department of Education in Denmark. Bente Elkjaer has within her research taken a special interest in developing a theoretical perspective on organizational learning inspired by American pragmatism (particularly the works by John Dewey), which she has called the 'Third Way'. This is an attempt to work with organizational learning as entangled processes of learning and organizing as well as processes of emotions and cognition in their mutual constituencies. Bente Elkjaer is currently working on a project on the problems of knowledge sharing when work is dispersed and knowledge is personal. She has published her work both within the educational research community in, for example, *International Journal of Lifelong Education* and in organization and management studies in journals such as *Human Resource Development International* and *Management Learning*. She is Emeritus Editor of *Management Learning* and former Head of a doctoral program on organizational learning as well as former Head of Department.

Ian Evans is a doctoral student in the Department of American and Canadian Studies at the University of Nottingham, UK. He has taught twentieth-century US intellectual and cultural history, including a healthy dose of pragmatism, at Nottingham and African American history at the University of Birmingham. His doctoral research examines the ways canons are formed within African American literary culture, paying particular attention to the ways high-profile figures such as Harvard's Henry Louis Gates, Jr. construct authoritative accounts of cultural value in their work, and what this means for African American writers who operate at the margins of the critical discourses they favor. He is an outsider to critical management studies (CMS) scholarship, but strongly believes that the theoretical and political questions raised by CMS scholars also have implications for the humanities.

Tore Hafting graduated in Sociology at the University of Trondheim, Norway. Tore is currently working as Associate Professor at the Department of Business Economics and Management, Hedmark University College. He is currently teaching theories of organization and management in the study of crisis management. Research interests include collaborative action research in the private and public sector. Tore has conducted and published research on the national research program Value Creation 2010 on innovation in business organizations. More recently, an evaluation was conducted on leadership training of unit managers in the municipal sector. Recent publications include a co-author piece, in Norwegian, on the identity of unit managers in municipalities with performance-based principles of organization.

Emily Kay Hanks is Assistant Professor at Texas State University, US. She began her professional journey as an actress, receiving her BFA in Fine Arts from The University of Texas at Austin. It was while working at the Texas Capitol, however, that she discovered politics was the greatest drama of all. She was hooked, not only because of the great performances but also because of what this passion-play meant to everyday Texans. Emily completed her master's degree at Texas State University and her PhD at The University of Texas at Austin.

Nathan Harter is Professor of Leadership Studies at Christopher Newport University in Newport News, Virginia, US, after having taught organizational leadership for the School of Technology at Purdue University in the state of Indiana. During that time, he served as chair of the scholarship section for the International Leadership Association (ILA) and also published *Clearings in the Forest: On the Study of Leadership* (2006) with the Purdue University Press. Prior to teaching, he practiced law for several years after having earned his AB from Butler University in Philosophy and Political Science and his JD from the Indiana University School of Law.

Peter M. Jackson is Director of Research and Enterprise for the College of Social Science at the University of Leicester and is Professor of Economics and Strategy in the School of Management. He was Dean of the Faculty of Social Science (2002/09) and Director of the University of Leicester's School of Management (1989/2003). Prior to that, he was Head of the Economics Department. He is a public sector economist with an interest in public sector management and has made contributions to these areas through over 200 publications including books, chapters and journal articles. In addition, he has served as an adviser to a number of international agencies including the OECD, EU and World Bank and was a specialist adviser to the Finance Committee of the Scottish Parliament. He is an Academician of the Academy of the Social Sciences and a member of the Chartered Institute of Public Finance and Accountancy.

David Jacobs is Associate Professor of Labor and Sustainability at the Graves School of Business at Morgan State University in Baltimore, Maryland, US. He has sought to bring a radical pragmatism based on an understanding of the capacity of ordinary people to the study of organizational theory. Jacobs has explored the relationship of pragmatism to business ethics, related questions of trade union strategy, pragmatism and politics, and pragmatist democracy. His teaching is informed by the concept of social invention, the application of an unconstrained imagination to the design of social institutions with positive consequences for society and the individual. Jacobs is a past Chair of the Critical Management Studies Division of the Academy of Management and an Editorial Board member for several journals.

Erik Lindhult is Senior Lecturer in Innovation Management and Entrepreneurship at Mälardalen University, Sweden. He received his doctoral degree in Industrial management, Royal Institute of Technology in Stockholm, in the area of Scandinavian dialog and democratic approaches to innovation and inquiry. His main area of research is participatory, collaborative and democratic innovation and change management as well as entrepreneurship for a sustainable development of society. His research interests also involve collaborative research methodology, including action research and interactive research where researchers and practitioners co-produce knowledge and change. He has been involved in a wide range of collaborative R&D projects in the private, public and cooperative sectors, in areas such as organizational development, service innovation, societal entrepreneurship and school development. Recent publications focus on subjects such as pragmatic versus critical action research, development partnerships and service innovation.

Philippe Lorino is Professor of Management Control and Organisation at ESSEC Business School and an adviser to the French Nuclear Safety Authority. He has held operational roles, first in the French government administration, then as a director in the finance department of an international computer company. Since gaining his PhD in Management he has developed a process view of organizing that draws from pragmatist philosophy and semiotics (Peirce, Dewey), activity theory (Vygotsky) and dialogism theory (Bakhtin), to focus on the ongoing entanglement of collective activities and dialogical inquiries, mediated by systems of signs such as languages, technical tools and management systems.

Patricia M. Shields is Professor of Political Science and Director of the Master of Public Administration program at Texas State University, US. She received her master's in Economics and PhD in Public Administration from Ohio State University. Her research interests include applying pragmatism to all facets of public administration including theory, research methods, and finance. She has taught public finance and has written extensively on public finance issues such as fiscal stress, user fees, and contracting. Her research interests also extend to include many aspects of civil military relation including the equity and effectiveness of recruitment systems, women in the military and women's contribution to the American Civil War. She has been the editor of the journal *Armed Forces & Society* since 2001. She is currently working on two research methods books as well as applying the ideas of John Dewey and Jane Addams to peacekeeping.

Barbara Simpson is Professor of Leadership and Organisational Dynamics at Strathclyde Business School in Glasgow. Her thinking about practice is driven by a desire to better understand what it is that managers actually do in their day-to-day activities. Theoretically, she is deeply informed by the American pragmatists who emphasise the intertwining of agency and temporality in practice. Her work is published in *Organization Studies*, *Organization*, *Journal of Management Inquiry*, *R&D Management*, and *Long Range Planning*. She is also an Associate Editor for *Qualitative Research in Organizations and Management*.

Rosa Slegers is an Assistant Professor of Philosophy at Babson College where she teaches courses in Ethics, Philosophy & Literature, and Existentialism. She received her

PhD in Philosophy from Fordham University and is currently completing an MBA degree at Babson College. Slegers' current research interests include philosophy of management, business ethics, ethics and the emotions, and Adam Smith.

Scott Taylor is Reader in Leadership & Organization Studies at Birmingham Business School, University of Birmingham, UK. He has researched and taught at Manchester Metropolitan, Open, Birmingham, Essex and Exeter universities. His research is an attempt to contribute to representing the individual and collective human experience of work and workplaces, in all their variety and richness, through interpretive analysis of qualitative data. Currently, he is working mostly on the interplay of religious and spiritual beliefs with organization, management and leadership. He has also published research that analyzes people management in smaller organizations, training and development initiatives, and the incorporation of employees into organizational branding.

Tony Watson is Emeritus Professor of Sociology, Work and Organisation at the Nottingham University Business School, UK. Recent and continuing work focuses on the sociology of the pub, 'entrepreneurial action' in a variety of settings and on 'pragmatic realism' in ethnographic and organizational studies. He is the author of *In Search of Management* (revised edition 2001) and his *Sociology, Work and Organisation* (6th edition) was published in 2012.

Travis A. Whetsell is currently the managing editor of the journal *Armed Forces & Society*. He has an MPA degree from Texas State University, US, and will be attending the John Glenn School of Public Affairs at The Ohio State University for doctoral study in the fall semester of 2012. He has recently published a journal article in *The American Review of Public Administration* titled 'Theory-Pluralism in Public Administration: Epistemology, Legitimacy, and Method'.

Acknowledgments

We are enormously grateful to our contributors, since it was their willingness to write about American pragmatism that helped to bring this edited volume to fruition. Copious thanks also to Martin West and his colleagues at Gower for supporting the publication of this book.

Mihaela

I have had a lovely time editing this book with Nick. Nick has given me incredible moral support throughout the darkest time of my life: that of losing my mother. Without his friendship and constant support, I would have not found the strength to go ahead with this worthwhile project. I'd like to also thank Dr Andrew Christmas for his contribution to summarizing the key works of the classics and for constantly asking the 'so what?' question, vis-à-vis many of the theoretical issues explored in the book (he would, being such an accomplished businessman). Many people attending the Fourth Nordic Pragmatism conference in Copenhagen were great in helping me to understand what pragmatism is all about, in particular David Pfeifer and Bjorn Ramberg. Many friends deserve warm thanks for their support and interest in my American pragmatist crusade, in particular Tuomo Peltonen, Paul Willis, Anita Mangan, Sue Moffat and Teresa Oultram. Last but not least, my husband, Csabi, and my two lovely kids, Michael and Amily, for making life so rich and worthwhile.

Nick

My heartfelt thanks and love to members of my immediate family and very dear friends who have supported me over the years. Those who deserve mention here include Peter, Susan, Gerald, Lady Buckley and Danny Macdonald.

PART 1

Theory and Context

1

American Pragmatism and Organization Studies: Concepts, Themes and Possibilities

NICK RUMENS AND MIHAELA KELEMEN

Introducing American Pragmatism

On 26 August 1898, in a speech to the Philosophical Union of the University of California, in Berkeley, US, an individual by the name of William James used the word 'pragmatism' to designate a philosophical position. This moment has come to be acknowledged as a significant milestone in the commitment toward the development of American pragmatism as a philosophical movement in the US, which emerged in the 1870s and flourished until the end of World War II. Summarizing the main thrust and merits of American pragmatist philosophies is difficult, not least because they are not a unified body of ideas, perspectives and theories. Still, put simply, American pragmatism may be described as a practical and anti-foundationalist philosophy that focuses on the future, concerned with improving the conditions that enable individuals to thrive in their everyday lives. It collapses not only the artificial division between theory and practice, emphasizing the link between theory and praxis, but also other restrictive dualisms (e.g. body-mind, subject-object), by a process of inquiry that understands knowledge as social phenomena and the value of theory by the consequences and actions it produces. That being said, we do not wish to provide essentialist definitions, acknowledging that other commentators may place emphasis on different qualities and characteristics associated with American pragmatism.

During its heyday, roughly from the 1890s to 1930s, American pragmatism established itself on the philosophical landscape in the US, influencing theory and practice within and across the realms of politics, psychology, education and religion, to name just a few. Yet in the years after World War II, the credibility American pragmatism had previously enjoyed began to wane. As analytical philosophies such as logical positivism gained the ascendancy, American pragmatist struggled to respond to the criticism leveled at it by its adversaries. Following the death of John Dewey in 1952, someone who is often credited with advancing the pragmatic approach within academic circles well into the early decades of the twentieth century, American pragmatism receded into the background. It is important to note that American pragmatism had been in trouble for some years prior to Dewey's death. Explanations for its alleged demise are varied and disputed, although we might point to the frequent charges levied by its critics of naiveté, idealism and romanticism. For example, while Dewey and his fellow pragmatists believed in the ability of the American 'civilization ... (to) ... establish and nourish institutions that will promote the liberation of the talents and potentialilites of all citizens' (Dewey 1928: 134), his opponents viewed this as an unattainable dream and criticised the simplicity of the proposed pragmatist methods by which such goal could be reached. This gave ammunition to critics who attacked American pragmatism for being vague, lacking clarity and robust philosophical foundations, for being deficient of grand themes and ideals as present in metaphysical philosophies. But the story does not end here.

American pragmatism did not disappear altogether, but it did suffer from marginalization for a number of years. It is in 1979 that we witness a marked reversal of pragmatism's fortune instigated, in part, by the publication of Richard Rorty's *Philosophy and the Mirror of Nature*. This was the beginning of a resurrection in pragmatist philosophies and, arguably, heralded the emergence of neo-pragmatism: informed by but distinct from classical American pragmatism. Philosophers such as Richard Rorty and Hilary Putnam helped to reinvent American pragmatism, restoring something of its former intellectual reputation and furnishing it with a new sense of direction. Since then American pragmatism has entered what we might dub a 'third phase', with new scholars reworking its concepts and ideals to maintain its contemporary vitality and relevance, of which the contributors to this edited volume are striking examples.

While it is relatively easy to chart the vicissitudes of American pragmatism, it is much harder to pinpoint exactly what it is. As with many philosophies, American pragmatism encompasses diverse positions, often competing and contradictory, and a range of founding figures who steered pragmatism in different directions. A key observation here is that American pragmatism does not cohere around a neat and tidy set of principles or distinctive doctrine. This is explained, in part, by the lack of general consensus among early pragmatists about what, exactly, pragmatism is – more on this later. As Peter Jackson rightly points out in this volume (Chapter 3), it is a 'tall order' to define American pragmatism, but it is a challenge that we confront over the pages of this introductory chapter.

One important reason for getting to grips with American pragmatism is the overarching argument, presented and developed across the chapters of this edited collection, that American pragmatism has much to offer organization studies. More specifically, we argue that, from one perspective, American pragmatism has already enriched organization studies but its influence and popularity is not widespread, seldom acknowledged and sometimes misunderstood. Put differently, the potential American pragmatism holds for informing how scholars and practitioners understand, analyze and 'improve' forms of organization and management to the benefit of human experience is, with some notable exceptions (Elkjaer and Simpson 2011; Watson 2010; Fontrodona 2002), largely unrealised. Indeed, from the perspectives of those who have contributed to this book, even those individuals who express scepticism, American pragmatism offers attractive modes of thought, positions and concepts that are not easily dismissed. This appeal is strong in a context of ongoing concerns about the role and 'value' of theory in 'improving' management, how some modes of organizing have detrimental effects for those who are 'managed' and the apparent lack of imagination to envision new, alternative ways of organizing and improving the human experience in organization (Delbridge and Keenoy 2010; Hambrick 2007; Markoczy and Deeds 2009; Parker 2002).

Over the course of this chapter, we provide background information about some of American pragmatism's key figures, major concepts and themes that, together, have shaped the content of the chapters in this edited collection. Collectively, these chapters aim to bring to the fore the relevance of American pragmatism for understanding organizational issues that relate to public administration, economics, finance, organizational learning, spirituality and emotion in the workplace. All contributions exhibit a passion for American pragmatism and evaluate whether American pragmatism can provide a different and constructive lens through which we may examine and alter contemporary organizational life.

Key Figures

In this section we provide background information about some of the key figures associated with American pragmatism. This is necessarily brief, not due just to the limits of space, but also because of the sheer number of people who, over the years, have shaped the course of American pragmatist philosophies. These include the early pragmatists such as Charles Sanders Peirce, William James, John Dewey, Jane Addams and George Herbert Mead, and those later associated with its resurrection such as W.V. Quine, Hilary Putnam and Richard Rorty. It is crucial to note this is by no means an exhaustive list, with much scholarly discussion having taken place about who is and who is not a 'pragmatist'. Not all this debate about who/does not qualify as a 'pragmatist' has been productive, revealing more about the fractured nature of pragmatism as a movement and the diverse array of people associated with it. For the purpose of this introductory chapter and the book more broadly, we focus on three major figures connected with what some call 'classical American pragmatism': Charles Sanders Peirce, William James and John Dewey; all of whom figure centrally in many writings on American pragmatism. However, we may also add Josiah Royce and George Herbert Mead to the canon of 'classical American pragmatists', although restrictions of space do not allow us to discuss the contributions of these figures further.

CHARLES SANDERS PEIRCE (1839–1914)

Charles Sanders Peirce is often regarded as the founding figure in pragmatism, coining its name as well as some of its ideals. Born in Cambridge, Massachusetts, US, in 1839, Peirce's fascination with logic and reasoning started at an early age. He graduated from Harvard University in 1859 and in 1863 he was awarded Harvard's first-ever summa cum laude chemistry degree. It was at Harvard where he met and began his lifelong friendship with William James. Peirce worked intermittently between 1859 and 1891 for the US Coast Survey. From 1879 to 1884 he was employed by Johns Hopkins University as a lecturer in logic (among his students was John Dewey). This was the only academic appointment that Peirce ever held. In 1887, Peirce received a modest inheritance from his parents and purchased a plot of land in Milford, Pennsylvania. It was here that he wrote prolifically, although much of this work was published posthumously. Peirce lived meagrely but he continued to write. Throughout this period the ever-faithful William James arranged occasional lectures for him in Cambridge. Peirce also relied on reviewing articles and writing encyclopaedia entries to supplement his income. Be that as it may, Peirce never attained the scholarly reputation enjoyed by William James and John Dewey, and he died destitute 20 years before his widow in 1914.

Peirce only ever had one book published in his lifetime, which was on astronomy: *Photometric Researches* (1878). His intellectual reputation rests on his prolific article writing in American scholarly journals and on the thousands of unsorted papers/documents sold to Harvard University by his wife after he had died. It is striking then that it did not become clear until 1967 that Peirce had left 1,650 unpublished manuscripts, equating to over 100,000 pages. Much but by no means all of Peirce's writing has been published in anthologies. From these volumes, it is clear that Peirce's work is diffuse in its coverage of topics and issues, not all of which directly relate to pragmatism, and his writing style obscure and dense, earning Peirce the reputation of not being the most accessible of the early pragmatists. Yet, these limitations notwithstanding, Peirce had an acute influence on what we currently understand as classical American pragmatism.

In order to provide some flavour of his thoughts and ideas on pragmatism, it is useful to refer to his often-cited articles ('The Fixation of Belief' and 'How to Make Our Ideas Clear') which appeared in a collection titled 'Illustrations of the Logic of Science', published in *Popular Science Monthly* (1877–78). These articles are considered by many to be pivotal in inaugurating the pragmatist movement (Bernstein 2010). Notably, in 'How to Make Our Ideas Clear', Peirce proposed a 'pragmatic' notion of clear concepts. Both papers, however, reveal that, for Peirce, pragmatism was a theory of standing in opposition to or questioning various strands of idealism. Significantly, Peirce did not use the term 'pragmatism' to identify his overall philosophical position and orientation. He proffered that theorising alone was unsatisfactory and that the effects of beliefs should be tested in the real world. Yet, as the term 'pragmatism' attracted more and more attention, Peirce became unhappy with the ways it was interpreted. It is notable then that, in 1905, Peirce coined the term 'pragmaticism' in an attempt to distance himself, and to distinguish his original conceptualization of the word 'pragmatism' from others' perceptions and from what it had become to be recognised as in the literary journals. He famously stated that pragmaticism was 'to serve the precise purpose of expressing the original definition', saying that it was 'ugly enough to be safe from kidnappers'.

WILLIAM JAMES (1842–1910)

William James was born in New York City on 11 January 1842, the son of Henry James Sr. who was a wealthy, eccentric, theologian and philosopher in his own right. In fact, the James family was marked by intellectual brilliance. His brother and sister were notable writers: Alice James was a diarist and Henry James is commonly regarded as one of the most acclaimed American novelists. William James could speak fluent French and German, and visited Europe many times as a child and throughout his life. From an early age, James was interested in becoming a painter and although his father initially resisted, James was permitted to study art under William Morris Hunt before enrolling at Lawrence Scientific School at Harvard to study chemistry in 1861. In 1864 he enrolled at Harvard's School of Medicine. He then studied physiology at Berlin University until 1868, before returning to Harvard to complete his MD degree in 1869. James never practised medicine and, in 1872, he accepted a role at Harvard to teach an undergraduate course in comparative physiology. James secured himself as an academic, spending almost his entire career at Harvard where he was eventually made a full professor in philosophy in 1885.

James wrote prolifically throughout his life, encompassing the disciplines of physiology, psychology and philosophy. His works are numerous and varied but he gained widespread recognition for *Principles of Psychology* (1890) which took him 12 years to write. Two years later, he wrote a condensed version, *Psychology: The Briefer Course* (1882). There were many influential concepts which came out of these books including his analysis of the 'stream of thought', his characterization of the 'self' and his theory of emotion. His ideas sometimes courted controversy. In 1896 he published 'The Will to Believe', a lecture in which he defended the concept of a belief without prior evidence of its truth, such as religious faith without sufficient evidence of religious truth. As one of the early pioneers of pragmatism, James is often noted for being the first to use the word in print in 1898, although he rightly credited its conception to Charles S. Peirce. Among his many intellectual endeavours, James criticised empiricism for being too dependent upon the elements and the origins of experience, and how it did not satisfactorily deal with the importance of how they related to or were used to determine future experience. James considered all knowledge as pragmatic: it is either true or right if it is to take its place in the world. Crucially, philosophical uncertainty can be addressed by determining what difference opposing answers would make to the lives of people who choose one option over another option. If two competing theories offer no practical differences, then the best theory can still be found by considering the outcome to the effects of successful living. James asked: 'What, in short, is the truth's cash value in experiential terms?' Different to other early pragmatist assertions that the truth of an idea cannot be proven, James changed the focus to the 'usefulness' of an idea or its 'cash value'.

JOHN DEWEY (1859–1952)

Like William James, John Dewey is often credited with popularizing American pragmatism. Born in Vermont, US, Dewey had an exemplary school record and enrolled at the University of Vermont at the age of 16. Dewey graduated from the University of Vermont and then spent two years as a high school teacher in Oil City, Pennsylvania. He then obtained a doctorate in philosophy from Johns Hopkins University where he met and studied with Charles Sanders Peirce. Dewey developed a successful academic career, teaching at the University of Michigan (1884–94), University of Chicago (1894–1904) and Columbia University (1904–30). Dewey was renowned for being one of the most controversial philosophy professors of his generation. His theories of progressive education have influenced the American system of education, initially tested in an experimental school which he founded in Chicago. In public affairs, he was one of the first to warn of the dangers of Adolf Hitler's rise to power in Germany and of the Japanese threat in the Far East.

Dewey published over 700 articles in 140 journals and wrote approximately 40 books in his lifetime. He wrote extensively on many different subjects including philosophy, psychology, political science, education, aesthetics and the arts. Dewey first became interested in the work of James in the 1890s, whilst he was trying to free himself of the restraints of the Hegelian influences he had adopted. Dewey also drew upon Peirce's work which concurred with his own individual thoughts. As with Peirce and James, Dewey also had an interest in analysing the consequences of human knowledge on people's lives, setting much store by the idea that human action can enhance the human condition. His pragmatist philosophy was developed over a number of critically acclaimed texts including *Essays in Experimental Logic* (1916), *Human Nature and Conduct* (1922) and *Logic: The Theory of Inquiry* (1938). Significantly, Dewey developed a perspective called instrumentalism in which the value of concepts and theories is assessed not on the basis of abstract epistemological principles, but in terms of their ability to respond to particular problems. In regard to pragmatism, Dewey referred to his framework of pragmatism as 'instrumentalism'. Dewey believed that only a scientific method of inquiry could increase knowledge. He believed that inquiry (scientific, technical, sociological, philosophical or cultural) is self-corrective over time, if it is openly put forward to other inquirers to test in order to clarify, justify, refine and/or refute the original proposition.

Dewey's principal contributions to philosophy are manifold, but in most of his work he wholeheartedly advocates democracy – a subject which occupied much of his thinking and writing. During the 1930s and into the 1950s a great deal of his writing and efforts were put into various causes championing humanism, equality and freedom. For instance, in 1935 he joined Albert Einstein and Alvin Johnson as a member of the US section of the International League for Academic Freedom. He was also involved in the organization which became the National Association for the Advancement of Colored People, he marched for women's rights and he defended the independence of teachers. He also headed up the Dewey Commission in Mexico 1937 which exonerated Leon Trotsky from the charges filed against him by Joseph Stalin.

Although we have roughly sketched out three major representatives of classical American pragmatism, it is crucially important to acknowledge the gender bias here. It is incorrect to suggest that women had no influence on classical American pragmatism, despite the impression given to the contrary in many texts on the subject. Although women's concerns and issues are not at the heart of classical American pragmatism, the contribution of female pragmatists such as Jane Addams (1860–1935) is truly remarkable. Acting in a corrective fashion, a growing number of scholars interested in Jane Addams's life and works have acknowledged her considerable achievements (Seigfried 1996; Shields 2006; Gross 2009; Deegan 2010). Addams was a close friend of John Dewey who greatly admired and supported her experiments in social reform, most notably the founding of Hull House in 1889: a 'pragmatist experiment' in neighborhood activism, which addressed vexing social and industrial problems such as poverty and poor education that were rife within impoverished urban communities in Chicago. Yet such projects have been played down by some as examples of female 'do-gooding'. In line with Seigfried (1996: 6) and others cited above, we wish to recognise a tradition of women pragmatists, not least by advocating that the well-accepted cabal of classical American *male* pragmatists is enlarged to include women like Jane Addams.

As mentioned previously, commentators such as Richard Rorty helped to rescue pragmatism from intellectual bankruptcy, revitalizing its currency following the 'linguistic turn' that started to gain momentum within the social sciences from roughly the 1950s onwards. This has led to the emergence of what some scholars see as new forms of pragmatism, such as Rorty's 'postmodern pragmatism'. These strains of pragmatism have been accommodated under the umbrella term 'neo-pragmatism' (Bernstein 2010), which is understood by some to be evidence of a 'New Pragmatism' which is conceptually distinct from classical American pragmatism (Malachowski 2010). However, such distinctions are by no means fixed or widely accepted within academic domains.

Skirmishes between commentators have erupted about the conceptual clarity and merits of neo-pragmatism or 'New Pragmatism', and while there is no obvious consensus about what neo-pragmatism exactly is, nonetheless, we are witness to a wave of fresh air which is ventilating the former ideals of classical American pragmatism. In that sense, and given the global reach of American pragmatism as evidenced by the diverse people currently involved in keeping it alive and relevant, one might reasonably ask: what is 'American' about contemporary pragmatism? As exemplified in this volume, the Anglo-European flavour of our contributions suggests that American pragmatism is being kept alive and channelled into different directions by scholars on both sides of the Atlantic.

Major Concepts and Themes

Having provided some detail about the lives and works of the main classical American pragmatists we turn to examine American pragmatism in terms of concepts and themes. Even from the brief discussion above, it should be clear that American pragmatism, as a philosophical movement with a long pedigree, is multi-branched and riven with conceptual differences, exerting influence well beyond the shoreline of the US. Although American pragmatism is far from unified, we outline some of the concepts and themes which, in our view, signify some of its noteworthy qualities. We accept that others may disagree with our selection and might prefer to highlight other concepts and themes. Acknowledging this is to recognise a 'pragmatic spirit' that runs throughout this text, so we would be concerned if others did not seek to contest and build on the approach we adopt here. However, our selection has been determined by what we have identified as recurrent concepts and themes within American pragmatism more generally, and those touched upon in the contributions to this volume. By drawing out some of the qualities of American pragmatism, we hope this will serve as a heuristic device and encourage organization studies scholars to engage with American pragmatism more widely. In what follows then we identify six concepts/themes that color American pragmatism, while recognizing its diverse mantra of ideas and perspectives.

TRUTH

Prior to pragmatism, philosophy held two significant views on truth. The first is 'the correspondence view', where theory reflects and therefore corresponds to a reality out there. The second is 'the coherence view', where truth is a coherent and plausible interpretation of the world. Pragmatism provides another view on truth, one that rejects any notion of absolute truth, suggesting instead that the meaning of truth is to be determined by its prediction of future experience. In that sense, some versions of events or accounts of the world are 'truer' than others. Therefore, the aim of truth is not to correspond to the world but to anticipate and shape future experience, taking as starting point day-to-day experiences. Truth cannot be defined a priori, for its value is always realised in its application to a concrete situation. As such, whether one account or theory is 'truer' than any other comes down to a matter of evaluating how it serves as a guide for action, especially in response to a problem that affects individuals and communities.

By couching it in this way, we are at risk of suggesting that American pragmatism has one view on truth. This is not the case, as the likes of Peirce, James and Dewey struggled with the notion of truth from the beginning. What is certain, however, is that early American pragmatists did not equate truth to a vulgar notion of utility, as suggested by populist accounts on pragmatism. Peirce contemplated the notion of truth in 'The Fixation of Belief' (1877), suggesting that continuous and intelligent inquiry will help fix and unfix belief (truth) in an evolutionary fashion. Truth is not static or universal. Its pursuit presupposes the application of formal logic and semiotic processes to check out hypotheses (ideas) and improve on them, in order to reach ever more meaningful levels. James (1907) also rejected the idea of universal truth and ideals that guide humanity, asserting that truth happens to an idea rather than being built in it. Dewey took this position further by emphasizing the centrality of inquiry in the pursuit of truth.

According to Capps (2000), there are two dilemmas with regards to the nature and meaning of truth that have polarised pragmatist opinions and are unlikely to be resolved easily. The first point of contention concerns the similarities or differences between truths across different contexts; in particular, the day-to-day life context as compared to the 'higher' context of science. The second relates to the dichotomy between what we *should* believe in (normative truth) and what we *do* believe in (explanatory truth). While there may be important differences between a scientific view of the world and that of ordinary experience, the former should not be upheld to be superior to the latter. Dewey (1938) argues that the difference between these two domains resides in their subject matter not in their basic logical forms and relations. The pragmatists see science and its associated methods deeply connected with day-to-day experience. Indeed, it is experience that spurs us on to 'investigate' and understand what is going on in the world. Accordingly, knowledge can deal only with various aspects of what experience reveals. Therefore, the starting point of any scientific pursuit of truth starts with experience and contributes in some form to that experience. There is no gulf between the problems of science and the practical problems of ordinary life. In fact, all of us are all inquirers, though only a minority of us are scientific inquirers (Paavola 2011).

For Peirce, James and Dewey, one of the most interesting questions about truth was 'what sorts of beliefs we should have?' In the 'Fixation of Belief' Peirce (1877) suggests that scientific truths may provide explanations (explanatory truth) but they fail to be of use in terms of helping us with our beliefs (with our normative truths) or, in other words, with the selection of ends worth pursuing. Scientific methods can describe 'what is the case?' but remain incapable of informing us what we ought to do and what we should believe in. No scientific explanation on its own can stand as a reason as to why we should do one thing or another. Moral deliberation requires more than scientific deliberation and is usually a collective and morally infused process. We return to the concept of morality later to unpack its social and practical nature and its relationship with 'truth'. For the moment, we turn our attention to inquiry, the process by which one pursues truth.

INQUIRY

In 'The Fixation of Belief' (1877), Peirce discusses multiple methods of inquiry to eventually settle on the scientific method as the most useful model of inquiry. For Peirce, the scientific method 'unlocks or at least leverages the power of individualism as people work together to address problems. Science is distinguished from all other methods of inquiry by its cooperative or public character' (quoted in Shields 2003: 512). Dewey's work conceptualises further the scientific method by suggesting that it is ultimately 'a technique for making a productive use of doubt by converting it into operations of infinite inquiry' (Dewey 1929: 228). While the universal quest for certainly is impossible and indeed destructive, the scientific method allows one to reach relatively settled mini-truths that speak to particular situations. Though neither Peirce nor Dewey privilege science, they both see it as the most successful intellectual enterprise which can help bring particulars together. The scientific model of inquiry upheld by the pragmatists sees knowledge as inextricably linked with experience and, as such, open to fallibilism and criticism. For Peirce, inquiry must be seen as never ending and absolutes and meta-narratives are to be rejected. Inquiry is processual and as it progresses more concepts will be known. In this vein, the road of inquiry ought to lead to *concrete reasonableness*; in other words, Peirce urges us to find explanations that are logically coherent and useful in terms of enhancing our experience.

Like Peirce, Dewey also applauded science for offering rigorous methods for solving problems and acquiring information about how the world works, but science was not regarded as the ultimate or the only way to know the world. According to Dewey, there may be other, equally valid, means of experience (such as common sense or art) and the activity of knowing through them could also enrich human understanding (Shields 2003). As Dewey writes: 'Inquiry is the controlled or directed transformation of an indeterminate situation into one that is so determinate in its constituent distinctions and relations as to convert the elements of the original situation into a unified whole' (1938: 319–20). In reading Dewey, and applying his notion of a community of inquiry to public administration, Shields (2003) suggests that it is the uncertainty of practice that triggers the need for inquiry. But there are no universal standards by which one could judge the outcome of inquiry: it is the actual community being affected and affecting the inquiry that will decide what 'counts' as moral and therefore as useful. As such, a 'community of inquiry' is a key pragmatist concept, first sketched out by Peirce and subsequently developed by Dewey.

Put simply, the 'community of inquiry' refers to any group of individuals involved in a process of empirical/theoretical inquiry concerning a problem. People belonging to such communities are connected by three elements: first, the existence of a problematic situation that needs to be solved; second, the science needed to resolve that problem; and third, the democratic values to be upheld in coming up with a practical solution. According to Dewey, the focus on a problematic situation is essential for it helps a community to form around the issue requiring resolution. Members of a community of inquiry must bring a scientific attitude to the problematic situation and view both theory and method as tools to address the problem. Crucially, communities of inquiries must be democratic. They must take into account values/ideals such as freedom, equality and efficiency in pursuing their goals and objectives (Evans 2000). The community of inquiry is a powerful concept (although not without its shortcomings (Shields 2003)) that recognises truth and knowledge are social phenomena, marked by contextual contingency.

EXPERIENCE

In pragmatism, the basic unit of analysis is experience. Experience is not antithetical to knowledge; rather, knowledge is part of experience and contributes to its enhancement. As such, experience is both embodied and rational, it is both thought and action. American pragmatists oppose the abstract epistemic notion of experience embraced by Western metaphysical philosophy, as something concrete, observable and outside of cognitive processes, in favor of a fluid, plural and ambiguous process.

In the *Principles of Psychology*, James (1890) argues that the starting point of experience is the individual's interaction with the environment. Experience, for James, is a sense of personal continuity enveloping external objects, their relationship to each other, and their relationship to the purposeful subject who both thinks and experiences at the same time. Out of this flow of interactions emerges a state of consciousness which allows the individual to respond satisfactorily to their environment. The individual does not just survive in a complex environment but does so on their terms. Therefore experience is progressive, containing the possibility of responding to the environment in new ways as well as the ability to evaluate the effectiveness of such responses. James makes experience the exclusive source of knowledge by arguing that experience is both open and continuous enough to allow people to make useful choices and shape society the way they hope for. Thought becomes the process of conceptualization, implied in the selection of future models of conduct and the rejection of alternatives. Truth is not an inherent property of certain correct ideas but the relationship of an idea to its consequences when acted upon. No truth is ever final or permanent since experience, the ultimate court of appeal, is ongoing and in flux. The process by which a concept becomes true, like experience itself, is progressive (James 1890).

Dewey (1929) also embraces the view that experience is active, enacted and oriented to the future. He sees knowledge as a series of practical acts judged by their consequences. Conversely, for Dewey, all judgements are practical in as much as they originate from an incomplete or ambiguous practical situation which is to be resolved. The aim of knowledge is not to correspond to the world but to anticipate future experience, taking as its material experiences the present and the past (Mounce 1997). While one must go through a logical process of reasoning to progress from prior ideas to new ones, new ideas do not owe their power to the prior ones, they are merely lucky variants that may catch on because they resonate with people's circumstances in useful ways. The truthfulness of knowledge is ultimately assessed by its usefulness, for if people do not find ideas useful for some purpose, they will simply discard them. For Dewey, thinking and acting are just the two names for the same process, the process of making our way as best we can in a universe shot through with contingencies and ambiguities (Menand 2001). Knowledge is not a copy of something that exists independently of its being known, but becomes an important instrument for successful action. The pursuit of pragmatist knowledge invokes the need for plural methodologies which place doubt rather than certainty at the heart of the inquiry process.

PLURALISM

Pragmatist philosophies are characterized by their embrace of pluralism, recognizing that there are multiple and diverse in values, experiences, meanings, perspectives and methodologies. American pragmatism 'gives us a pluralistic restless universe in which no single point of view can ever take in the whole scene' (James 1897/1956: 177 quoted in Kelemen and Rumens 2008). Pragmatists recognise that there are many ways of interpreting and engaging with the world and some are better than others. However, one can recognise the superiority of one way over another thanks to practical experience and serious dialog. The pragmatist's interest in what works and how and why it works (or does not) translates into a notion of knowledge which is anti-foundational, directed towards problem-solving using the data and the understandings available at the time. The researcher is permitted (indeed encouraged) to use indeterminate truth values in the attempt to handle situational indeterminacy. The quest for pragmatic certainty sensitises the researcher to multiple realities, paradox and ambiguity. Doubt rather than certainty is central to the methodological process:

> A disciplined mind takes delight in the problematic, and cherishes it until a way out is found ... The questionable becomes an active questioning, a quest for the objects by which the obscure and unsettled may be developed into the stable and clear. The scientific attitude may almost be defined as that which is capable of enjoying the doubtful. (Dewey 1929: 228)

From a pragmatist perspective, doubt is seen to originate in and find resolution by experience. Doubt arises when our normal ways of doing things are disrupted because of surprises or unusual events that are difficult to comprehend and deal with. Doubt, experienced as a state of not knowing, is a motivator for our search for knowledge. Dewey (1938) refers to such disruptions as problematic situations in which habits and routines are not enough to explain what is going on and to offer a way out. This becomes the starting point of reflexive inquiry.

Reflexive inquiry relies on abduction, a form of reasoning that searches for possible explanations to an experienced anomaly (Locke et al. 2008). Abduction is a form of guessing that requires creativity and imagination. It helps one infer explanations for what is being observed in the world; therefore, preconditions may be inferred from consequences. There are multiple possible explanations (preconditions) for what we observe but there is a tendency to 'abduce' a single or a few explanations, in the hope that we can better orient ourselves and cope with the ambiguity present in the world. Thus, abduction is a link between the empirical and the logical or between events/facts and theory. It serves as a hypothesis that explains our observation and gives us a starting point to think about the approach a problematic situation, a sort of working hypothesis that will be constantly revised in light of new evidence.

Abduction is powered by the existence of doubt:

> Doubt is an uneasy and dissatisfied state from which we struggle to free ourselves and pass into the state of belief; while the latter is calm and satisfactory state ... The irritation of doubt causes a struggle to attain a state of belief. I shall term this struggle Inquiry. (Peirce 1877: 99)

According to Peirce, abduction is the only form of reasoning that makes novelty and imagination possible. Induction and deduction do not serve such processes for they follow well-trodden paths. Indeed, deduction allows us to derive consequences of what is assumed while induction allows us to make general statements based on what we observe in practice. Abduction, however, generates 'inventive solutions, explanatory propositions and theoretical elements' (Locke et al. 2008: 908–9) in a speculative way, without which the door to our imagination would be closed and no scientific progress would be possible. Abduction does not apply only to scientific inquiry, but it is also central in the course of day-to-day life (Joas 1996). Both belief and doubt are necessary to progress our everyday understandings and practices. Doubt helps us to question our beliefs in light of new experiences. At the end of this process, new beliefs are formed but they themselves may be eventually questioned when they no longer serve to explain what is going in day-to-day practice. A pragmatist stance assumes that the inquirer operates in a social world and his/her inquiry is active and experimental and, therefore, must be open to pluralism and embodied in social practice.

EMBODIMENT

For Pierce, inquirers are embodied human beings. What inquirers know about the world is influenced by what they do, can do and want to do in the world, as individuals and as collectivities. As such, knowledge is not a mere individual achievement but a social one, and the validity of a theory is assured when the theory makes sense to a certain collectivity that engages with certain practices, be they day-to-day or scientific. Groups are bound together by similar or shared experiences and are able to reflect on new knowledge via dialog and deliberation. At the heart of a pragmatist epistemology is the interactive flow between the individual, the group and the environment. The quest for certainty is achieved practically and consensus around what counts as truth is established communicatively.

For the pragmatists, inquiry must be embodied if it is to be able to cope effectively with the perennial indeterminancy and contingency with which humans have to struggle in their everyday existence. Dewey puts it thus:

> The senses are the organs through which the live creature participates directly in the on goings of the world around him. In this participation the varied wonders and splendour of this world are made actual for him in the quality he experiences ... . (1934: 22)

To think means to experience the world in one way or another and not accounting for this experience means escaping into abstract and useless theory. Experience means not only what had happened in the past but our visceral and embodied response to the immediate context. In *Experience and Nature* (1925: 8), Dewey writes that experience is about what:

> men [sic] do and suffer, what they strive for, believe and endure, and also how men act and are acted upon, the ways in which they do suffer, desire and enjoy, see, believe, imagine ...

In a similar vein, doubt is a living sensation not a rational, logical state of mind. Doubt is a sensation one feels in one's body, the experimental signal that one needs to reconsider one's way of understanding and engaging with the world (Hildebrand 1996).

PROSPECTIVE FUTURES

Pragmatism, in its focus on the future, upholds the promise and the possibility of social reform. The classical American pragmatist version of theory might be regarded as distinct from any previous philosophical stance on theory: one purpose of pragmatist theory is to meet people's needs, to help them deal with problems as they arise without necessarily making recourse to the Cartesian and Platonic dilemmas. The reciprocity between theory and praxis is pivotal in this endeavour. Indeed, classical American pragmatists often criticised traditional philosophy for its over reliance on and obsession with abstraction, its aloofness and reflective isolation and its apparent incapacity to engage with the public in general and to innovate in the pursuit of social reform. Or, as Rorty (1998: 19) writes, making much the same point: 'pragmatists think that if something makes no difference in practice, it should make no difference to philosophy'. Rather, the task of the philosopher is a *practical* one bearing on social, economic and political problems with the view to ensure that individuals and communities live richer and more fulfilling lives (Wicks and Freeman 1998). As Shields (2003) notes, Dewey links social progress and social science through the instrument of the scientific method:

> *Every step forward in the social sciences – the studies termed history, economics, politics, sociology – shows that social questions are capable of being intelligently coped with only in the degree in which we employ the method of collecting data, forming hypotheses, and testing them in action which is characteristic of natural science, and in the degree in which we utilize in behalf of the promotion of social welfare. (Dewey 1916: 333, quoted in Shields 2003)*

Dewey worried about the effects corporate life would have on its members and the dangers of technocracy. He addressed some of these issues in *Liberalism and Social Action* where he criticised the hidden power asymmetries present under existing social arrangements:

> *It is not surprizing in view of our standing dependence upon the use of coercive force that at every time of crisis coercion breaks out into open violence. (1935: 64)*

Moreover:

> *... the issue is not whether some amount of violence will accompany the effectuation of radical change of institutions. The question is whether force or intelligence is to be the method upon which we consistently rely and to whose promotion we devote our energies. (1935: 78)*

Dewey sees critical intelligence and social dialogs as the response to this dilemma. The method of intelligence includes open deliberations, problem-solving, organizational democratization, movement building and direct challenges by the majority to the privileges of economic and political elites. What we may take from Dewey is a sense of the significance attached to the aim of revisioning and creating new futures, in order to improve the human experience and condition.

What Can American Pragmatism Offer Organization Studies Scholars?

Organization studies has not been impervious to the influence of American pragmatism, although it is reasonable to assert that its influence is rarely acknowledged. Management textbooks of the standard fare that one might expect to find in mainstream high-street bookshops, for example, seldom introduce American pragmatism to their readers, but they are likely to discuss organization theories that have been shaped by the writings of pragmatist philosophers. As discussed earlier, one aim of this edited volume is to examine what American pragmatism can offer organization studies scholars. In so doing, we join a growing number of writers for whom American pragmatism is relevant to organization and management scholars concerned with understanding the dynamic processes and practices of organizational life (Elkjaer and Simpson 2011). Such discussions are starting to gather momentum, evident amidst a rash of organizational scholarship that derives insight from the canon of American pragmatist literature (Evans 2000; Jacobs 2004; Elkjaer 2004; Simpson 2009; Whetsell and Shields 2011). As we see it, these contributions add to the vitality of the field of organization studies which is not always curious and open in its scope, ambition and concerns.

For example, ontological debates in organization and management studies have seen an increased polarization of structuralist positions, where organizational life is seen in terms of objective entities with clear attributes that can be quantified and classified according to some general model, on the one hand, and social constructivist perspectives where ideas and meanings are central to what constitutes organizational reality, on the other hand. According to Thompson (2011), the epistemological response to such ontological divides has been to adopt positions that embrace an objective and evolutionary perspective on organizations while at the same time acknowledging the role played by inter-subjective factors. Such mid-range theories (Weick 1989) build on the idea that general principle and abstractions are necessary, despite the fact that they cannot cope fully with the singularities and complexities of organizational life. As Thompson (2011) argues, mid-range theories also embrace the view that there is a continuum between entity and process forms of organizational reality and any ontological movements researchers make on this continuum will represent an epistemological trade-off that could have positive or negative consequences on the theory developed. Ontological shifts are associated with positive theory outcomes while ontological drifts are seen as leading to bad theorizing.

With this in mind, we suggest that American pragmatism provides a useful platform for making ontological shifts and preventing the occurrence of ontological drifts. Such drifts refer to reification, a process that happens when a social construct is turned into an objective phenomenon with an undeniable objective existence (e.g. markets, institutions). Ontological drifts can also lead to processification, a situation which may be encountered when the attributes of a process are relegated to an entity. Pragmatism encourages us to make two types of ontological shifts which are crucial to developing theories that are both rigorous scientifically and relevant to the communities of practice affected. Abstraction takes place when the complexity of organizational processes is simplified and translated into an isolable entity whose characterization could be used to advantage. Conjunction is the situation when one shifts from an entity-driven view of the world to one that seeks to acknowledge the processual dimensions of a construct. These shifts are at the heart of pragmatist theories, the tension between them encouraging researchers to change mental gear and see the world in its multitude of potentialities, in order to arrive at a workable solution and an acceptable explanation.

It is widely accepted that managers and other practitioners from organizational worlds prefer entative constructs for they are more likely to be expressed in a transparent language and hence easier to implement. However, the subtleties and complexities present in organizations require a more processual understanding and a treatment that, although may not yield quick solutions and *a la carte* management recipes, will lead to real dialog amongst the affected parties and ultimately to effective problem-solving. Pragmatism is not against scientific rigour per se but redefines it in ways that are more relevant to the world of practice. As Schultz (2010) reasons, scientific rigour, in its most traditional sense, emphasises standardization, quantitative methods, testing and generalization and leads to well-crafted studies of minor issues that may not be important for practitioners. These studies, while methodologically complex and cleverly written up, tend to be just some kind of intellectual acrobatics that serves no purpose beyond academia. Academic careers are propelled by a drive to discover and institutionalise new concepts in order to achieve recognition from peers, rather than by the wish to engage with significant problems rooted in the practice of day-to-day life. According to Schultz (2010: 275):

> *the virtue of the pragmatist tradition has been its ability to address issues in organizations that matter to people and point to different ways of organizing.*

This takes us back to a central question in the social sciences and in management especially: what is a good theory? In an incisive article, Hambrick (2007: 1344) states that 'theories are not ends in themselves', a view that finds deep resonance with the pragmatist tradition. However, there is lack of consensus as to what theories are, let alone the purpose they may serve.

Sutton and Staw (1995: 277) take an objective entity-driven view of the world and a deductive approach to theory, suggesting that theory is about connections among phenomena, a story about why acts, events, structure, and thought occur. Theory emphasises the nature of causal relationships identifying what comes first as well as the timings of such events.

In a related vein, Zahra and Newey (2009) argue that theory is about generating interesting findings by combining theories from various disciplines. Without such syntheses, scholars develop only partial views of complex phenomena and theories will fail to have an all rounded impact. Their fivefold impact model refers to impact on pre-existing theories, on field development, on discipline development, on researcher's development and external stakeholder development. At pains to oppose the view above, Markoczy and Deeds (2009) take a processual view of the world and an inductive view on theory, arguing that theory is about explaining empirical findings and anomalies. It is about making sense of the world without superimposing our presuppositions and pre-existing meta-narratives. Where does American pragmatism stand in relation to such views?

Pragmatism does not see such views as totally opposed to one another or, indeed, as incommensurable. As introduced earlier, the pragmatist abductive way of theorizing looks for the most plausible explanations to a problematic situation by using creativity and insight. Such insight could come from the anomalies present in the real world or from combining theories from different fields to come up with a workable answer to an existing problem. Creativity could be the result of deductive or inductive logic: what matters then, not least for organization studies scholars, is that the resultant explanation is useful to the community of practice affected by the issue at hand. This is one but crucially not all the appealing insights American pragmatism has to offer organization studies.

The Chapters that Follow

The main body of this book aims to give readers a strong sense of what might be learned when organization studies scholars draw inspiration from American pragmatism. The volume is organized into two parts: 'Theory and Context', and 'American Pragmatism Applied'. Chapters are organized into these sections for the sake of convenience and appeal to readers, especially for those practitioners who might dip into the pages of this volume, but we have no intention of creating a false divide between theory and practice. As readers will discover, chapters emphasise the relation between theory and praxis, undermining the theory-practice dualism. Chapters can be read as stand-alone contributions but they are connected and permeated by the pragmatist concepts and themes outlined in the previous section. A summary of each chapter follows next.

In Chapter 2, Patrick Baert extends our discussion of classical American pragmatism by focusing on neo-pragmatism. Specifically, Baert elaborates on the precise nature of the neo-pragmatist agenda for the social sciences, suggesting that a neo-pragmatist agenda changes our priorities about social research. Baert, a distinguished scholar in social theory, is not situated in or directly concerned with organization studies. Yet his chapter demonstrates contemporary attentiveness to the significance of neo-pragmatism from which organization studies may draw inspiration. As Baert argues, there is much to be gained by integrating insights from American neo-pragmatism and, in particular Emmanuel Levinas, Hans-Georg Gadamer and Jean-Paul Sartre. Such explorations are likely to hold promise for revisioning organization and management theories, which we leave to others more qualified than ourselves to develop, revise and critique.

In Chapter 3, Peter M. Jackson examines a problem with the current state of economic knowledge and how American pragmatism might offer a way forward. Jackson's argument starts from the point of view that although economics has been transformed over the past 40 years, from the earlier narrow set of interests of neoclassical economics to become more pluralistic, it remains imprisoned within an 'iron cage' of assumptions about the nature of the socioeconomic reality that it seeks to explain. Jackson extends Lawson's assertion that it is necessary to reorientate economic theory by reintroducing an examination of its ontological foundation. Developing the references Lawson makes to John Dewey, Jackson reasons that within the canon of American pragmatism is a powerful critique of the way in which economists today conceive social reality and hence the way in which they conduct their economic analyses. Jackson is hopeful that, by yoking together the scholarship of Lawson and the American pragmatists, economists will take more seriously the institutions and mechanisms which generate the economic realities currently experienced and which shapes lives.

In Chapter 4, Tony Watson, a sociologist and pragmatist, reflects upon his own practice and learning over a number of decades as a sociologist who teaches, researches and writes about organizations, management and entrepreneurship. What Watson offers in this chapter is, to coin his own terms, 'a pragmatist's use of pragmatism'. This is elaborated in a series of reflections about why Watson has increasingly turned much more directly and explicitly to the pragmatist tradition to help develop a clear rationale and justification for conducting ethnographic research on management and organization. Readers of Watson's chapter stand to gain insights into how a pragmatist mood and style of thought has been present and influential in the social sciences for some considerable time, even if it is only recently that its importance is being fully acknowledged. Furthermore, Watson shows how pragmatist thinking can help organization studies scholars reconsider the effectiveness and relevance of organizational research and theorising.

In Chapter 5, Nathan Harter continues to explore the contribution American pragmatism can make at a theoretical level, focusing on leadership. Harter takes an interesting entry point into the subject, grounded in Eric Voegelin's reading of the work of William James. Taking James's ideas about a pluralistic universe, Harter argues that one of the tasks of leadership is to encourage a culture of openness and to transcend its long-standing concepts, largely by challenging their ongoing utility. For Harter, pragmatism promises to help organizations live within that tension and possibly flourish in a pluralistic universe. Harter outlines how Eric Voegelin interpreted James's lectures on both pragmatism and pluralism at various stages in his life, before setting forth the implications for leadership today, when so many tensions and 'wicked problems' threaten to overrun our mental models and decision trees. For Harter, pragmatism offers to help leaders function, if not thrive, under such circumstances.

In Chapter 6, David C. Jacobs examines what the pragmatism of John Dewey has to offer contemporary organization theory. Jacobs draws on a number of Dewey's key concepts and arguments, in order to explore the democratic core of pragmatist organizational theory as well as the emphasis on experimentation. Contrasting Deweyan pragmatism with organizational behavior contingency theories, which superficially resemble pragmatism, Jacobs argues that Deweyan pragmatism locates agency in individuals and groups and not managers. For Jacobs, Dewey was sufficiently engaged in the public sphere to understand the myriad hierarchies and authoritarian systems that constrained democratic reform. Jacobs argues that Dewey's conception of human capacity, his understanding of social intelligence, and his assessment of the role of publics constitutes a robust basis for an organizational theory of democratic reform and experimentation.

In Chapter 7, the last in this section, Ian Evans provides a polemic account of the potential utility of American pragmatism within the branch of organization studies known as 'Critical Management Studies' (CMS), specifically in regard to internecine debates about its ability to influence public policy and real-world management practices. Put differently, Even's crucially considers whether pragmatism (as both critical method and, in a sense, a way of operating within and beyond institutional contexts) offers a viable means by which CMS scholars might overcome the institutionalization of the movement which many see as debilitating. Notably, Evans questions if American pragmatism is really the 'best place' to turn to help us break out of this institutionalization, or is it just another 'approach' to add to the already burgeoning bag of critical tools CMS makes use of. As such, this chapter provides an important and provocative counterpoint in this section of the book.

The second section of this volume, titled 'American Pragmatism Applied', focuses on how pragmatist perspectives may help us to understand organizational life differently. Notably, in this section some of the chapters use pragmatist concepts and themes to frame empirical data gathered within organizations. In Chapter 8, Patricia M. Shields, Travis A. Whetsell and Emily Kay Hanks provide a useful account of how classical American pragmatism has, over the years, influenced the field of public administration. According to the writers, public administration appears to lack an overarching intellectual identity, to which American pragmatism has provided a remedy. The central argument presented by Shields et al. is that classical pragmatism furnishes public administration with an intellectually sustaining philosophy that focuses on practitioner experience while incorporating social ethics, participatory democracy, and a flexible research tradition that integrates theory and practice. The chapter examines the public administration literature and discusses five interconnected themes:

1.   the practice perspective;
2.   the rediscovered historical connection;
3.   the ideas of Jane Addams as a feminist/pragmatist/public administrator;
4.   the debate between varieties of pragmatism in public administration;
5.   the role of pragmatic inquiry in research methods.

In Chapter 9, Diane-Laure Arjaliès, Philippe Lorino and Barbara Simpson propose that American pragmatism, especially the works of Charles Sanders Peirce, John Dewey and George Herbert Mead, offer fruitful ways of understanding creative practice as a dynamic social process. Drawing on empirical data gathered from a three-year ethnographic study carried out in a small French asset management company, the researchers argue that pragmatism provides a very practical perspective on creativity by locating it in the everyday human practices by means of which people make sense of their situations. This chapter elaborates on pragmatist ideas of abduction, habit, inquiry, transactional meaning-making and semiotic mediation, all of which are deemed pivotal in coming to an understanding of creative action in organizations. This chapter demonstrates how creativity cannot be explained simply in terms of the application of preplanned techniques and formulae. Rather, it arises as a response to uncertain and unanticipated situations that call out changeful actions.

In Chapter 10, Ulrik Brandi and Bente Elkjaer propose a theoretical framework for organizational learning anchored in American pragmatism. They address two interrelated conceptual issues: the relationship between pragmatism and organizational learning; examining the organizing element in organizational learning. Acknowledging Herbert Simon, Chris Argyris and Donald Schön as founding figures in organizational learning, Brandi and Elkjaer find their conceptions of organizational learning grounded too firmly in an understanding of organizations as rational systems and individuals as cognitive beings. This means that organizational learning becomes a question of individuals' adaptation, detecting and correcting dysfunctional behaviors leaving out the organizing of enterprises. Drawing on a case study of organizational change in a Danish biotech/pharmaceutical company, Brandi and Elkjaer turn towards a pragmatist inspired understanding of the sociology of work, in order to overcome the separation between individuals' learning and organizational systems.

In Chapter 11, Scott Taylor and Emma Bell seek inspiration from William James's writing on pragmatism and his desire to construct an epistemologically credible framework for analysis of the wider social significance of practising religious belief, in order to analyze the contemporary interplay of religious belief, organization and ethics. Taylor and Bell observe how pragmatism has been interpreted within the field of business ethics, primarily as a philosophical underpinning for stakeholder analysis, arguing that this version of pragmatism neglects a key task, the assessment of the meaning of a proposition. To address this shortcoming, a Jamesian pragmatist perspective on the ethical implications of managing and organizing is advanced, one that involves at least as much focus on meaning as on the purpose or use-value of an action or principle. James's work is used as a resource to analyze a particular case, the approach to business ethics promoted by the City of London-based Christian Association of Business Executives. Implications are drawn out of a revised pragmatist perspective for the theory and practice of business ethics, concentrating on James's stated desire for scholars to focus on melioration in applied settings such as workplaces, with the aim of improving lived human experience.

In Chapter 12, John R. Bartle and Patricia M. Shields suggest that since pragmatism is a philosophy that emphasises learning through action, and building a knowledge base from experience and reflection, it is a potentially compelling approach for understanding government finance. Underpinning this chapter is an argument that the goal of positive social science theory should be to explain social actions and advance a framework so an observer can develop a model that allows for description and understanding to a broader audience. To advance practice, the theory must first take into account practice. Bartle and Shields suggest that the overarching framework of pragmatism allows for this. This potential is explored and its implications articulated over the course of this chapter.

In Chapter 13, Rosa Slegers picks up on the theme of ethics again, in regard to the concept of 'emotional intelligence' as it is commonly understood in organizational contexts. Slegers explores the temptation to use this concept to simplify, categorise or even reject vague and unruly sensations as they occur in the work place. A particular kind of regret is used as an example of such unwelcome sensations. Mobilizing William James's pragmatism, specifically his work on emotion, Slegers goes on to show that the acknowledgement of 'emotional vagueness' in general, and a type of regret in particular, both make a difference in our experience and enriches the decision-making process in a way that benefits the organization. The chapter suggests that a pragmatist approach to the emotions, which allows room for the vague and on occasion resists the intellect's simplifying, labor-saving inclinations, can only be put into practice by managers with 'tough-minded, empiricist temperaments'.

In Chapter 14, the last in this section of the book, Tore Hafting and Erik Lindhult address the oft-neglected and under theorized concept of power in American pragmatism. In a bold move, Hafting and Lindhult argue that American pragmatism can inspire and support an important shift in prevailing social science discourses on power, towards non-coercive, collaborative understandings of power consistent with a participatory democratic politics and way of life. This chapter draws out a pragmatist understanding of power in the domain of action research in the Scandinavian tradition. Notably, Hafting and Lindhult focus on two thinkers: John Dewey and Mary Parker Follett. It is argued that Follett can and should be counted as one of the leading figures in American pragmatism, a female counterpart to Dewey in terms of making pragmatist points of departures relevant for a progressive and participation-based democratic society. Follett is shown to be more specific in focusing on and working out a non-coercive conception of power, and can be said to address specific dimensions not worked out by Dewey from a pragmatist point of view. Follett's conceptualization of power as 'power-with' is said to make significant contributions to a pragmatist understanding of the concept and its practices within organizations.

References

Bernstein, R.J. 2010. *The Pragmatic Turn*. Cambridge: Polity.

Capps, J. 2000. Naturalism, pragmatism, and design. *The Journal of Speculative Philosophy*, 14(3), 161–78.

Deegan, M.J. 2010. Janes Addams on citizenship in a democracy. *Journal of Classical Sociology*, 10(3), 217–38.

Delbridge, R. and Keenoy, T. 2010. Beyond managerialism? *The International Journal of Human Resource Management*, 21(6), 799–817.

Dewey, J. 1925/1953. *Experience and Nature*. London and Chicago, IL: Open Court.

Dewey, J. 1928. A Critique of American Civilization, in *John Dewey The Later Works*, vol. 3, (ed.) Boydston, J.A. Carbondale, IL: Southern Illinois University Press, 133–44.

Dewey, J. 1929. *The Quest for Certainty: A Study of the Relation of Knowledge and Action*. New York: Minton, Balch & Co.

Dewey, J. 1934. *Art as Experience*. New York: Minton, Balch.

Dewey, J. 1935. *Liberalism and Social Action*. New York: G.P. Putnam's Sons.

Dewey, J. 1938. *Experience and Education*. London and New York: Macmillan.

Elkjaer, B. 2004. Organizational learning: 'The third way'. *Management Learning*, 35(4), 419–34.

Elkjaer, B. and Simpson, B. 2011. Pragmatism: A lived and living philosophy. What can it offer to contemporary organization theory?, in *Philosophy and Organization Theory* (Research in the *Sociology of Organizations*, vol. 32), (ed.) Tsoukas, H. and Chia, R. London: Emerald Group Publishing Limited, 55–84.

Evans, K.G. 2000. Reclaiming John Dewey: Democracy, inquiry, pragmatism, and public management. *Administration & Society*, 32(3), 308–28.

Fontrodona, J. 2002. *Pragmatism and Management Inquiry: Insights from the Thought of Charles S. Peirce*. Westport, CT: Quorum Books.

Gross, M. 2009. Collaborative experiments: Jane Addams, Hull House and experimental social work. *Trends and Developments*, 48(1), 81–95.

Hambrick, D. 2007. The field of management's devotion to theory: Too much of a good thing. *Academy of Management Journal*, 50(6), 1346–52.

Hildebrand D. L. 1996. Genuine doubt and the community in Peirce's theory of inquiry. *Southwest Philosophy Review*, 12(1), 33–43.

Jacobs, D.C. 2004. A pragmatist approach to integrity in business ethics. *Journal of Management Inquiry*, 13(3), 215–23.

James, W. 1890/1950. *The Principles of Psychology*, 2 vols. Mineola, NY: Dover.

James, W. 1892/1985. *Psychology: A Briefer Course*. Notre Dame, IN: University of Notre Dame Press.

James, W. 1897/1956. *The Will to Believe, and Other Essays in Popular Philosophy*. New York: Dover.

James, W. 1907/1981. *Pragmatism: A New Name for Some Old Ways of Thinking*. Indianapolis, IN: Hackett Publishing.

Joas, H. 1996. *The Creativity of Action*. Cambridge: Polity.

Kelemen, M. and Rumens, N. 2008. *Introduction to Critical Management Research*. London: Sage.

Locke, K., Golden-Biddle, K. and Feldman, M.S. 2008. Perspective-making doubt generative: Rethinking the role of doubt in the research process. *Organization Science*, 19(6), 907–18.

Malachowski, A. 2010. *The New Pragmatism*. Durham, MD: Acumen.

Markoczy, L. and Deeds, D. 2009. Theory building at the intersection: Recipe for impact or road to nowhere? *Journal of Management Studies*, 46(6), 1076–88.

Menand, L. 2001. *The Metaphysical Club: A Story of Ideas in America*. New York: Farrar, Straus, and Giroux.

Mounce, H.O. 1997. *The Two Pragmatisms: From Peirce to Rorty*. London and New York: Routledge.

Parker, M. 2002. *Against Management*. Cambridge: Polity.

Paavola, S. 2011. Deweyan abduction, paper presented at the *Fourth Nordic Pragmatism Conference*, Copenhagen, 22–24 August 2011.

Peirce, C.S. 1878. *Photometric Researches*. Leipzig: W. Engelmann.

Peirce, C.S. 1877. The fixation of belief. *Popular Science Monthly*, 12, 1–15.

Peirce, C.S. 1878. How to make our ideas clear. *Popular Science Monthly*, 12, 286–302.

Rorty, R.M. 1979. *Philosophy and the Mirror of Nature*. Princeton, NJ: Princeton University Press.

Rorty, R.M. 1998. *Truth and Progress: Philosophical Papers*, vol. 3. Cambridge: Cambridge University Press.

Schultz, M. 2010. Reconciling pragmatism and scientific rigour. *Journal of Management Inquiry*, 19(3), 274–7.

Seigfried, C.H. 1996. *Pragmatism and Feminism: Reweaving the Social Fabric*. Chicago, IL: University of Chicago Press.

Shields, P.M. 2003. The community of inquiry: Classical pragmatism and public administration. *Administration & Society*, 35(5), 510–38

Shields, P.M. 2006. Democracy and the social feminist ethics of Jane Addams: A vision for public administration. *Administrative Theory & Praxis*, 28(3), 418–43.

Simpson, B. 2009. Pragmatism, Mead, and the practice turn. *Organization Studies*, 30(12) 1329–47.

Sutton, R. and Staw, B. 1995. What theory is not. *Administrative Science Quarterly*, 40(3), 371–84.

Thompson, M. 2011. Ontological shift or ontological drift: Reality claims, epistemological frameworks and theory generation in organization studies. *Academy of Management Review*, 36(4), 754–73.

Watson, T. 2010. Critical social science, pragmatism and the realities of HRM. *The International Journal of Human Resource Management*, 21(6), 915–31.

Weick, K. 1989. Theory construction as disciplined imagination. *Academy of Management Review*, 14(4), 516–31.

Whetsell, T.A. and Shields, P.M. 2011. Reconciling the varieties of pragmatism in public administration. *Administration & Society*, 43(4), 474–83.

Wicks, A.C. and Freeman, R.E. 1998. Organization studies and the new pragmatism: Positivism, anti-positivism and the search for ethics. *Organization Science*, 9(2), 123–40.

Zahra, A.A. and Newey, L.R. 2009. Maximising the impact of organization science: Theory-building at the intersection of disciplines and/or fields. *Journal of Management Studies*, 46(6), 1059–75.

2 Neo-Pragmatism and Phenomenology: A Proposal

PATRICK BAERT

Introduction[1]

In this chapter, I will elaborate on the precise nature of the neo-pragmatist agenda for the social sciences which I have been developing over the last couple of years, and which I have tried to crystallise in *Philosophy of the Sciences: Towards Pragmatism* (Baert 2005) and a number of other publications (e.g. Baert 2006, 2007). I will argue that this neo-pragmatist agenda changes our priorities about social research. Its significance can be shown especially in relation to the writings of a number of authors, who engage with Husserl's phenomenology. There is much to be gained by integrating insights from American neo-pragmatism and, in particular Emmanuel Levinas, Hans-Georg Gadamer and Jean-Paul Sartre. Although prima facie very different, these three Continental European authors have a non-representational view of knowledge and language in common, as well as a commitment to putting the ongoing engagement with difference at the center of philosophy. I will argue that this new way of thinking about philosophy has repercussions for how we conduct social research in ways that tie in especially neatly with the recent debates around, for instance, public sociology.

By pragmatism I refer to the distinct philosophical tradition, initially set in motion by Charles Peirce, later developed by William James and John Dewey, and further articulated by Richard Bernstein and Richard Rorty. This philosophical tradition is often portrayed as quintessentially American, and for very good reasons. Not only did the major pragmatists live and work in the US. Their philosophical works emerged in response to distinctly American problems and concerns; they expressed distinctly American sentiments, hopes and anxieties. This is not to say that pragmatism is solely an American enterprise. Some European philosophers of the nineteenth century, like Henri Bergson and Friedrich Nietzsche, developed views which were remarkably close to those of pragmatism, as did the Oxford-based philosopher F.C.S. Schiller at the beginning of the twentieth century. Some of the older generation of American pragmatists studied in Europe, had regular intellectual exchanges with European intellectuals and were very much indebted to them. More recent exponents of pragmatist philosophy, like Rorty and Bernstein,

1   I thank Alan Shipman and Bruno Frère for reading this text and commenting on it. This chapter has been previously published as: Baert, P. 2011. Neo-Pragmatism and phenomenology: A proposal. *European Journal of Pragmatism and American Philosophy*, 3(2), 24–40.

engaged with and saw affinities with a number of Continental European authors who were considered seriously out of line within the analytical tradition. The multiplicity of influences is not surprising, given that American pragmatism has always portrayed itself as non-doctrinaire, open and receptive to new ideas, in contrast with the boundary-consciousness of analytical philosophy and its general disdain towards much written in the German and French tradition.

If American pragmatism has been shown to be open to European philosophy, the latter has been less receptive towards the former. There are notable exceptions like Jürgen Habermas (1981a, 1981b, 1994[1968]), whose critique of positivism and theory of communicative action drew on Peirce and the pragmatist tradition. All too often, however, pragmatism has been discarded as a parochial endeavour, too deeply ingrained in American society and its problems to appeal to a broader philosophical audience. Underlying my contribution is the conviction that this picture of pragmatism is deeply misleading. By integrating American neo-pragmatism and phenomenology, I will demonstrate not only the bearing of pragmatism on contemporary philosophy of social science, but also the fruitfulness of a continued dialog between the two traditions which on the surface look so different.

Although the argument which I will develop here is inspired by pragmatist philosophy, notably by Bernstein and Rorty's neo-pragmatism, this is not to say that either of them would endorse the views that I develop, let alone express them precisely in the way in which I do. Although generally sympathetic to their outlook, the problems addressed in this chapter and the questions asked are quite different from those of the neo-pragmatists, and the argument elaborated stands very much on its own. This chapter consists of six parts. The first section discusses which components of pragmatist philosophy are central to my proposal for the philosophy of social science, and the second section demonstrates how my perspective differs from the two approaches that dominate the philosophy of social science and social research. The third section explores the relationship between my agenda and Sartre's ontology, in particular his distinction between being-in-itself and being-for-itself. The fourth section explains how my approach draws on Levinas' conceptualization of otherness, and the fifth shows how my pragmatist-inspired proposal ties in with Gadamer's dialogical notion of understanding. Finally, this chapter shows the contemporary relevance of my proposal by focusing on the significance of social research for society.

Pragmatism and Pragmatisms

Before we proceed further, it is important to gain clarity as to the meaning of 'pragmatism' and a 'pragmatist agenda' as opposed to the employment of the term in everyday language. People often equate 'pragmatism' with a 'pragmatic' attitude, according to which action ought not to be guided by a priori principles but primarily by an assessment of the actual constraints and opportunities of a given context. In foreign policy, the label 'pragmatism' refers precisely to this non-ideological stance, whereby political actors routinely seek to gauge and take advantage of what comes their way. Likewise, when social scientists label research as 'pragmatist', sometimes they mean that it does not follow rigid methodological principles and instead exhibits an eclectic or opportunistic choice and application of method. In those circumstances, I prefer to term this a 'pragmatic' attitude to distinguish it from the 'pragmatist' argument developed here. So a pragmatic stance implies that the choice of theories or techniques depends on the particular topic of investigation or situation at hand rather than on a well-articulated philosophical or theoretical position.

My argument for a pragmatist stance has little in common with the methodological opportunism that characterises a pragmatic attitude. Firstly, I am not arguing that social researchers should pick and choose the theoretical framework or technique that somehow 'fits' or 'corresponds' best to the data or that seems opportune given the circumstances. I am actually sceptical of this view, not least because it draws on a problematic metaphor of vision as if social research is meant to mirror the external social world as accurately as possible (of which more in section two). Secondly, whilst a pragmatic attitude questions the usefulness of *any* philosophical account for social research, pragmatism questions the value of *some* philosophical debates, in particular about essences or ontology, and it also doubts the merit of *some* philosophical views, for instance, foundationalism. Pragmatism is sceptical of intellectual disputes if taking one or another position has no practical consequences for anyone (James 1907). For pragmatists, questions about inner essences or ontology are such scholastic enterprises because answering them in one way or another makes no practical difference.

What is the common ground which pragmatist philosophers share? What distinguishes the pragmatist outlook from those of other philosophical traditions? And which of the pragmatists' ideas have influenced my own agenda for the philosophy of the social sciences? To identify which ideas are shared by pragmatists is not a *sinecure* because pragmatism was, and still is, a heterogeneous entity. From the beginning, pragmatism entailed competing branches and antithetical positions, even to the extent that Charles Peirce, who coined the term, later distanced himself from 'pragmatism' because he felt that some of the beliefs carried under this banner were so alien to his. It is ironic that some philosophers, whom we now regard as iconic figures of the pragmatist movement, occasionally invoked other labels to refer to themselves, with Peirce's 'pragmaticism' and Dewey's 'instrumentalism' being particularly poignant examples. More recently, Richard Bernstein, Donald Davidson, Nelson Goodman, Hilary Putnam and Richard Rorty have taken pragmatism into uncharted territories (such as literary criticism and critical theory). This has led commentators to question whether some of those contemporary developments can be as easily reconciled with earlier forms of pragmatism as the likes of Rorty would have us believe.

Nevertheless, it would be a mistake to infer from this that pragmatists have little in common. Most pragmatist philosophers – old and new – share a number of key ideas, which makes it possible to talk about a pragmatist movement. It is particularly important to illustrate a number of these ideas here because they underscore my perspective on the philosophy of the social sciences. To start with, few commentators mention the humanist tendencies of pragmatism, which is surprising given how pervasive humanism is amongst classical and contemporary pragmatists and how essential it is to their intellectual project. William James (1911: 121–35), John Dewey (1994) and F.C.S. Schiller (1903, 1907) occasionally used the term to contextualise their own work, though they attributed different meanings to it. By humanism I refer to a particular perspective according to which cognitive, ethical and aesthetic claims, including claims about those claims, are intertwined with human projects and are predominantly human creations. Not only ought those claims to be judged on their practical contribution to society, they are also social and cultural in nature, often entailing the cooperation of many individuals and drawing on a complex web of symbols and cultural codes. The social and cultural dimension of those claims has, in turn, a number of repercussions, of which the rejection of both foundationalism and objective knowledge are particularly important.

By foundationalism one refers to the belief that philosophy can establish a-temporal, universal foundations that secure aesthetic, ethical or cognitive claims. Historically, a significant number of philosophers conceived of their work as primarily a foundational enterprise. To be foundational in this sense, philosophy ought to be able to step outside history – outside culture or language – so as to adopt a 'neutral' position from which the right kind of prescriptions can be made. Most pragmatists take an anti-foundationalist stance. They believe that philosophical reflection cannot achieve this position of neutrality because it is, like other intellectual accomplishments, a *human* activity; and as a human activity, a *social* activity; and as a social activity, a *situated* activity (see, for instance, Peirce 1877, 1878; Dewey 1938; Rorty 1982: xiiff; Bernstein 1991: 326ff.). This means that philosophical knowledge, like any other kind of knowledge, is always partial: it takes place from a certain vantage point. Pragmatists call for humility amongst philosophers, because, no matter what the amount of cleaning work they do, philosophy can never remove those human stains. As such, it cannot obtain the neutral stance which foundationalism requires.

A similar argument applies to other forms of knowledge, including scientific knowledge (Dewey 1929; James 1907). Scientific knowledge, too, is situated, partial, enacted from a particular viewpoint. Logical positivists spent a great deal of effort showing that scientific knowledge is superior to other forms of knowledge because it supposedly meets stringent criteria of objectivity. In this context, one talks about objective knowledge if it is not affected significantly by the attitudes and values of those who obtain this knowledge. In contrast, pragmatists insist that scientific knowledge is an intervention in the world and that, as an intervention, it is necessarily shaped by the interests or focus of the researchers involved. This does not mean that knowledge is necessarily always subjective, if by subjective we mean that it fails to represent the external world accurately. In fact, pragmatists avoid using the label 'subjective' altogether; firstly, because it implies the possibility of objective knowledge in the way in which logical positivism postulated it; and secondly, because it mistakenly assumes that knowledge has something to do with the copying of the external world.

Descartes' method supposedly provided philosophical foundations that ensure infallible knowledge. In contrast, the pragmatist world is indicative of what Hilary Putnam called the 'democratization of inquiry': devoid of foundations, people are encouraged to re-assess their views in the light of new empirical evidence (Putnam 2004). Various pragmatists might interpret this fallibilism differently. For the older generation of pragmatists, like Peirce, Dewey and Mead, scientific conjectures are empirically tested and, if necessary, replaced by superior scientific conjectures. It is the confrontation with new empirical phenomena that precipitates doubt, which only subsides once the old theory has been adjusted. Neo-pragmatists are less concerned with scientific discovery and change. They are more interested in how communities can adopt new vocabularies, re-describing themselves in the light of the new information provided. Rich, vital cultures are confident enough to exhibit openness towards uncomfortable experiences. As such, they are well-equipped to re-describe and reinvent themselves. However, in both cases, anti-foundationalism goes hand in hand with a genuine fallibilist attitude whereby people are willing to question entrenched beliefs and replace them with more useful ones.

I already hinted earlier at the pragmatist rejection of the mirror view of knowledge (see, for instance, James 1907; Dewey 1929; Rorty 1980, 1999: 47–71). This mirror view conceives of knowledge in terms of passive and accurate recording of the essence of the external world. In this view, the external world is taken to be independent of human experience, waiting to be discovered. This pictorial view has its intellectual origins in the Platonic perspective on knowledge. Plato took knowledge as passive contemplation as opposed to active involvement; only the philosophers' contemplation would allow proper and unmediated access to the real world. The mirror view is widespread both in philosophical and scientific circles, and it assumes an opposition between theory and knowledge on the one hand, and practice and action on the other. Knowledge is taken to be passive and instantaneous, whereas action is, by definition, active and proceeds through time. One of the upshots of this view is that knowledge should no longer be judged on the basis of its isomorphic relationship to the external realm, but on the basis of what kind of contribution it makes to our world. For too long, the dualism between theory and practice and its attendant preoccupation with accurate representation has led Western philosophers to ignore the practical difference knowledge can make. Pragmatism breaks with this dualism and takes seriously the notion of scientific engagement.

Pragmatist-Inspired Philosophy of Social Science

Pragmatism, as outlined above, has significant repercussions for the philosophy of the social sciences. The philosophy of social science is a meta-theoretical enterprise which reflects on the nature and workings of social research, often leading to recommendations about which methodology or theory should be used. My pragmatist-inspired perspective on the philosophy of social science draws on the insights illustrated in the previous section and on the integration of pragmatism and continental philosophy (infra). This perspective, centerd around the notion of self-understanding, is diametrically opposed to two perspectives which have dominated the mainstream of the philosophy of social science, and which I call 'representationalism' and 'methodological naturalism'. In what follows I describe and criticise these two perspectives, and this will allow me to discuss in more detail the contours of my perspective.

To start with, 'representationalism' is a widespread position in meta-theoretical reflections on the social sciences, though more implicit than overtly defended or propagated. Representationalists presuppose that social research aims to map or depict the social world as accurately and completely as possible, with social theory providing the necessary building blocks for this social cartography. Empirical research is regarded as fruitful if the theory used is shown to be eminently applicable and to allow for the social cartography to take place effectively. Amongst those who adhere to this philosophical outlook are structuralists, structuration theorists and critical realists, although most do so implicitly rather than defending it explicitly. The problems with representationalism are twofold: one referring to the mechanical and repetitive nature of the research conducted under its banner, and the other referring to its flawed notion of knowledge. Firstly, it makes for repetitive and uninspiring research, whereby a particular theoretical framework, to which a group of researchers is committed, is habitually applied to new settings, and thereby continually used and reproduced. In this social cartography model, empirical research reinforces the theory that is used, rather than checking its validity. As empirical research is no longer seen as a testing device but as providing instantiations of a given theory (and so yielding yet further evidence that the theory 'fits' various situations), the possibility of theoretical innovation is very limited and operates only within the contours set by the theory. Secondly, representationalists assume what John Dewey facetiously called the 'spectator theory of knowledge' according to which knowledge mysteriously captures the inner essence of the external world (Dewey 1929). As seen in the previous section, the spectator theory of knowledge is problematic, relying as it does on a passive notion of knowledge acquisition as if it is a flaccid mirroring of the outer world (Rorty 1980; 1999: xvi–xxxii, 23–46). Also, it fails to grasp the temporal dimension of knowledge acquisition, the extent to which it is the outcome of a process rather than an instantaneous occurrence. In this context, it is worth invoking Dewey's distinction between 'knowledge' and 'experience': whereas the latter alludes to a passive and immediate sensation of the outer world, the former refers to the outcome of an active process of reflection (Dewey 1910, 1929).

The spectator theory of knowledge erroneously conflates the immediacy and passivity that is characteristic of experience with that of knowledge, thereby promoting a flawed notion of 'immediate knowledge'. More generally, influenced by Darwinism, the early generation of pragmatists already conceived of knowledge in terms of process and action, insisting that knowledge is one of the tools people use to adjust, cope and interact with their external surroundings (Mead 1936, 1938). While from an evolutionary point of view, the intricate link between knowledge, process and action is imminently plausible, it is more difficult to see how, through time, people would have managed to develop knowledge that represents the world as it really is. Similar to Gadamer, for whom any act of description or making sense of the external world draws on a variety of presuppositions which give the representation direction and shape, pragmatists are committed to a holistic perspective according to which so-called statements of fact always tie in with theoretical presuppositions.

Moving to the second meta-theoretical perspective, a significant number of philosophers of social science are committed 'methodological naturalists', searching for a unifying scientific method which would be applicable to both the natural and social sciences. Within the discipline of philosophy, falsificationists and critical realists subscribe to methodological naturalism, whereas in the social sciences diverse research programs, ranging from rational choice theory to Durkheim-inspired structural analysis, accept this philosophical position albeit often implicitly rather than discursively formulated. Methodological naturalism should not be confused with 'ontological naturalism', which assumes that the social and the natural sciences are comprised of the same substance. Methodological naturalism assumes that a distinctive method underlies most, if not all, successful scientific activities, and that philosophical reflection can show why this method is so superior to others. This means that methodological naturalists hold two distinct, though related views, one being philosophical and the other historical. On the one hand, they are wedded to a foundationalist outlook which supposedly captures the essence of science – that which distinguishes it from lesser forms of knowledge acquisition like religion, ideology or pseudo-science. On the other hand, they hold a particular historical view according to which the natural sciences have employed this successful methodological strategy for quite a while whereas the social sciences, being too close to their subject matter, have consistently failed to do so. Unsurprisingly, naturalist philosophers of social sciences often make recommendations for social research, urging it to grow up and emulate the 'mature science' which can be found in the departments of physics and chemistry.

As indicated in the earlier section, pragmatists tend to question the virtues of foundationalist reasoning in general, and in this case the empirical studies of science seem to confirm this scepticism. Contrary to the naturalist agenda, studies in the history and in sociology of science show that the closer we look at the actual workings of scientists, the less support emerges for a unifying methodology within the natural sciences, let alone across the natural and social sciences (e.g. Latour and Woolgar 1979). There is a growing awareness that scientific research does not fit neat, objectivist criteria, that various disciplines operate quite differently, and that within each discipline there are national and local traditions which culminate in distinct methodological practices to such an extent that it is no longer warranted to talk about a unifying method.

Whereas naturalist philosophies of social science take for granted that social research is primarily an explanatory (and possibly predictive) endeavour, a pragmatist-inspired perspective explores the intricate relationship between method and cognitive interests and refuses to take for granted that explanation and prediction are the only legitimate cognitive interests (see also Rorty 1982: 191–210). Besides explanation and prediction, pragmatists also consider other cognitive interests to be integral to the social sciences, amongst which are meaningful understanding, social critique and emancipation, and (importantly for my argument) self-understanding (Baert 2005: 146–69). Whereas classical pragmatists focused on the problem-solving qualities of science, my neo-pragmatist perspective, influenced by Rorty's appropriation of the German notion of *Bildung* or self-edification, underscores the importance of the notion of self-understanding. This concept refers to the process by which knowledge can help groups of people re-describe, re-evaluate and reconceptualise themselves. Major breakthroughs in science have often been accompanied by substantial changes in the way in which people conceptualized themselves. In some cases, such as with Darwinism, this even led to a radical rethinking of the position of humanity as a whole.

Self-understanding occupies a particularly central place in the humanities and the social sciences, serving as they do to encourage groups of people to rethink who they are in the face of a confrontation with other forms of meaningful activity. This explains why some commentators go as far as arguing that the emergence of sociology or the social sciences is itself a sign of increasing collective self-knowledge under conditions of modernity (Wagner 1994). Crucially, when academics in the humanities and social sciences are asked to list the intellectual milestones of their discipline, they tend to select works which bring about this *Gestalt*-switch. Whereas self-understanding might be an interesting corollary of significant transformations in the natural sciences, the case of the humanities and social sciences is quite different as self-understanding is absolutely integral to what makes for a substantial work in this area of the academy. Key contributions to social research might obtain other cognitive interests – for instance, they might exhibit strong explanatory or predictive power – but ultimately, I argue, self-understanding remains the key criterion by which the significance of a piece of research will be judged (Baert 2007). Self-understanding does not imply that people necessarily agree on how to reconceptualise themselves in the light of a new or established framework, and indeed there is often substantial disagreement on this score. But whether or not there is agreement, a significant contribution in the humanities and the social sciences forces individuals to reconsider some of their presuppositions about themselves in the face of the new narrative presented.

In what follows, I discuss particular aspects of the work of Jean-Paul Sartre, Emmanuel Levinas and Hans-Georg Gadamer. By doing so, I will demonstrate that a dialog between neo-pragmatism and European phenomenology is possible. More importantly, this fruitful dialog leads to an identification of the key features of a method (and an ethos) of social research which revolves around the idea of self-understanding and which bears more promise for the social sciences than the current fixation on representationalism and methodological naturalism.

While Sartre, Levinas and Gadamer all engage with Husserl's phenomenology, each takes it in a direction different from Husserl's that is convergent with mine. What follows is not an attempt to rediscover or resuscitate Husserl's philosophy (which in crucial respects is diametrically opposed to my neo-pragmatist argument), but to show how subsequent developments within phenomenology help enrich a neo-pragmatist perspective on the philosophy of the social sciences. There is, however, one important link between my argument and Husserl's which is worth mentioning at this stage. For Husserl, philosophy is not merely an intellectual enterprise without external value; it is also a means for obtaining self-knowledge or self-discovery. Philosophy enables the individual to create a useful distance towards him- or herself and to conceptualise the self differently. This, so Husserl argued, would eventually help to create a form of freedom. The neo-pragmatist argument, which I have been developing, takes equally seriously this notion of self-knowledge and recognises the important role philosophy may play in achieving it. There are differences, though, between the neo-pragmatist use of self-knowledge and that of Husserl. Essential to my argument is that the social sciences – not philosophy – are particularly well-placed for achieving it. Also different from Husserl's individualist reading is the neo-pragmatist argument that self-knowledge is a collective achievement; it is something shared by members of a community.

Sartre and Epistemological Authenticity

My neo-pragmatist philosophy of the social sciences shows striking affinities with the existentialist phenomenology as it was developed by Martin Heidegger and Jean-Paul Sartre. Both Heidegger and Sartre engage critically with Husserl's writings and take phenomenology in a new direction, which I would argue is closer to pragmatist philosophy. Firstly, like pragmatists, existentialist phenomenologists recognise the quintessentially human nature of cognitive, ethical and aesthetic claims. This position leads, amongst other things, to the questioning of both the possibility of objectivity and of the viability of epistemology, because it is no longer held possible for philosophers and scientists to decipher a neutral algorithm that would allow them to escape history and culture. Secondly, like pragmatists, existential phenomenologists reject the opposition or dualism between the subject and an independent external world. As people's knowledge is seen as inevitably embedded in and practically engaged with the world, the opposition between the knower and known, assumed by both realism and idealism, becomes a mere artificial intellectual construct. Thirdly, both philosophical strands – pragmatism and existential phenomenology – reject the spectator theory of knowledge according to which knowledge mirrors or captures the external world. Indeed existentialist phenomenologists distanced themselves from Husserl whose notion of the transcendental ego – a disembodied, detached ego – was indicative of the way in which he was still wedded to a spectator theory of knowledge. In contrast with the spectator theory that conceives of objects as *vorhanden* ('present-at-hand', detached), existentialists emphasise that people encounter objects first and foremost as *zuhanden* ('ready-to-hand', like a tool). Pragmatists and existentialists argue that the form of reflexive intelligence, which is characteristic of *vorhanden*, only arises when people are confronted with unexpected experiences. Fourthly, whereas Husserl's phenomenology conceives of meaning in terms of essences and senses of words, existentialist phenomenology resembles pragmatism in promoting a holistic picture and in demonstrating the intricate link between understanding and purposive action. So in contrast with Husserl, pragmatists and existentialists subscribe to Wittgenstein's later views about meaning and how it is embedded in larger systems or 'forms of life'.

In clarifying the connections between the neo-pragmatist agenda and existentialist phenomenology, Sartre's *L'être et le néant* (1943) and *L'existentialisme est un humanisme* (1996) are particularly instructive. Sartre's anti-essentialism manifests itself in his refusal to accept that human beings – *any* human being, as a matter of fact – can be defined in terms of a set of fixed characteristics. However subtle a description of an individual, he or she is always able to overcome this account and prove otherwise through his or her actions. Ultimately, people are nothing but the sum of their actions, so it is a fallacy, for instance, to say that a person who acted cowardly all his life was deep down truly courageous (Sartre 1996: 26–7, 29–30). People might adopt strategies to deny their intrinsic freedom, and there are indeed various instances of this bad faith, but a genuinely full life requires that one acknowledges the freedom which one has and makes choices whilst ensuring that others are free as well. Freedom is also at the heart of Sartre's distinction between being-in-itself and being-for-itself. Whereas being-in-itself exists independent of consciousness and can therefore only be what it is, being-for-itself refers to the fluid aspect of human existence. It was Hegel who initially coined the term 'being-for-itself' to refer to the uniquely self-conscious dimension of human being, the extent to which individuals are, unlike objects, able to reflect on the conditions of their existence and to act accordingly. Likewise, Sartre's notion of being-for-itself centers round the reflexive component of human existence, capturing as it does the ability of human beings to transcend the most structurally constraining of circumstances and ultimately their capacity to exercise genuine freedom even in the face of severe adversity (Sartre 1943: 109–41).

Sartre focused on individuals and individual decisions but his arguments can be translated into a social vocabulary, a move which helps to further clarify the neo-pragmatist proposal which I have been advocating. Just as Sartre argued that individuals have the freedom to define themselves and to deny the categories that are imposed on them, a given social setting does not necessitate a specific account, descriptions or explanation. Just like individuals who, by virtue of their self-consciousness, escape fixed descriptions, any social setting can be re-described and rearticulated ad infinitum and there is no a priori reason to rule out any of those accounts on epistemological grounds. Both representationalists and naturalists are mistaken in searching for a final vocabulary that would mysteriously 'fit' a given social situation because the epistemological or theoretical justifications provided have been shown to be flawed. For social researchers to search for such a final vocabulary is basically to act in what Sartre would call bad faith

(Sartre 1943: 81–106): that is, for them to deny their own undeniable freedom to present new, exciting narratives, to string together the kind of storylines which makes us look at old themes in novel, interesting ways (see also Rorty 1980: 365–79). There are various academic, institutional forces that entice social researchers to deny their own freedom, be it the urge for 'scientific' recognition or the loyalties to established academic clans and their patriarchs. Firstly, whether positivist or falsificationist, researchers often allude to 'science' or 'scientific procedures' to justify the methodological decisions they make. However, as I have pointed out in the above and elsewhere, references to '*the* scientific method' are always problematic given the methodological diversity between scientific disciplines and even within them. Secondly, institutionalized loyalties towards an intellectual school (or towards a mentor) risk culminating in repetitive practice whereby empirical research is seen simply as an instantiation of the theoretical framework or general orientation that is being adopted. It is difficult to break those loyalties given the power relations involved and the extent to which they are tied in with academic job prospects and career progression.

In a nutshell, my argument for a neo-pragmatist perspective, with its acknowledgement that there is no neutral algorithm that will help us decide which theories or methods to adopt, calls on researchers to escape those epistemological and institutional constraints and to acknowledge the freedom to construct innovative narratives and help communities redefine themselves. Following on from Sartre's notion of 'authenticity' (as the mirror image of bad faith) (Sartre 1943: 70–71), what I am proposing could be described as 'epistemological authenticity', by which I mean that researchers ought to cast off epistemological shackles, recognising their intellectual ability to shatter established storylines and their moral responsibility to do so.

Levinas and the Encounter with the Other

My argument for a pragmatist-inspired philosophy centers on the idea of self-understanding, which ties in with Emmanuel Levinas' arguments put forward in his *Théorie de l'intuition dans la phénoménologie de Husserl* (1970[1930]), *Le temps et l'autre* (1991[1947]), *Autrement qu'être ou au-delà de l'essence* (1974) and in particular in his magnum opus *Totalité et infini* (1961). Compared to other French philosophers referred to as operating neatly within the phenomenological tradition, like Maurice Merleau-Ponty, Paul Ricoeur or Jean-Luc Marion, Levinas occupies such a distinctive position and his central claims are so strongly opposed to Husserl's philosophy that it is difficult to justify labelling his work as unambiguously phenomenological. Influenced by Franz Rosenzweig and Martin Buber, Levinas' divergence from Husserl and other phenomenologists stems from their failure to recognise the distinctiveness and irreducibility of the Other, and Levinas tries to show the implications of that failure for philosophy. From his early writings onwards, Levinas shows interest in the notion of escape, which refers to the positive need of the individual to avoid the facticity of existence and in particular to break with the sheer individual experience of being oneself. From the point of view of the later Levinas, the individual can only achieve this distantiation towards the self by engaging properly with alterity. In this regard, Levinas' position heralds those of Edward Said and Homi Bhabha developed half a century later. They denounce a large proportion of Western thought and literary criticism for not engaging sufficiently with different cultures and for imposing their own dichotomies on what is by all accounts a radically different cultural landscape.

For Levinas, Western philosophy, and indeed Western thought in general, promotes a distinctive and ultimately problematic relationship between the Same (or the self or the subject) and the Other, and phenomenology is no exception in this regard. In this dominant view, otherness might provisionally appear as differentiated from sameness, but this is only a temporary phase as the former can always be reinterpreted in terms of the latter and be assimilated to it. The metaphor of light plays an important role in this philosophical tradition: once otherness is illuminated, it loses its 'alterity' (Levinas 1978: 74ff.). Hence, there is an inability on the part of Western thought to experience, engage with and learn from something that is truly different from itself.

Husserl's phenomenology is a case in point, arguing as he does that any encounter with the external world takes place through acts of meaning bestowed by the subject onto it. The subject can only encounter otherness in so far as it is articulated and rearticulated in terms of that which is familiar to the subject, but by doing so, the very nature of otherness is negated (Levinas 1967, 1970). In contrast, Levinas wants to safeguard the unfamiliarity of the Other against the invasions of the Same, and like Heidegger, he finds it necessary to create a new terminology – a new language, one might say – to bring this project to fruition. Rather than attempting to gain knowledge about the Other so as to submit it to the logic of sameness, Levinas' project entails that otherness is, by definition, outside the grasp of the self. Otherness is not to be understood simply as that which is 'other than me'. To do so would be to downgrade it to something that is relative to me or that I can articulate in terms of my vocabulary. For Levinas, the Other remains absolutely external to me and, by virtue of its radical difference, resists conceptualization and intelligibility (Levinas 1961, 1967).

As many commentators have pointed out, a significant part of Levinas' work consists of an ethical shift in existential phenomenology, exploring as he does the extent to which the confrontation with others imposes a variety of obligations on the individual. However, for my purposes, Levinas' attention to the relationship between alterity and dialog is more important. While Levinas wants to hold onto Husserl's position that intentionality represents the world through the mediation of consciousness, he is very keen to emphasise that the encounter with the external world makes for a dynamic exchange whereby the subject engages with and is affected by the Other. Comparably to Gadamer's dialogical notion of understanding, Levinas sees the confrontation with alterity also as an opportunity for the self to reassert, re-evaluate and redefine itself. In the face of otherness, the self can undergo change while still retaining its sameness (Levinas 1961: 5–10).

Despite his notoriously nebulous language and his lack of interest in the status and objectives of contemporary social research, Levinas' treatment of the complex relationship between self and alterity is relevant here because of its substantial bearing for a pragmatist-inspired philosophy of social science. Few social researchers and indeed even fewer philosophers of social science show a genuine interest in the concept of otherness, let alone incorporate it into their writings. In their particular endeavours to obtain reliable knowledge of the social world, neither the representationalist nor the naturalist perspective on the social sciences engages properly with otherness. Wedded to a spectator theory of knowledge, the social cartography model treats the encounter with otherness in a way that reinforces the theoretical framework in operation, thereby replicating familiar theories and undoing the unfamiliarity of empirical experiences. Likewise, naturalists tend to use metaphors and analogies with well-known phenomena to explain and possibly predict new, unfamiliar phenomena, thereby again failing to engage properly with, and learn from, what is being studied. In both cases, the methodology is used as a strategic weapon to negate a genuine encounter with different forms of life – to ensure, in other words, that no real surprises are in store. The pragmatist-inspired philosophical project, on the other hand, conceives of the encountering of different forms of life as an enormous opportunity to re-describe, re-assess, and re-create ourselves (Rorty 1999: 87–8). In Levinasian parlance, one of the central tenets of my proposal is to conceive of social research as a proper engagement with otherness, refusing to reduce alterity to sameness. The key to this research program is a dialogical model, which cuts right across the traditional dichotomy between the knower and the known. For this, it proves particular useful to draw on Gadamer's account of understanding, which is more developed than Levinas'.

Gadamer and the Pursuit of Self-Understanding

Whereas Levinas' thought is embedded in the phenomenological tradition, Gadamer's central arguments, as developed in *Wahrheit und Methode* (1975), are often seen as entrenched in hermeneutics. It is indeed true that Gadamer situates himself very much in relation to the 'romantic hermeneutics' of Wilhelm Dilthey and other nineteenth-century authors. However, Husserl and Heidegger's influences loom large, especially where Gadamer decides to deviate from nineteenth-century hermeneutic authors. Gadamer shares Dilthey's critique of positivist attempts to model the *Geisteswissenschaften* onto the natural sciences, but disagrees with Dilthey's project to put the social and historical sciences on as secure, objective a footing as the natural sciences (Gadamer 1975: 162–250). Central to Gadamer's position is Husserl and Heidegger's argument that the objective natural sciences can only emerge within a historically engraved 'life-world'. Parallel to my own rejection of naturalism, Gadamer argues that the standards of 'objectivity', which are associated with the natural sciences, ought not to be seen as norms for knowledge *tout court* because those 'scientific' yardsticks, like any criteria, have developed within a particular tradition. Similarly to the pragmatist call for methodological diversity, Gadamer insists that to treat 'scientific' criteria of 'objectivity' as *the* standards of knowledge is to neglect other historically situated norms and criteria. In opposition to the Cartesian preoccupation with a method of objective understanding, Gadamer's 'philosophical hermeneutics' explores the conditions of possibility of understanding. This philosophical project puts him on a collision course with the Enlightenment orthodoxy which conceives of tradition and prejudice (*Vorurteil*) as impediments to proper understanding. For Gadamer, nothing could be further from the truth because understanding cannot take place without tradition and prejudice. Resembling the pragmatist critique of the Enlightenment search for a neutral algorithm for knowledge (Rorty 1999: xii–xxxii), Gadamer argues that any appeal to reason and method also necessarily draws on tradition and prejudice and thereby inevitably invokes what was meant to be eradicated. However, if Gadamer claims that tradition and prejudice are a *sine qua non* for understanding, he does not mean that understanding is an individual or arbitrary accomplishment. Mirroring the pragmatist insistence on the social and historical nature of knowledge claims, Gadamer treats tradition as a shared experience, rooted in and developed within a long historical trajectory. Gadamer coins the term 'effective history' (*Wirkungsgeschichte*) to refer to the way in which tradition and its history affects us even when we try to shed their power (Gadamer 1975: 250–360).

It would be easy to misinterpret Gadamer or to infer the wrong conclusions from his work. From Gadamer's assertion that understanding is always socially and historically constituted, we should not infer that researchers, like other individuals, have a philosophical licence simply to impose their categories and presuppositions on what they study. We have seen earlier how the social cartography model adopts this erroneous view of research, projecting as it does theoretical categories onto the empirical material, and thereby replicating and reinforcing them. As I have indicated in the above, the upshot of this representational perspective is a peculiar form of theoretical ossification whereby empirical material is devalued and treated as simply an instantiation of the theoretical framework to which the research is wedded. In contrast, Gadamer's notion of genuine understanding is quite different because it ties in with what I called self-understanding: that is with the recognition of one's own fallibility and a willingness to learn and see things differently. Just like an authentic dialog whereby participants are treated on an equal footing and are prepared to find out about other points of view, genuine understanding or *Verständigung* involves openness towards the unfamiliar and a willingness to learn from it in the hope of reaching an agreement.

In a move which is particularly relevant to my argument about the significance of self-knowledge in social research, Gadamer contends that, in the case of genuine understanding, people are willing to recognise the validity and coherence of what is being studied to such an extent that this recognition might undermine some of their own presuppositions. In Gadamer's terminology, understanding eventually leads to 'self-formation' or *Bildung*, the process by which individuals and communities take on a larger perspective and realise the fallibility or parochial nature of beliefs they have hitherto cherished. Eventually, self-formation does not simply imply that people obtain knowledge of new forms of life but also that they acquire deftness in obtaining that type of knowledge. The *gebildete* culture is one in which people have acquired the ability to judge and discern (Gadamer 1975: 7–16, 77ff.).

Following on from Levinas' mission to preserve the distinctiveness of the Other against ongoing attempts to assimilate it to the familiar, Gadamer's dialogical perspective on understanding and his notion of *Bildung* tie in neatly with the concept of self-understanding that occupies such a central role in my pragmatist-inspired perspective. However, whereas Gadamer considers the relationship between understanding and self-understanding in ontological terms, my pragmatist-inspired perspective wants to exploit it *methodologically*. The question, then, is no longer whether understanding necessarily entails an element of self-understanding, but how to use this notion of self-understanding as a criterion to evaluate and judge social research, and, conversely, which methodological strategies can be conceived to bring about this reflexive stance. As shown elsewhere, genealogical historians, post-processual archaeologists and the exponents of the critical turn in anthropology have been effective in pursuing self-understanding in this sense (Baert 2005: 157–65). However, it is worth emphasising they have done so within the specific intellectual climate in which they were writing, and that there is no guarantee that their methodological orientations will remain equally successful in the future or in a different context. So to appeal for a methodological reading of the dialogical notion of understanding is not to invoke yet another elusive neutral algorithm, but it is to be sensitive to the cultural importance of self-knowledge and the central role the social sciences can play in this, and to reflect on the methodological strategies which in a given context are well suited for this purpose. The picture that emerges is one in which social research is seen as an encounter with otherness, potentially facilitating or encouraging a community to reflect on its presuppositions, including those that underlie the research. In contrast with traditional philosophy of social science that has little regard for self-edification, my appeal for a *gebildete* research revolves around the importance of the broadening of people's perspectives.

Social Research, Reflexivity and Societal Engagement

In contrast to their contemporaries in Vienna and Cambridge, classical pragmatists, like Dewey and Mead, wanted philosophy and the social sciences to engage with the social world, to make it a richer, more diverse and altogether more interesting place. Dewey's contributions to educational theory are a case in point, and so is the sociological research conducted by members of the Chicago School (see, for instance, Abbot 1999, Joas 1993). These examples show philosophy and the social sciences at their best, interacting with and learning from the external world, and attempting to give something back to the communities that are being studied. Since then the further institutionalization of academics within university establishments and the intense professionalization of the social sciences has led to quite a different set-up (see, for instance, Jacoby 1986). This shift has certainly not been altogether negative, bringing legitimacy and outside recognition, securing improved work conditions and setting rigorous standards of intellectual quality. However, in relation to the initial pragmatist ambitions about the relationship between knowledge and practice, those institutional transformations have meant that intellectual legitimacy and academic recognition have become stronger priorities than practical engagement. Whereas earlier sociologists addressed significant political and social concerns, the upshot of the structural changes is that social scientists increasingly address other social scientists and that their language and intellectual interests reflect and reinforce this narrowing of horizons.

Against this backdrop, my argument for a new way of thinking about social research, which centers on an integration of American neo-pragmatism and Continental philosophy, acquires an element of urgency. In contrast with the academic setting today, social research in pursuit of self-understanding encourages researchers to be sufficiently open to the unfamiliar, to take a broader perspective and reflect on the world we took for granted hitherto. This type of research is about expanding our imaginative canvas and practical reach, something to be achieved by learning from and reaching out to those beyond the safe contours of the academy.

My argument in particular shows affinities with Michael Burawoy's recent plea for a 'public sociology', which uses expert knowledge to promote debate with and amongst various non-academic publics, thereby responding and adjusting to their demands and ultimately providing 'dialog' and 'mutual education' (Burawoy 2004, 2005). Burawoy compares his notion of 'organic' public sociology with 'traditional' public sociology: whereas the latter addresses an amorphous, invisible and mainstream public, the former actively engages with a specific, visible and politically organized group of people. Both forms of public sociology can perfectly coexist and indeed feed into each other, but Burawoy argues particularly in favor of the organic version because its political mandate is better articulated, it has clearer direction and its practical pay-off is less ambiguous. Public sociology, he argues, is not only different from mainstream 'professional sociology' but also from 'policy sociology'. While policy sociology attempts to provide technical answers to questions provided by an external client, public sociology develops a 'dialogic relationship' between sociology and the public whereby the issues of each partner are brought to the attention of the other, and each adjusts or responds accordingly. Whereas both professional and policy sociology construct 'instrumental knowledge', public sociology shares with 'critical sociology' a preoccupation with 'reflexive knowledge' or 'dialog about ends'. However, public sociology should not be conflated with critical sociology. Whereas both professional and critical sociology target an academic audience, public sociology, like policy sociology, embarks on a dialog with non-academic publics about the 'normative foundations' of society.

While Burawoy's passionate argument for a more socially engaged sociology is appealing and indeed has obtained worldwide attention, he focuses mainly on the actual practical engagement of sociologists with their publics. Less attention is given to exploring the type of knowledge acquisition involved in the kind of reflexive sociology which he promotes. Following the distinction by the Frankfurt School between substantive and instrumental rationality, Burawoy differentiates reflexive sociology from policy sociology on the basis that it establishes goals and values rather than means. But this definition remains notoriously vague, especially given that what counts as a value in one context can be a means for acquiring a value in a different context. Meta-theoretical discussions about the future of the discipline of sociology, as the debate around public sociology certainly is, need to be accompanied by philosophical explorations of the methodological issues involved. Otherwise the arguments presented have a hollow ring to them and can easily be dismissed as mere statements of intent, devoid of any substance.

The pragmatist-inspired proposal, outlined here – with its rejection of foundationalism, naturalism and representationalism, its emphasis on self-understanding, and its exploration of the link between knowledge and action – provides the right philosophical backing to support and define the type of social scientific knowledge that engages with groups and communities outside the safe contours of the ivory tower. However, this is not to say that the Gadamerian dialogical model of knowledge, for which I have been arguing, is solely relevant for non-academic publics. Social research in the pursuit of self-understanding cuts right across Burawoy's distinction between critical and public sociology because the reflexivity that is built in affects presuppositions that are held within academic as well as non-academic communities.

This is particularly clear in the case of Zygmunt Bauman's *Modernity and the Holocaust* (1989) – a prime example of the type of research I have in mind. This not only invites a broader non-academic audience to rethink the nature of the atrocities during the Third Reich, but also challenges some of the presuppositions sociologists and philosophers hold about the value, the possibilities and the dangers of the transition towards modernity. Challenging the *Sonderweg* thesis and opposing the orthodox view that modernity and the Holocaust are antithetical, Bauman persuasively argues that key features of modernity – the 'garden' notion of the nation state, and a process of bureaucratization with its increasing instrumental rationality and decreasing sense of individual responsibility – were necessary conditions for the emergence of the Holocaust. By doing so, Bauman goes further than arguing against the popular conception that the atrocities committed during that period were somehow irrational outbursts or indicative of the fact that the project of modernity had not quite been accomplished. Crucially, his analysis also implies that sociologists ought to re-assess their views about the project of modernity itself, a reassessment which ultimately affects how they conceive of their own discipline, entrenched as it is in the Enlightenment vision. In short, this example indicates that, in practice, the rigid distinction between Burawoy's critical and public sociology may be less relevant than he assumes it is. This is because any substantial dialogical knowledge, of the kind I have been arguing for and which Bauman epitomises, will be relevant to both academic and non-academic communities.

Conclusion

This chapter has sought to demonstrate the fruitfulness of an ongoing dialog between American neo-pragmatism and Continental philosophy which, for far too long, have been regarded as addressing irreconcilable intellectual concerns. It has explored the affinities which exist between my own neo-pragmatist agenda in the field of philosophy of the social sciences, and the philosophical outlook developed by Sartre, Levinas and Gadamer. Rather than conceiving of social research as, primarily, an explanatory or predictive endeavour, I have shown that this neo-pragmatist view promotes social research in terms of an ongoing engagement with otherness, a process which ultimately contributes to the pursuit of richer forms of collective re-description. In this view, research takes a central role in the ability of communities to distance themselves from their hitherto unacknowledged presuppositions, to assume different points of view and, ultimately, to make a difference to the social world which those communities have helped to create and which they inhabit. This neo-pragmatist approach, I have argued, presents a philosophical basis for the reflexive knowledge entailed in both critical and public sociology.

One final issue needs to be addressed. As my neo-pragmatist perspective aims to contribute to the philosophy of the social sciences, the question inevitably arises which theories are well (or ill-) suited to bringing about the reflexivity which I have been advocating? From the above, it should be clear that my answer is that, unlike other philosophies of social science such as falsificationism or critical realism, this pragmatist-inspired proposal is neutral *vis-à-vis* theory choice in so far as it refuses to invoke external criteria – such as falsifiability, explanatory power or predictive success – to decide on the value of a given theory. Instead, it suggests that we should take into account the context of the dominant presuppositions of the discipline or indeed of a community at large before evaluating the theory under consideration because it is only against this background that such an evaluation can be achieved. Alfred Schutz's notion of 'stock of knowledge at hand' is particularly applicable here because it captures very well how, in their everyday life, people approach the social world in terms of 'familiarity and pre-acquaintanceship' (Schutz and Luckmann 1973). Just as everyday life is embedded in the *Lebenswelt* – a world of everyday life governed by the 'natural attitude' – social researchers take for granted a number of theoretical and metaphysical beliefs and methodological strategies.

It follows from the above that theories ought to be evaluated on the basis of how much of a *Gestalt*-switch they manage to bring about – how much they could bring researchers to rethink those hitherto deeply entrenched and often unacknowledged presuppositions. In opposition to the ritualistic hero-worship, which is so endemic in the social sciences today and which is tied in with the representational model of social researcher, the pragmatist-inspired perspective calls for less deference and bolder claims – an intellectual iconoclasm of sorts. The question should no longer be how we can apply the works of our intellectual heroes or preferred models (whatever they are) to the empirical data, but how we can learn from the encounter with the unfamiliar to challenge them and think differently.

References

Abbott, A. 1999. *Department and Discipline: Chicago School at One Hundred*. Chicago, IL: University of Chicago Press.

Baert, P. 2005. *Philosophy of the Social Sciences: Towards Pragmatism*. Cambridge: Polity Press.

Baert, P. 2006. Social theory and the social sciences, in *Handbook of Contemporary European Social Theory*, (ed.) G. Delanty. London: Routledge, 14–24.

Baert, P. 2007. Why study the social, in *Pragmatism and European Social Theory*, (ed.) P. Baert and B.S Turner. Oxford: Bardwell Press, 38–52.

Bauman, Z. 1989. *Modernity and the Holocaust*. Cambridge: Polity Press.

Bernstein, R.J. 1991. *The New Constellation: The Ethical-Political Horizons of Modernity/Postmodernity*. Cambridge: Polity.

Burawoy, M. 2004. Public sociologies: A symposium from Boston College. *Social Problems*, 51(1), 103–30.

Burawoy, M. 2005. 2004 Presidential address: For public sociology. *American Sociological Review*, 70(1), 4–28.

Dewey, J. 1910. *The Influence of Darwin on Philosophy*. New York: Henry Holt.

Dewey, J. 1929. *The Quest for Certainty*. New York: Henry Holt.

Dewey, J. 1938. *Logic: The Theory of Inquiry*. New York: Holt, Rinehart and Winston.

Dewey, J. 1994. *Religious Faith and Democratic Humanism*. New York: Columbia University Press.

Gadamer, H.G. 1975/1960. *Wahrheit und Methode: Grundzüge einer philosophischen Hermeneutik*, Tübingen: Mohr.

Habermas, J. 1994/1968. *Erkenntnis und Interesse*. Frankfurt am Main: Suhrkamp.

Habermas, J. 1981a. *Theorie des kommunikativen Handelns; Bd 1. Handlungsrationalität und gesellschaftliche Rationalisierung*. Frankfurt am Main: Suhrkamp.

Habermas, J. 1981b. *Theorie des kommunikativen Handelns; Bd 2. Zur Kritik der funktionalistischen Vernunft*. Frankfurt am Main: Suhrkamp.

Jacoby, R. 1986. *The Last Intellectuals: American Culture in the Age of the Academe*. New York: Noonday Press.

James, W. 1907. *Pragmatism, a New Name for Some Old Ways of Thinking: Popular Lectures on Philosophy*. London: Longmans, Green & Co.

James, W. 1911. *The Meaning of Truth*. New York: Longman Green.

Joas, H. 1993. *Pragmatism and Social Theory*. Chicago, IL: University of Chicago Press.

Latour, B. and Woolgar S. 1979. *Laboratory Life: The Social Construction of Scientific Facts*. London: Sage.

Levinas, E. 1961. *Totalité et infini; Essai sur l'extériorité*. Librairie général Française.

Levinas, E. 1967. *En découvrant l'existence avec Husserl et Heidegger*. Paris: Bril.

Levinas, E. 1974. *Autrement qu'être, ou, au-delà de l'essence*. La Haye: Martinus Nijhoff.

Levinas, E. 1978/1947. *De l'existence à l'existant*. Paris: Vrin.

Levinas, E. 1970/1930. *Théorie de l'intuition dans la phénoménoloie de Husserl*. Paris: Vrin.

Levinas, E. 1991/1947. *Le temps et l'autre*. Paris: Presses Universitaires de France.Peirce, C. 1877. The fixation of beliefs, *Popular Science Monthly*, 12, 1–15.

Mead, C.H. 1936. *Movements of Thought in the Nineteenth Century*. Chicago, IL: University of Chicago Press.

Mead, G.H. 1938. *The Philosophy of the Act*. Chicago, IL: University of Chicago Press.

Peirce, C. 1878. How to make our ideas clear, *Popular Science Monthly*, 12, 286–302.

Putnam, H. 2004. *The Collapse of the Fact/Value Dichotomy and Other Essays*. Cambridge, MA: Harvard University Press.

Rorty, R. 1980. *Philosophy and the Mirror of Nature*. Oxford: Blackwell.

Rorty, R. 1982. *Consequences of Pragmatism*. Hempel Hempstead: Harvester Wheatsheaf.

Rorty, R. 1999. *Philosophy and Social Hope*. Harmondsworth: Penguin.

Sartre, J-P. 1943. *L'être et le néant: Essai d'ontologie phénoménologique*. Paris: Gallimard.

Sartre, J-P. 1996. *L'existentialisme est un humanisme*. Paris: Gallimard.

Schiller, F.C.S. 1903. *Humanism: Philosophical Essays*. London: Macmillan.

Schiller, F.C.S. 1907. *Studies in Humanism*. London: Macmillan.

Schutz, A. and T. Luckmann 1973: *The Structures of the Life-World*. Chicago, IL: Northwestern University Press.

Wagner, P. 1994. *A Sociology of Modernity: Liberty and Discipline*. London: Routledge.

3 *The Economic Crisis and the Crisis in Economics: Pragmatism and the Ontological Turn*

PETER M. JACKSON

Introduction

The post-2008 global economic crisis has undoubtedly raised many questions about the current state of economic knowledge. Whilst economics has been transformed over the past 40 years from the earlier narrow set of interests of neoclassical economics to become more pluralistic; nevertheless, it remains trapped in an iron cage of assumptions about the nature of the socioeconomic reality that it seeks to explain. This is the view strongly held by Lawson (2003) who is a severe critic of modern economics and whose quest is to reorientate economic theory by reintroducing an examination of its ontological foundations. Without doing too much violence to Lawson's intricately woven and extensive thesis, his perspective can be summarized as follows. The social realm, of which economics is a part, is inherently an open system, which implies that event regularities over a long period of time are rare and that predictive statements of the kind 'if X then Y' are impossible. Near stable relationships can exist under specific circumstances at a specific time in history but they are subject to change in the long run. That is they are contingent upon a highly specific set of circumstances. For Lawson, research based upon closed system modelling is inappropriate if the objective is to gain insight into and understanding of social problems. Social structures are not reducible to individuals. There are internal relationships between individuals within society and institutions are structured processes of social interaction. Lawson favors retroduction (abduction) rather than deduction. This dialogical reasoning is based upon contrastive explanation. Observed contrasts are used to gain insight into the underlying mechanisms that explains their occurrence.

The argument presented in this chapter is that whilst there is not a perfect correspondence between Lawson's claims about the nature of social reality and those held by the American pragmatists; still, there is a close match. Lawson does not acknowledge this link. Whilst he makes a passing reference to Dewey he does not refer to the vast literature of the American pragmatists. Lawson is not alone amongst economists. American pragmatism does not feature in the literature of economics. Frank Knight in the 1920s and 1930s, and the early Herbert Simon in the 1950s, referred, usually in a critical fashion, to the work of Dewey and James, but since then neither notable economists nor economic philosophers and methodologists have made reference to the debates that were central to the American pragmatists. This chapter seeks to begin to rectify this deficit. Lying within the canon of American pragmatism is a powerful critique of the way in which economists today conceive social reality and hence the way in which they conduct their economic analysis. By bringing together the literatures of Lawson and the pragmatists the hope is that economists will take more seriously the institutions and mechanisms which generate the economic reality that is experienced and which shapes lives.

The Confused State of Economics

Over the past 40 years and more, there has been a growing groundswell of discontent about the way in which economics is practiced within the academy; the nature of the advice that is given to policy makers and the general status of the corpus of economic knowledge. This discontent transcends the use of elaborate mathematics in economics or the positivism of econometrics. It is much deeper and, moreover, the critique comes from some of the high priests of the subject. Take, for example, a comment made by Frank Hahn (1970), a leading edge economic theorist, who has made more significant contributions to the theoretical infrastructure of mathematical economics than most:

> it cannot be denied that there is something scandalous in the spectacle of so many people refining the analysis of economic states which they give no reason to suppose will ever, or have ever, come about. It is probably also dangerous. Equilibrium economics ... is easily convertible into an apologia for existing economic arrangements and it is frequently so converted. (1970: 1)

Wassily Leontieff, an economics Nobel laureate, writes:

> page after page of professional economic journals are filled with mathematical formulas leading the reader from sets of more or less plausible but entirely arbitrary assumptions to precisely stated but irrelevant theoretical conclusions. (1982: 104)

Ariel Rubenstein (1995), a world class game theorist, also writes:

> economic theory lacks a consensus as to its purpose and interpretation. Again and again, we find ourselves asking the question, 'where does it lead? ... economic theory has not delivered the goods ... the link between economic theory and practical problems ... is tenuous at best. (1995: 12)

The French economist, Edmond Malinvaud argues that:

> ... today much praise is given to building and solving models of disputable relevance: too little is given to good pieces of economics as long as they contain no mathematical model. (1997: 149–65)

Finally, Mark Blaug, a seasoned economic methodologist and historian of economic thought, believes that:

economics is sick. Economics has increasingly become an intellectual game played for its own sake and not for its practical consequences for understanding the economic world. Economists have converted the subject into a sort of social mathematics in which analytical rigor is everything and practical relevance is nothing. (1997: 4)

Economics is sick; it lacks relevance; it is devoid of realism; it is possibly dangerous and it is confused about its purpose. Nonetheless, economists in the academy can point to a number of successes. Economics provides an analytical framework that enables clarification of socioeconomics issues and helps to identify problems more clearly. That is not denied. What is, however, in question is whether that framework is itself too constraining by only framing particular questions at the exclusion of other significant features and dimensions of the social realm. Might it be that this framework has left too much out of the picture and that one of the consequences of this has been the 2008 economic crisis? Could it be that if economists had incorporated the American pragmatists' conception of the socioeconomic realm then their framework could have been more effective in avoiding crises?

What is Pragmatism?

In the early twentieth century, pragmatism was the dominant American philosophy and it left an indelible trace upon philosophy and social theory. Whilst pragmatism was eclipsed by logical positivism during the 1940s and 1950s, there is now a revival of interest in it as scholars turn to the literature of the American pragmatists for inspiration and insights about how to understand better current socioeconomic issues. This revival is part of the post-Cartesian (post-positive) tradition. Those early writers who are acknowledged to be members of the school of American pragmatism include John Dewey (a philosopher, educator and a public intellectual), William James (a psychologist and popularist) and Charles Sanders Peirce, a physical scientist whom Einstein and Popper regarded as a genius. Others who shared a number of the insights and methods of these earlier pragmatists are G.E. Mead, A.N Whitehead and H. Bergson. More recently, Sidney Hook, Hilary Putnam, Willard Quine, Richard Bernstein and Richard Rorty have been regarded as radical pragmatists.

To summarise the main arguments of pragmatism is a tall order. John Dewey's career spanned many decades and his thinking developed and changed over that time. Pragmatism is committed to holism, consequentialism, fallibilism and the primacy of practice. Holism requires the inquirer to examine a problem in general rather than partially. This means that any phenomenon should be treated as an interdependent whole rather than being divided into a number of elements, which are then studied separately. Holism underpins the Duhem–Quine thesis in philosophy and also the theory of the 'second best' in economics. Pragmatists argue that in order to discover meaning the inquirer should examine the consequences of any action. Pragmatism turns its back on a priori reasoning and turns towards concrete facts and consequences (Dewey 1938). Dewey argued for a material logic rather than the formal logic of analytical relations suggested by Kant and embodied in Russell and Whitehead's *Principia Mathematica*. Material logic looks at how things are and tries to explain them. The role of philosophy, Dewey argued, was not to dictate what should be but to illuminate what is – to tackle and resolve real rather than logical problems. Russell (1908, 1909) vigorously attacked this view. The pragmatist's reply is that whilst deductive inferences can be logically correct, in terms of the internal rules of logic, they can, nevertheless be empirically false. Strongly held beliefs may turn out to be false. Any belief is subject to revision. This is the basis of fallibilism. John Maynard Keynes is famously supposed to have remarked:

When the facts change, I change my mind. What do you do sir?

Pragmatists are concerned with practical inquiry and seek to break down the boundaries between normative and factual inquiry. They emphasise a problem-solving approach and believe that their ideas have practical, political and ethical consequences. This is clearly evidenced in their work which seeks to design more democratic institutions. In much of his writing, Dewey attempts to reconnect philosophy with practical affairs. He wanted to engage with compelling scientific and social problems and not only acknowledged a difference between knowing and acting (practice) but collapsed them, thereby, indicating that philosophy has the potential to change the world. Because social science/social philosophy offers hypothetical solutions which, if adopted, might resolve a problem, it opens itself to the charge of 'social engineering', a criticism that was made of Dewey by Frank Knight, C. Wright Mills, Bernard Crick and George Santayana. Social engineering is intrusive and state intervention requires control over social affairs. Those with technical knowledge (sapiential authority) become powerful and pragmatism can become identified with a strong centralising state of technocrats. Pragmatists regard human action as a creative force. Dewey went beyond the instrumentalism of naïve means/ends relations: '... the functions of mind is to project new and more complex ends – to free experience from routine and caprice'. Human action can be liberating.

Pragmatism is essentially an anti-reductionist philosophy. Experience is regarded to be the site of knowledge and meaning. This anti-Cartesian perspective maintains that there are no transcendental truths. The world of everyday reality is, according to the pragmatists, the only reality we have access to. The world presents itself as a series of problems of everyday life and the role of the inquirer is to look behind experience to find a fundamental enduring reality. Education in Dewey's world is a process of 'continual reorganization, reconstruction and transformation of experience' (Dewey 1916: 349). The early pragmatists, especially Dewey when he was writing his *Logic* in the 1930s, appear to have been unaware of the debates that were raging in the field of quantum physics. Quantum reality transcends our experiences and we can only gain glimpses of it through the consequences of actions taken within an experimental setting, such as the Hadron Collider.

Ontological Reflections

Those who engage in modelling economic behavior or who investigate the economy empirically using econometric techniques implicitly subscribe to some premodel conception of the 'reality' of the economy. These foundational properties of economic reality are rarely revealed, discussed or acknowledged by mainstream neoclassical economists. They are hidden from view. An ontological approach seeks to surface the premodel foundational conceptions with a view to exploring how they constrain the results of the modellers and the econometricians. Ontology, which is the 'science of being', of *ouisa*, seeks to establish what is. Ontology precedes epistemology, which is the science of knowledge, i.e. the theory of how we know what we know. Economic ontology is part of a much wider embracing ontology of the social realm. What is the foundational nature of the social reality? If ontology precedes epistemology then it shapes and constrains the economic models that are constructed. Schumpeter (1954), in his history of economic analysis, whilst not referring to matters ontological did talk about 'vision', which captures similar ideas to the fundamental world view (*Weltanschauung*) which is presupposed, is not derived and which is incorrigible. Buchanan points out that these fundamentals lie at the heart of all research programs and are seldom challenged by those who work inside the intellectual tradition of the program.

> *These central elements are taken as presuppositions, as relatively absolute absolutes, and, as such, they become themselves, the constraints (the constitution) within which the scientific discourse is conducted. (1991: 14)*

Wittgenstein (1969) referred to these presuppositions as 'hinges' on which our thoughts and judgements hang and turn, likening them to a riverbed within which our thought flows.

Ontological reflections establish how the researcher thinks about the 'reality' (material, biotic or social) that is being investigated. They influence what is modelled, what is searched for, what is ignored and what remains hidden from view. The long-standing debate about whether or not there is a reality which is mind independent has long since run into the sand. Quantum reality resides within the models of the quantum scientists. No one has seen an electron or any other fundamental particle. They exist within the reality of a model and provided the model works well by providing insights and explanations then the model is said to be a reasonable representation of what physical or material reality might look like. Hawking and Mlodinow (2010: 58) refer to 'model-dependent realism'. Few physical, natural or social scientists today take seriously the 'mirror view' or 'God's eye' view of reality, i.e. there is an external objective knowledge that science strives to find. Rorty's (1979) powerful rejection of the correspondence theories of truth held by Locke, Kant and Carnap is today generally accepted. Interestingly Sir Arthur Eddington, the leading cosmologist and physicist of his day, presented in 1928 a powerful metaphor which also rejected the correspondence theory of truth. For Eddington, 'the stuff of the world is mind stuff'. That is, our view of the world is invented (constructed); it is not discovered. Whilst Eddington believed in an external world (reality), he argued that the way we view the world is limited and that science is partly subjective. To illustrate his point, Eddington invites us to imagine an ichthyologist studying what exists in the ocean. He puts in a net – mesh size two inches – and the fish he catches are more than two inches in size. The ichthyologist, therefore, concludes that no sea creature is less than two inches long. In other words, we ignore that which we cannot observe/see.

> *Anything uncatchable in my net is, ipso facto, outside the scope of ichthyiological knowledge and is not part of the kingdom of fishes ... in short what my net does not catch isn't fish. (Eddington 1928: 184)*

Whilst A.N. Whitehead and E.A. Milne agreed with Eddington, he was ridiculed by his fellow scientists. Yet Eddington's fish net metaphor has important messages for epistemology (what we find depends upon the effectiveness of our techniques and measuring instruments), but it also speaks to ontological reflection. The way in which we model reality is shaped by the premodel foundational conceptions which frame the model reality which emerges. These basic conceptions represent the size of the net's mesh. If we presuppose that fish much smaller than two inches exist then we shall design a net that will capture them. How do these general reflections about ontology relate to the ontology of the American pragmatists? This is the subject of the next section.

Pragmatist Ontology

Although Dewey did not explicitly outline his ontological beliefs, it is possible to distil these from his general writings but especially *Logic* (1938) and *The Quest for Certainty* (1929). Dewey, and later Rorty, rejected the notion that reality is radically external, complete and determinate and mind independent. He regarded it as meaningless to ask the question of whether objects have an existence independent of mind. Instead, he preferred the question, 'how shall we read reality?' Dewey, therefore, recognises the importance of cultural and historical bound specific meanings rather than timeless universal truths (Dewey 1925). As such, Dewey rejected the idea that knowledge is universal, certain and fixed: that there is an absolute epistemic truth which is invariant to personal and cultural perspectives, as claimed by the correspondence theory of truth. For Dewey pragmatism is interested in building intelligence and meaning rather than truth. He, thus, rejects the Cartesian approach to scientific method: the idea that the objective of scientific inquiry is to produce something which represents an independently external reality, which exists prior to the inquiry. This is also a rejection of philosophical realism or the spectatorial account of knowledge, which Kant referred to as 'the eye of the mind'. Cartesians also sought 'certainty' in their knowledge claims, another notion which Dewey rejected. As such, he did not think in terms of universal laws:

> Nature is not an unchanging order unwinding itself majestically from the reel of law under the control of deified forces. It is an infinite congeries of changes. Laws are not governmental regulations which limit change, but are convenient formulations of selected portions of change followed through a shorter or longer period of time and then registered in statistical forms that are amenable to manipulation. (Dewey 1910: 71)

He argued that generalizations are:

> not fixed rules ... but instrumentalities for investigation, methods by which the net value of past experiences is rendered available for present scrutiny of new complexities ... they are hypotheses to be tested and revised by their further working. (Dewey 1925: 240)

Pragmatists hold an 'escatological' view of history. Both Dewey and Mead referred to the 'emergent present' and Mead to the 'incurable contingency of the future'. In other words, the future is not closed – it is made by agency. We can make the future more or less just or fair. Agency is not dominated by the iron laws of history, which Hegelians believed in.

In this regard, individuals are understood as knowing subjects who make history through choices. This notion of emergence will be of importance later, when economic ontological reflection is considered in more detail. For instance, Bergson talked about 'duree': that is, individuals are in a state of becoming – lived time. An open emergent future implies that knowledge is dynamic and unfolding. There is no supreme reality and knowledge is a means not an end. Knowledge changes that which is already known; it is instrumental in enabling becoming, it redirects action and it is a means of liberation. Knowledge is never complete; it grows and develops through interaction within a changing environment. Discovery never ends. Looked at in this way, knowledge is dynamic and evolutionary.

Pragmatists believe in the fallibility of knowledge. No knowledge claim is free from the possibility of revision. Dewey in *The Quest for Certainty* (1929) argues against the Cartesians' seduction for certain knowledge by rejecting the idea that there is a foundation to certainty. All knowledge should be considered as hypotheses that are to be tested against experience. As such, knowledge is ephemeral and is continuously updated in the light of radically new experiences. To repeat an earlier point, knowledge is always in a state of becoming. Instead of truth, Dewey prefers the notion of 'warranted assertability', which is the outcome of inquiry. At the time of writing *The Quest for Certainty*, Dewey would only have been vaguely aware of the developments that were taking place in quantum physics. If he had been aware then he would have acknowledged that notions such as Heisenberg's uncertainty principle in the quantum world had done violence to the belief in certain knowledge. In a world of emergence, given the infinite number of combinations (different worlds) that could arise, it is only possible to speculate in probabilistic terms about what might be. Even that is too strong a statement because it assumes knowledge about all possible future worlds in order to calculate probabilities. Where there is radical uncertainty and no knowledge of the unknown unknowns, then there is ignorance of the future. Whilst we might see through a glass darkly, we cannot see through one that is opaque.

It is generally acknowledged that Dewey and other classical pragmatists were not systematic in their treatment of ontological issues. A summary of their ontology can be expressed as follows:

- Reality is change and dynamism.
- The world is open-ended.
- The world is one of creative opportunities.
- The world is relational – relations are temporal and exist within specific contexts.
- The world is emergent/evolutionary – it is characterized by an emergent process of becoming.
- Through emergent processes new forms of organization and novel new 'plateaus of existence' become.
- All experiences are influenced by prior experiences.
- No process is deterministic – there is no preordination.

The process ontology of Dewey, James and Peirce was developed further by Whitehead, who became a pragmatist in his later years at Harvard. Whitehead had come to realise that the closed axiomatic method of David Hilbert and Gottlob Frege, which he had systematized along with Bertrand Russell in *Principia Mathematica*, was not so much a mistake but a highly constrained view of reality because it could not deal with processes and that which had still to become. Dewey's earlier relational ontology was subsequently developed in Dewey and Bentley (1949), through the notions of interaction and transaction. Interaction is thought of as balanced or causal interconnection whilst transaction acknowledges that things are not independent, but acquire their identity through relations such as those in networks. Actors plus patterns of relationships imply dynamic relationships. Relational ontology is also found in the writings of Marx, Simmel and Bordieu. The nature of the causality that Dewey and Bentley refer to, when discussing interaction, is not a mechanistic type. Elsewhere throughout his writing Dewey is careful not to talk about causality preferring instead to refer to 'tendencies' or about means producing 'consequences', which is much more speculative and contingent. Associated with a relational ontology is the pragmatists' belief in holism, that the web of belief is fallible and interconnected – no part of the whole can be ring fenced from corrigibility.

Dewey's Post-Positivism

Dewey was not a positivist though some have misinterpreted and misrepresented him as one. In *Logic and the Theory of Inquiry* (1938) he denounced the scientific objectivity and certainty which had been the quest of the Cartesians; he claimed that there is no neutral observational language and that language distorted understanding. Whilst post-positivism is a vague term, it is normally understood to reject nomological explanation (i.e. the logic-deductive approach, which is privileged by physicists and neoclassical economists). Post-positivists also reject falsificationist strictures and the correspondence theory of truth. Instead, post-positivists privilege speculation and experimentation, which includes experimentation of thought, and emphasise that experience is ephemeral, specific, singular, historical and neither general nor universal. For Dewey the ultimate objective of scientific enquiry is to shape the disordered materials of a problematic experience into a 'unified existential situation' (Dewey 1938: 500). Method should not be seen as enabling the inquirer to see things as they really are; rather, method is about a set of inter-related practices that transform indeterminate situations. The social realm is haphazard, 'confused and chaotic'. Social science is not about observation, organization and causal explanation of the 'facts'. It is about shaping the disorganized material into something intelligible. Dewey argued strenuously against positivist views and the notion of determinism. He was also careful not to suggest that the social sciences adopt the methods of the physical and natural sciences (see *Social Science and Social Control*, Dewey 1931). Social actors bestow meaning on 'facts' and concepts are built out of subjective meanings constituted within the social actor and within the process of social interaction as, for example, in epistemic communities.

Dewey favored the denotative method, whereby an investigator should acknowledge the problem that is presented or perceived rather than a problem that is preconfigured by theory. Inquiry is a meeting of theory and practice. It is a means of problem identification and problem-solving in which meaning is created within the process of the inquiry. The outcome of all inquiry is subject to continuous revision (fallibilism) until a settled belief emerges but the existential situation continuously challenges belief because we always remain in doubt. This is the basis of reflective thought. If problems are not to be prefigured by theory, then how are they identified and posed?

Abduction

An important contribution to the pragmatists' set of ideas is Peirce's notion of abduction, which has significant consequences for social science methodology. Many regard Peirce to be the founding figure of the pragmatic movement but for many reasons he is something of the forgotten man, who resides in the shadows. Karl Popper regarded him as a most formidable thinker. One instance of this is that the complexity of the social world implies that the methodology of social science demands meta-abductions.

> *Theory becomes a replacement for experiments and in such a way it assumes an experimental character: it becomes counterfactual. (Bertilsson 2004: 384)*

As Peirce (1901) argued, abductive inference gives a clue to reality, that is, it is a may be.

> *Abduction seeks a theory, it also suggests a theory. Induction seeks for facts. In abduction the consideration of the facts suggests the hypotheses. In induction the study of hypotheses suggests the experiments that bring to light the very facts to which the hypotheses had pointed. (Peirce 1901)*

Peirce (1905) saw that there are three steps in any inquiry process: abduction, deduction and induction. Induction is based on experiential research – a move from specific observations to the construction of empirical generalizations. For example, if all swans that have been observed are white then it is asserted that the next swan which is observed will also be white. Deduction applies general statements to specific situations. These general statements are a priori and are based on mathematical and logical processes derived from axioms. Abduction examines a mass of facts and lets these facts suggest a theory. Abduction operates on all levels of inquiry. It facilitates induction and deduction; it is a link between the empirical and the logical and it is a link between events and theory. For C. Wright Mills the challenge of abduction was the 'sociological imagination'. Peirce distinguished between over coded and under coded abduction. Over coded abduction referred to vague interpretations and assertions held with certainty. Cautious abductions are under coded. These notions were extended by Eco (1988).

Induction tests the conclusion of some abduction. Beliefs are fixed on a particular hypothesis. If that hypothesis is verified time and time again, and not refuted, then a strong belief in its truth value is established. But it is only a belief. Even if, after a million tests, it remains unrefuted this does not prove that it is true. The hypothesis is not contained in the data. The data give a clue about the appropriate representation; for example, is it linear or curvi-linear? Any curve can be fitted to the data. Many years previously, Hume (1975) concluded that any claim to derive universal laws from data runs into problems. To derive laws from specific observations is to assume that laws exist. This implies that we cannot use induction to prove that laws exist. The importance of abduction will become more apparent when the ontological turn in economics is discussed. In particular, the notion of retroduction will be examined when considering the nature of causation.

In summary, the discussion above has argued that American pragmatists have a view of the world that is open, processual, emergent, relational, ephemeral, non-general and non-deterministic but one, nevertheless, in which there exist tendencies which are discernible over reasonably lengthy periods of time. This view stands in sharp contrast to the closed, axiomatic and deductive modelling of much of mathematical physics and neoclassical economics. Many American pragmatists emphasise the importance of abduction and do not confine themselves to inductive or deductive reasoning. How does this analytical perspective compare to the dominant ontology of economics? This question is addressed in the next section.

The Ontological Turn in Economics

Milton Friedman pointed out that 'more than other scientists, social scientists need to be self-conscious about their methodology' (1953: 34). The philosophy of economics has been dominated, especially during the 1970s and 1980s, by the Popperian literature on epistemological issues such as falsificationism and, also, by Milton Friedman's infamous 1953 essay in which he argues that whether or not the assumptions of a model are realistic is of little importance provided it is able to predict accurately. Popper's standards were overly strict and most of the propositions of neoclassical economies, as presented in General Equilibrium Theory (GET) are not testable (Blaug 1992) because it is like super-Euclidean geometry. Leijonhufvud (1973) caricatures economists as belonging to the 'Econ' tribe who are engaged in ceremonial worship at the totem of mathematics. Economists pursue 'scientism' through their physics envy, but it is more classical Newtonian mechanics than modern quantum theory. Few economists have spent time thinking about the nature of the economic reality that they are studying. Indeed, most economists become rapidly irritated by such questions and are dismissive of those who adopt this line of inquiry. Put differently, discussion of methodology is the ghost at the table of economic theory. Frank Hahn, an outstanding theoretical economist, is representative of the vast majority of economic theorists when he says that economists 'should give no thought at all to methodology' (1992: 5). Many methodological discussions within economics have been undoubtedly misplaced and fruitless, such as whether or not economics should use mathematical reasoning. That discussion misses the point. Of course economics should use mathematics. It helps to clarify, gives precision of thought and ensures cohesive and consistent argument. The deeper issues are concerned with questioning whether mathematics is the only form of reasoning that should be used; which kind of mathematics should be used for which problems; and are some problems simply not amenable to mathematical approaches? To answer these questions depends upon the nature of the economic problems under review and how they are structured. This is surely a methodological issue.

Amongst those few economists who have risked the opprobrium of their theoretical colleagues because they have faced methodological issues head on is Tony Lawson, the leader of the Cambridge ontology group, who has challenged his fellow economists to think deeply about the nature of the economic and social realms. As Lawson points out, if you have a hammer then you see the world as made up of nails. The hammer is a tool just as mathematics is a tool. Economists, therefore, tend to see problems that are amenable to mathematics. What about those social phenomena that are not? Along with Lawson, the philosophers Uskali Maki (2001) and Nancy Cartwright (2001) have worked to get ontological issues onto economists' agendas. Each economist adopts a particular ontological perspective but, together, they constitute an 'ontological turn' that has taken place in economics over the past 15 years. Others whose contributions to the philosophy of economics have an ontological dimension are Paul Davidson, Duncan Foley and Robert Heilbroner. Economics is a modelling science (Krugman 1995; Gibbard and Varian 1978; Jackson 2008, 2010).

> *Much of economic theorising consists not of an overt search for economic laws, nor of forming explicit hypotheses about situations and testing them, but of investigating economic models. (Gibbard and Varian 1978: 676)*

Models are 'structured stories'. They are not like laws but are more like history (Schabas 2009), and the practice of modelling enables 'what if' simulations to be performed. Some models (especially macro forecasting models) attest to be approximations of the 'real' world but many others are just caricatures; in other words, an acknowledged distortion to highlight a specific feature. The assumptions that lie at the foundations of economic models are highly stylised (all individuals are assumed to be identical; individuals are under socialized; choices are made over two time periods or individuals are assumed to be infinitely lived).

Economics is almost hermetically sealed off from the other social sciences. It has its own self-assured confidence that its models will provide insight and explanation, despite them being devoid of psychological, social or cultural features other than the most primitive. Economists' approximations, caricatures or structured stories capture the complexity of the social realm. The economists' method does not provide engineering solutions, which signals clearly that economists should not build bridges nor should they design aircraft! A phrase which emerged during the 1990s was 'financial engineering', to describe the use of economic models supplemented by financial mathematics to design highly complex and risky financial instruments. Many of the problems that arose in financial markets can be traced back to the failure of economics to be a design science. In economics (and social science generally) the facts to be explained are not generated by the theory in the same way as they are in physical science. The economy does not repeat or replicate itself in the same way as in the physical world. Instead, it is adaptive and emergent in the sense of the early pragmatists. Friedman's insistence on prediction is plain wrong.

Economists, as already indicated, spend much of their lives in the fictional worlds of their models. Such models are false by definition, so it is trivial to criticise them for not being real – there is no pretension to be otherwise. Are they abstractions of the real world; are they analytical representations; or are they analytical heuristic fictions? So the question is how closely do these models resemble or approximate the real world? Is there a 'model reality' in the sense used by quantum physicists? Not all models are believed to be surrogates for reality; rather the majority of the models are heuristic devices which enable the economist to explore the internal structure and consistency of the model itself. These tend to be elaborate and technical exercises in mathematical logic. Also, economic models (as is true in all social sciences) contain artificial analytical concepts, which are constructed by the analyst (for example, the consumer; the firm; the state; prices and so on). Unlike physicists, economists' models do not predict the existence of unobservables such as the electron, the neutrino or the Higgs Boson ('God particle'). Economists introduce unrealistic assumptions for their tractability not for their epistemic virtue. All sciences use false assumptions but some are more ridiculously far off the mark than others, and to criticise economists for failing to predict the future really misses the point. Given the complexity of the phenomena that economists, and other social scientists, study it would be surprising if economic models enabled prediction with any accuracy. Geologists and volcanologists are unable to predict eruptions or tsunamis but that does not make the effects experienced of these phenomena any less real. A textual analysis of many economists' writings does, however, suggest that a large number of them do believe that there exists a mind independent social reality, which their models are attempting to capture, albeit imperfectly. So what might that reality look like? This is the ontological question which most economists ignore.

The majority of economists are unaware of their ontology and think it has nothing to do with their research. They seldom call into question the foundations of their theories and remain within a vice of metaphysical theory. Ontologies frame our research questions and our interpretations of results. A more useful approach to the design of research would be to discuss first the nature of social reality and then to consider the appropriate methods to investigate it. This, however, is challenging because every day phenomena are hard to see because they surround us and we are immersed in them and have no background against which to see them. Similar ideas were expressed by Mead (1934), who saw the individual and the environment within which the individual is placed being constitutive of one another. It is interesting to note that Peirce's ontology is similar to Heidegger's (1927) existential ontology. Individuals (the subject) are part of the world and are not disconnected as in the Cartesian epistemological subject-object relation. Being in the world ('Dasein') means the subject is not separated from the object, but is instead part of the object.

Economic Reality

Heterodox economists (for example, Commons, Hayek, Kaldor, Keynes, Shackle) tend to share similar, but not identical, ontological positions. These amount to a dismissal of the strictures of the neoclassical model as presented in general equilibrium theory. The thread that unites the heterodox economists, who have been banished to the outer reaches of the discipline, is their search for a more relevant economics for decision-making, policy making and explanation. And yet the ontological foundations of this relevant economics have been available for decades. They are the foundations established by the early pragmatists, who emphasised open systems, emergence, fallibilism, complexity, adaptation and the importance of abduction. A sketch of an alternative social ontology to that which is dominant in the closed logical deductive models of current economics is now presented. This alternative is based on the work of Tony Lawson (2003) and the many recent discussions following in the wake of the 2008 global financial crisis. As a sketch it leaves out much detail, which will be filled in later, but it does demonstrate a strong complementarity and overlap with the early pragmatists.

For Lawson and others, formal mathematical deductive modelling presupposes a closed system. In natural science, event regularities arise from being able to conduct controlled experiments that isolate the mechanisms that are of interest. The social realm (domain) is open and internally related. Any observed event regularities (correlations) are a rare special case and are transitory. Moreover, they refer to surface level phenomena. The social realm is structured. It has features that cannot be reduced to human activities (agency) such as social rules, positions, powers, social mechanisms and tendencies. This means that economists should seek the underlying causal mechanisms which give rise to economic phenomena and focus less on correlating surface phenomena. Looking at the deeper social mechanisms is an attempt to make the invisible visible and to go beyond surface descriptions. It requires identification of non-empirical causal mechanisms that govern (not cause) events and affairs. Such an approach seeks explanation and requires a discursive fallible account of the causal interplay between social structure (antecedent) and human agency (subsequent) in historical time. Lawson, like the early pragmatists, is a fallibilist. Knowledge develops, 'by getting things knowledgeably wrong' (2003: 101).

In Lawson's world, the social domain is emergent. Social structures have emergent properties and causal powers. They emerge out of social interactions whilst having properties that are independent of agents. This 'critical realist' position is half way between the reification of social structure (where social structure determines agency) and methodological individualism. Social structures are not exogenous nor are they reducible to individual action. Structure and agency are mutually constitutive entities. They are ontologically distinct but mutually dependent. This implies that the social realm is holistic and relational. Social networks are complex networks of highly inter-related internal positions. The social realm is also processual. It is a dynamic process of interaction and emergence. Social structures are continuously reproduced or transformed as they are used. The basic units of social science are individuals (agents) but, unlike atoms or the fundamental particles of physics, they are strategic. Strategic agents increase the degree of complexity and uncertainty. The combinatorial possible interactions among a large number of strategic agents is immense, and results in an even larger number of possible outcomes. Not only does this require a great amount of computing power, but it also implies that forecasting outcomes is a very difficult (if not a foolish) activity. The processual and relational nature of social reality means that coordination is problematic. Few economists, with the exception of Robert Clower and Axel Leijonhufvud, have examined the concept of 'coordination failure' and its significance. The positive and negative feedback within complex systems can generate interesting outcomes. The dominant logic in economics is to model the macro-economy as a set of mechanical laws (rules). Strategic behavior, however, undermines any knowable law. Currently there is very little understanding of the nature of the complex dynamics of socioeconomic systems. Emphasis is given to seeking equilibrium solutions following an external shock or perturbation. What, however, about the processes on the way to the new equilibrium if agents are strategic? Does an equilibrium exist–did one exist in the past? These dynamics are so complex that we do not know, as yet, how to model them. The dynamics embodied in DSGE (dynamic stochastic general equilibrium) models, whilst complicated, do not embrace the strategic behavior and emergence described above.

The social realm of economic reality is a complex system. Such systems are different from complicated or difficult systems and are characterized by a population of diverse agents, who are connected through behaviors and actions that are strategic and interdependent. Moreover, the behaviors of the agents adapt. Complex systems are unpredictable because of their openness. It is difficult to explain the underlying mechanisms of complex systems. Complex systems lie somewhere between highly ordered and chaotic systems. They are open, processual, emergent, nonlinear and path dependent (history matters), and little understood in the context of social reality. Traditional economics does not incorporate these features but instead emphasises closedness, rationality, equilibrium, situations of risk and expected utility. Individual preferences are exogenous. Institutional structure, other than the market, is ignored. Consumption defines welfare and individual preferences are aggregated into a social welfare function. Such restrictive assumptions make the traditional model a special case.

The social realm is one of radical uncertainty. Knight (1921), almost a hundred years ago, drew the sharp distinction between situations of risk and uncertainty. Risk is actuarial in the sense that probabilities (objective or subjective) can be assigned to the occurrence of future events. This is the basis of statistical decision theory and expected utility theory, and is used in DSGE models. Uncertainty refers to situations of ignorance where it is impossible to assign probabilities. Keynes expressed this as follows:

> By uncertain knowledge I do not mean to distinguish what is known for certain from what is only probable ... About these matters there is no scientific basis to form any calculable probability. We simply do not know. (1938: 113–14)

Finally, economists, such as Lawson, seek to establish a retroductive approach in economics. This is similar to Peirce's notion of abduction. Deductive reasoning is forward looking and predictive. Retroduction is backward looking and seeks to explain events a posteriori. It doesn't answer the question 'why?' Instead, it examines why X rather than Y? This is contrastive explanation. Keynes was implicitly acknowledging abduction when he wrote to Roy Harrod:

> Good economists are scarce because the gift of using 'vigilant observation' to choose good models, although it does not require a highly specialized intellectual technique, appears to be a very rare one. (1938: 207)

The features and characteristics captured by complex systems embedded in a world of radical uncertainty reflect many aspects of the collective ontology of the American pragmatists. Modelling complex, adaptive, non-equilibrium systems characterized by uncertainty represents a new dawn for economics, one which has partial origins in the writings of Marshallian, pre-Marshallian and Austrian economic traditions prior to the logico-deductive, mechanical physics approach that Samuelson introduced in 1947, and which took economics down a road to beautiful but fictional worlds that were eventually a dead end. Some believe, and indeed hope, that economics will return to an earlier literary approach. That is most unlikely. To understand complex systems more mathematics will be required and it will be difficult mathematics. After all, mathematics is a language and one which offers precision and clarity of thought. Like any other language, it has its limitations and constrains thinking and modelling. It is to be hoped that in future economic practitioners will be much more aware of these limitations.

Conclusion

McCloskey (1985) argues that, 'good science is good conversation'. The conversations in economics have for decades been highly distorted because of the peculiar ontological foundations of its dominant deductive models, which are more an exercise of mental gymnastics than a science of the economy. Any attack upon the citadel of traditional economics is bound to be repelled. In that inevitable case, it is important to remember the framework of norms (called 'Sprachethik') that McCloskey advocates to guide conversations:

don't lie; pay attention; don't sneer; cooperate; don't shout; let other people talk; be open minded; explain yourself when asked; don't resort to violence or conspiracy in aid of your ideas. (1985: 24)

Only if economics has such a civilised conversation, in which all ideas count from the outset, is there the prospect that economic's useable knowledge will contribute to improvements in human happiness, which was Dewey's general objective. That conversation must include the American pragmatists and the heterodox economists who, like Lawson, have an interest in ontology. They provide solid intellectual foundations for a new and potentially productive set of complex, adaptive and non-equilibrium models. It is to be hoped that these new models will provide the insights, understanding and explanations that are absent from the existing dominant economic models.

Note

In preparing this chapter, I have benefited from the work of Patricia M. Shields, especially her numerous articles in *Administration and Society*. The work of Patrick Baert (especially Baert 2005) has helped to shape my thinking. I am also pleased to acknowledge the helpful comments that I received from Emmanual Haven, Phil Marsh, Terry Robinson and the editors of this volume. All errors are the responsibility of the author.

References

Baert, P. 2005. *Philosophy of the Social Sciences*. Cambridge: Polity Press.
Bertilsson, T.M. 2004. The Elementary Forms of Pragmatism: On Different Theories of Abduction. *European Journal of Social Theory*, 7(3), 371–89.
Blaug, M 1992. *The Methodology of Economics*. Cambridge: Cambridge University Press.
Blaug, M. 1997. Ugly currents in modern economics. *Options Politiques*, September: 3–8.
Buchanan, J.M. 1991. *Constitutional Economics*. Oxford: Blackwell.
Cartwright, N. 2001. Ceteris paribus laws and socio-economic machines, in *The Economic World View*, (ed.) Maki, U. Cambridge: Cambridge University Press, 275–92.
Dewey, J. 1910. *The Influence of Darwin on Philosophy*. London: Bell.
Dewey, J. 1916. Democracy and education, in *John Dewey: The Middle Works*, vol. 9, (ed.) Boydston, J.A. Carbondale and Edwardsville, IL: Southern Illinois Press.
Dewey, J. 1925. *Experience and Nature*. Chicago, IL: Open Court (later revision 1929, George Allen and Unwin).
Dewey, J. 1929. *The Quest for Certainty*. London: George Allen and Unwin.
Dewey, J. 1931. Social science and social control, in *John Dewey: The Later Works*, vol. 6, (ed.) Boydston, J.A. Carbondale, IL: Southern Illinois University Press, 64–8.
Dewey, J. 1938. *Logic: The Theory of Inquiry*. New York: Holt, Rinehart and Winston.
Dewey, J. and Bentley, A.F. 1949. Knowing and the unknown, in *John Dewey: The Later Works*, vol. 16, (ed.) Boydston, J.A. Carbondale and Edwardsville, IL: Southern Illinois University Press.

Eco, U. 1988. Horns, hooves, insteps, in *The Sign of Three*, (ed.) Eco, U. and Sebeok, A. Bloomington, IN: Indiana University Press, 199–219.

Eddington, A. 1928. *The Nature of the Physical World*. Cambridge: Cambridge University Press.

Friedman, M. 1953. *Essays in Positive Economics*. Chicago, IL: University of Chicago Press.

Gibbard, A. and Varian, H.R. 1978. Economic Models. *Journal of Philosophy*, 75(11), 664–77.

Hahn, F. 1970. Some Adjustment Problems. *Econometrica*, 38(1), 1–17.

Hahn, F. 1992. Reflections. *Royal Economic Society Newsletter*, 77: 5.

Hawking, S. and Mlodinow, L. 2010. *The Grand Design*. London: Bantam Books.

Heidegger, M. 1927/1962. *Being and Time*, translated by MacQuarrie, J. and Robinson, E. London: SCM Press.

Hume, D. 1975. *Enquiry Concerning Human Understanding*, (ed.) Selby-Bigge, L.A. Oxford: Clarendon Press.

Jackson, P.M. 2008. Knowledge bases: The academy and practice, in *Evidence Based Policy Making*. London: Public Management and Policy Association.

Jackson, P.M. 2010 Econophysics: Models and metaphors, in *Proceedings of the First Interdisciplinary CHESS Interactions Conference*, (ed.) Rangachuryula, C. and Haven, E. Hackensack, NJ: World Scientific.

Keynes, J.M. 1938. Letter to Roy Harrod, 4th July, *Collected Works*, vol. 14. London: MacMillan.

Knight, F. 1921. *Risk, Uncertainty and Profit*. Boston, MA: Houghton Mifflin Co.

Krugman, P. 1995. *Development, Geography and Economic Theory*. Cambridge: MIT Press.

Lawson, T. 2003. *Reorienting Economics*. London: Routledge.

Leijonhufvud, A. 1973. Life among the Econ. *Western Economic Journal*, 11(3), 327–37.

Leontieff, W. 1982. Letter in *Science*, 217: 104–107.

Maki, U. 2001. Economic Ontology: what? why? how?, in *The Economic World View*, (ed.) Maki, U. Cambridge: Cambridge University Press, 3–14.

Malinvaud, E. 1997. The proper role of theory, in *Economic Science and Practice*, (ed.) Bergeijk, P.A.G. Cheltenham: Edward Elgar, 149–65.

McCloskey, D.N. 1985. *The Rhetoric of Economics*. Cambridge: Cambridge University Press.

Mead, G.H. 1934. *Mind, Self and Society: From the Perspective of a Social Behaviourist*, (ed.), with an Introduction, by Morris, C.W. Chicago, IL: University of Chicago Press.

Peirce, C.S. 1898/1992. *Reasoning and the Logic of Things: The Cambridge Conferences Lectures of 1898*, (ed.) Ketner, K.L. Cambridge, MA: Harvard University Press.

Peirce, C.S. 1901. Reasoning Baldwin's Dictionary, in *Collected Papers of C.S. Peirce*, vol. 2, 773–8.

Peirce, C.S. 1905. What pragmatism is, in *Collected Papers of C.S. Peirce*, vol. 5, 411–37.

Peirce, C.S. 1934–63. *Collected Papers of Charles Saunders Peirce*, vols 1–7, (ed.) Hartshorne, C. and Wiess, P. Cambridge, MA: Belknap Press of Harvard University.

Rorty, R. 1979. *Philosophy and the Mirror of Nature*. Princeton, NJ: Princeton University Press.

Rorty, R. 1989. *Contingency, Irony and Solidarity*. Cambridge: Cambridge University Press.

Rubenstein, A. 1995. John Nash: The Master of Economic Modelling. *Scandinavian Journal of Economics*, 97(1), 9–13.

Russell, B. 1908. Transatlantic Truth. *Albany Review*, January: reprinted in Russell, B. 2009. *Philosophical Essays*. London: Routledge.

Russell, B. 1909. Pragmatism. *Edinburgh Review*, April reprinted in Russell, B. 2009. *Philosophical Essays*. London: Routledge.

Schabas, M. 2009. Constructing the Economy. *Philosophy of the Social Sciences*, 39(1), 3–19.

Schumpeter, J.A. 1954. *History of Economic Analysis*. London: George Allen and Unwin.

Wittgenstein, L. 1969. *On Certainty*, (ed.) Anscombe, G.E.M. and von Wright, G.H. Oxford: Blackwell.

4 *Pragmatism, Organizations and Getting to Grips with Reality*

TONY J. WATSON

Introduction

Pragmatism is concerned with how knowledge, ideas, institutions and practices are developed through the creativity of human beings as they struggle to cope with a world which is never fully knowable. It applies to human activities at the most general level and it applies to the everyday practices of every single person in the world. In the present chapter I shall reflect upon my own practice and learning over a number of decades as a sociologist who teaches, researches and writes about organizations, management and entrepreneurship in a way which might be relevant to the lives of the people who are involved in and affected by the activities which go on in organizations. Pragmatist principles have shaped my thinking and practices from the earliest days of my sociological learning – even before I could have clearly articulated just what pragmatism is. In the process of producing a reflexive account of what might be called 'a pragmatist's use of pragmatism', I shall explain what I mean by this expression and also reflect upon the way I have found it necessary in more recent years to turn much more directly and explicitly to the pragmatist tradition to help develop a clear rationale and justification for the ethnographic work which has been at the heart of my research work in and around organizations. I am not, however, simply telling a personal story about social science and pragmatism. My first intention is to reinforce the argument which is implicit in what I have said so far: that the pragmatist mood and style of thought has been present and influential in the social sciences for a long time, even if it is only recently that its importance is being fully acknowledged in volumes like the present one. My second intention is to demonstrate the very significant contribution that pragmatist thinking can make to the effectiveness and relevance of organizational research and theorising.

A Sociologist's 'Take' on Pragmatism

At this stage I must say a little more about what I take 'pragmatism' to be. The history and the basic principles of American pragmatism have been usefully outlined by the editors in the introductory chapter to this volume. A problem that must be overcome, however, is that of the way in which the tradition has often been misunderstood and marginalized, sometimes with its being crudely dismissed as some kind of nineteenth-century ideological justification of American capitalism and money-making. This problem of marginalization and dismissal as a short-lived philosophy is now disappearing as the considerable continuities between pragmatism and other traditions are being identified by writers such as Bernstein (2010) – these traditions including, perhaps surprisingly, those taking the 'cultural turn'. The latter commentator also points out the extent to which pragmatism is no longer a primarily American tradition, noting the way that four 'outstanding German thinkers' (Apel, Habermas, Joas and Honneth) have not only taken a sophisticated grip of pragmatism but have 'critically appropriated pragmatic themes' (2010: 23).

As Misak (2007) emphasises, the writing of the classical pragmatists, Peirce, James and Dewey, has come to have a growing and fruitful influence over philosophers, whether or not they have been 'influenced' by pragmatism or see themselves in the pragmatist tradition. As a social scientist who looks to philosophy as a vital means of clarifying the assumptions with which I work, I see the power of the classical pragmatist intervention in philosophy in its provision of an alternative, first, to Cartesian scepticism, with its pursuit of absolute certainty through the application of reason, and, second, to empiricism, with its aim to achieve the same end through processes of empirical investigation. For Peirce, Haack (1996), points out, knowledge is advanced pragmatically by confronting practical difficulties and dealing with situations in which existing beliefs are interrupted 'by recalcitrance on the part of experience' (1996: 646). It is this principle which underpins my opening characterization of pragmatist thinking and it is something which informs the arguments which are to follow.

It is necessary for each of us to clarify what pragmatism means for our work given that, from early on, there have been a considerable variety of different emphases within the philosophical literature (Lovejoy 1963; Mounce 1997; Schiller 1907) as well as in the very use of the term 'pragmatism'. To sharpen what I have said so far, and to connect it to a concern with the purposes of the social sciences, I will turn to a figure who has been an important bridge between pragmatist philosophy and sociology. Charles Wright Mills is best understood as the creator of a 'sociologized pragmatism' (Delanty and Strydom 2003: 284). In his *Sociology and Pragmatism* (1966) Mills says that although the original pragmatists 'gave it a varied form', it is nevertheless possible to 'catch the pragmatic mood and style of thought' within which they all worked. I suggest that social scientists generally and organization theorists in particular would be unwise, 'unpragmatist' even, to attempt to 'follow' the precepts of any particular pragmatist thinker. They can utilise pragmatist thinking much more fruitfully by attempting to work, as Mills did, within a 'pragmatic mood and style of thought' and then developing concepts and theories which are most appropriate to the human problems with which they are concerned. Part of the inspiration of pragmatism, identified by Mills in his essay 'The social role of the intellectual' (1967), is pragmatism's 'emphasis upon the power of man's intelligence to control his destiny'. Horowitz connects Mills' concern here with the fact that 'mainstream pragmatism' had always addressed itself to the 'great dualism between theory and practice' (1966: 24). And this dualism, of course, is one with which all organization theorists must be concerned. I will return to this point later. For the present, I shall turn to my personal account of learning to be a sociologist and theorist of work and organization, all the time working within a pragmatist style of thought.

Social Science Learning within a Pragmatist Mood and Style of Thought

From very early in my sociological studies, I recognised that it would be difficult either to evaluate the various social science approaches and disciplines which were on offer or to decide on what one's own later research practices might be, if one did not think hard about the assumptions that one was making about the nature of the social world and the knowledge about the social world which that research might develop. This meant that it was vital to pay attention to what philosophers had to say, and philosophers of science in particular. To do this is to follow what I later learned was Locke's (1689) principle of philosophy acting as an under-laborer; helping us to clear the ground and remove the rubbish that might get in the way of advancing what we might call more substantive forms of knowledge. At this time, the mid-1960s, there was little, if any, talk of ontology, epistemology or multiple 'paradigms' in either sociology or organization theory. But a central figure in my first term undergraduate curriculum was Karl Popper, a philosopher of science who identified the weaknesses in those same two traditions against which Peirce had gone into battle: the rationalist and the empiricist. Bernstein tells us that Popper was a considerable admirer of Peirce and he argues that Popper's (1959, 1963) emphasis on *falsifiability* and on critical inquiry as involving 'making bold conjectures and then criticizing, testing, and seeking to refute them' he is 'reaffirming Peirce's own understanding of critical inquiry' (2010: 33).

It was with a strong awareness of this critical and refutationalist set of criteria for evaluating social science that I read and took delight in the work of the Marx, Durkheim and Weber. My learning from the first two members of this classic triumvirate was enormous and continues to inform all my work. But the earlier 'under-laboring' work that I had done left me uneasy with aspects of both Durkheimian positivism and Marxian political economy. Although I found reading Weber something of a struggle, it was in his work that I found the basic ideas which have been the foundation of my own sociological work ever since. It is only with hindsight that I recognise that this was probably because of an affinity between Weber's thinking and pragmatist philosophy. Re-reading one of my favorite undergraduate books *Max Weber: An Intellectual Portrait* (1966), I have discovered that Bendix brings together Weber and Dewey as two thinkers who were determined to defy the determinism which was so prevalent in their time, and to insist on a role for what we might call human creative agency in shaping history. I have also discovered that Weber and James spent time together when the former visited New York (Hennis 2000). But the most important affinity between Weber's work and pragmatism lies in the way they each take a realist view of the world whilst recognising the vitally important part that processes of interpretation play in the creation and maintenance of that reality. Van de Ven (2007: 56) notes that James was emphatic about the need for a realist ontology. He insisted upon the 'existence of a reality independent of our cognition' and quotes James' statement that the notion of an independent reality 'lies at the base of the pragmatist notion of truth' (James 1908: 455). And a reading of Radkau's biography of Weber makes it very clear that reality was 'a central concept for Weber' (2009: 72) in both his life and his scholarly work'. At various points in the book we see reference to Weber striving to 'get to grips with reality'. And the idea of a 'science of reality' (*Wirklichkeitswissenschaft*) shaped many of his endeavours (Radkau 2009: 79). To point this out is not to ignore the fact that Weber labelled part of his work 'interpretive sociology'. However, his intention 'was certainly not to assign a higher place to interpretation than to explanation' (Freund 1972: 91):

> He took the view that to study the development of an institution solely from the outside, without regard to what [the human being] makes of it, is to overlook one of the principal aspects of social life. (Freund 1972: 89, my emphasis)

Weber, like the pragmatists, gave primacy to neither the objectively existing 'real' world nor to subjective meaning-making subjective factors processes.

As with many of my contemporaries in late 1960s sociology classes, Charles Wright Mills was a key figure. He was not only the main channel bringing pragmatism into sociology, as we have already seen, but he was a key translator and user of Weber's ideas. His most influential book was *The Sociological Imagination* (1959) and, at the core of this book, is a concern with relating the 'personal troubles' of the individual (being made redundant by a work organization, say) to relevant 'public issues' (the state of an economy, the role of unemployment in economic policy and so on). The social sciences should help people 'grasp what is going on in the world, and to understand what is happening in themselves at minute points of the intersection of biography and history within society' (1970: 14). This takes up the classic pragmatist interest in encouraging human creative action (agency) in coping with the world and the importance of democratic institutions within this. We cannot have a democratic order if those participating in it are unable to make *informed choices*. A key role for social science is thus envisaged. It is one of getting to grips intellectually with the social world so that people can act more successfully in the world. Certain difficulties arise here with the extent to which different groups in society will become 'informed' in this way and I will take this up in my concluding comments. At the personal level, though, I would like to comment that it was about the same time that I was reading this pragmatist-oriented work of Mills that I came across a very early discussion of industrial sociology (within which organization studies tended to be located at that time) in which Burns (1962) argued that it is the sociologist's business 'to conduct a critical debate ... with the public about its equipment of social institutions'. I have never let go of this essentially pragmatist conception of social science. Often, in my writing about and teaching the sociology of work and organizations I combine it with a later discussion of industrial sociology by Eldridge et al. (1991) in which they say, 'To show what possibilities may exist for political choices in an active democracy is to exercise the sociological imagination'.

Although, as a student, I was very happy with a notion of sociology as the study of social institutions and was inspired by Mills' emphasis on the relationship between individual lives and their societal context, I felt that it was vital to think all the time about 'what it is to be human'. But I was also conscious of the enormous dangers of falling into a reductionist style of analysis which crudely explained structural and institutional patterns in terms of something called 'human nature'. The most helpful ideas here, I found, were those of various social scientists associated with the Chicago school of sociology. There is an insistence in the work of people like Cooley, Thomas, Mead, Hughes, Strauss and Becker that the human being is an essentially social creature whose meaning-making endeavours and social actions must always be situated in their interactions with others (Blumer 1969). This work, I suggest, was all inspired by the pragmatist mood prevalent in Chicago intellectual circles at that time. This is most obviously the case with regard to Mead, who worked closely with Dewey. And there are, as Simpson points out, many parallels in [the] intellectual trajectories' of the two men (2011: 1333). However, whilst there were invaluable insights here, I found it difficult, as a student, to link this interactional emphasis with the 'bigger' institutional, historical or social structural level of social life. And this is where, towards the end of my undergraduate studies, a book was published which I and my fellow student theory-enthusiasts leapt upon. We saw it as a work which would help us, as we moved towards our final exams, to pull together the various strands of our sociological studies, integrating ideas from Marx, Durkheim and Weber with the social psychology of Mead and the social phenomenology of Schutz. The book was Berger and Luckmann's *The Social Construction of Reality* (1967).

Pragmatism and the Social Construction of Reality

At this point, I must briefly suspend the personal narrative about how my ideas developed early on and jump forward to 'where I am now' and how, with my much greater consciousness of the importance of pragmatist philosophy, I link certain ideas from Berger and Luckmann with my self-consciously pragmatist sociological theorising. To qualify what I am going to say, however, I need to comment that I see *The Social Construction of Reality* as a work in the Weberian/ institutionalist tradition of sociology and not in the non-realist tradition of post-structuralist-inspired 'social constructionism' (Watson 2008, 2012a). The book deals with realities which have 'a being independent of our volition' (Berger and Luckmann 1967: 15). This realism strongly echoes pragmatist interest in 'brute force' realities which Peirce argued are 'forced upon cognition' (Mills 1966: 158). The key link between my reading of the work of Berger and Luckmann (writing separately and together) is the emphasis on human beings having actively to create a social world in the face of brute realities and in the face of the fact that their species-based physical and mental capacities force them to construct institutions, cultures, discourses and all the rest.

Vital to Berger and Luckmann's thinking here is Gehlen's (1940) development of Nietzsche's notion that humans are 'not yet finished animals'. Unlike other animals, members of the human species cannot rely on a set of instincts to guide them through life. They have to rely on norms, rules, social values, knowledge, narratives and institutional logics – which only they themselves can create (or socially construct) as they struggle to deal with ontological frailty and existential precariousness. As Berger puts it, 'the individual is provided by society with various methods to stave off the nightmare world of anomy and to stay within the safer boundaries of the established nomos' (1973: 33). Each of us is born into what Luckmann (1983) calls a 'socio-historical a priori' – 'a socially established nomos' (Berger 1969: 31) or a 'socially constructed reality' (Berger and Luckmann 1967) – which enables us to act much of the time in a habitual manner. But human circumstances are always changing and there are continuous clashes of human interests which push us off the rails of habitual behavior. Hence the need for the constant application of basic human creativity, the recognition of which is central to pragmatist thinking.

Putting Pragmatism to Work

So far, I have used my own early social science learning to make the case for an affinity between pragmatist philosophy and important parts of the sociological mainstream. I have then reinforced this argument with some more recent thinking about pragmatism and the social construction of reality. And, more than once, I have referred to the fact that it is only in recent years that I have turned directly and explicitly to pragmatism to help me in my work on various aspects of organizational work. To explain how this happened, I must revert to the earlier personal narrative mode. I do this not just in the spirit of reflexive analysis, but in the spirit of a pragmatist consciousness which treats ideas as resources for overcoming problems that habitual procedures cannot handle. This is what I referred to earlier as a pragmatist's use of pragmatism. I shall look at three problems within organizational studies which I have found amenable to pragmatist thinking. The first is about giving legitimacy to organizational and, especially fieldwork-based, research. The second is about resisting the pressure to make an either-or choice between critical realism and 'interpretivism'. And the third problem is that of how we might bring a consideration of entrepreneurship into organization studies, something with the potential to increase our sensitivity to creative and innovatory aspects of organizational practice.

Pragmatism and Overcoming Problems in Organization Studies: (1) Truth and Organizational Research

I first found myself turning to pragmatist philosophy to help me with a quite troubling epistemological challenge with which I was presented. I found myself needing to justify the 'truthfulness' of the ethnographic study of managerial work which I had carried out and which I wanted to be read by a much bigger audience than that of interpretively oriented organizational theorists. This latter group of people would not necessarily challenge the validity of a reflexively written participant observation study of a year in the life of a group of industrial managers in the English East Midlands. However, some of the managers with whom I had been working as a participant observer challenged me to explain the compatibility between 'telling the truth about management' in the book I was going to write and fulfilling my promise to my colleagues and informants to maintain confidentiality by 'disguising the details' of events and 'changing any details which would embarrass anyone'. I needed an answer to these questions from managers, who were educated and trained in traditional scientific and engineering thinking. And, for an academic audience, I had to explain the compatibility between my concern for seeking truths about the social world and my recognition that any piece of research writing involves considerable deployment of rhetorical devices and the artful manipulation of information in order to produce a meaningful narrative for the reader (Watson 1995a).

It was clear to me that with regard to each of these audiences I could not deploy the 'truth theory' to which people routinely – habitually indeed – turn when asked to establish the 'truth' of something. This is the *correspondence* theory of truth. Little of what I wrote about happened exactly as I described it. So what about the other popular 'truth theory': the *coherence* or plausibility theory. This was inappropriate, partly because science often produces knowledge which is, in contemporary jargon, 'counter-intuitive' (i.e. implausible within taken-for-granted thinking) and partly because a plausibility justification is precisely what the world's most effective liars and confidence tricksters depend upon to 'have their wicked ways'. So, my epistemological reading suggested, I was left with the *pragmatist* theory of truth (Urmson 1989). To put this simply, a pragmatist epistemology rejects the possibility of any final or absolute truth about the world that one can work towards (cf. Popper, above). An account of the world can, however, be judged to be more or less true to the extent to which it provides understandings which will be more or less effective in informing the practices of people pursuing their projects (whatever these might be) in the aspect of life covered in the account. To the pragmatist, Joas explains, truth is not to do with producing a correct 'representation of reality in cognition'. Instead, it 'expresses an increase of the power to act in relation to an environment' (1993: 21). Or as Mills reports James as saying: 'all our theories are instrumental, are mental modes of adaptation to reality, rather than revelations [about the world]' (Mills 1966: 227). What I have been able to say all readers of my *In Search of Management* is that my book is not 'the last word on what managerial work is or how it is experienced'. The claim I do make, however, is that 'anyone will be better placed to cope successfully with a practical involvement in managerial issues (whatever form that involvement might take) if they take into account the insights of this account than if they base their action on much of the standard material to be found on the management shelves of our libraries and bookshops' (2001a: xv–xvi).

Pragmatism thus encourages us to engage with reality in our pursuit of knowledge and understanding, all the time recognising that the social world, in its complexity and its emergent nature, is only partly knowable. We seek knowledge about 'how the social world works', aware that whatever knowledge we produce is fallible and open to improvement – in so far as we can develop knowledge which more effectively informs human practices than what preceded it. This way of thinking I call *pragmatic realism*.

Pragmatic Realism and Overcoming Problems in Organization Studies: (2) Beyond the Critical Realism/ Interpretivism Choice

Although Rescher (2003) has suggested the term 'realistic pragmatism', I believe it to be more helpful to think in terms of *pragmatic realism*. A similar label is applied by Putnam (1990) to his notion of 'realism with a human face'. His usage is different from mine (but wholly compatible with it). However, I have favored the term because it helps me place my approach alongside 'critical realism' (Bhaskar 1978, Sayer 1992) and evolutionist 'scientific realism' (McKelvey 2001). There is a particularly close relationship between pragmatism and critical realism. This is reflected in the way Van de Ven incorporates pragmatist thinking into his version of what he calls 'a critical realist philosophy of science' (2007: 70). We also see it in the way Johnson and Duberley bring the two approaches together to advocate a 'pragmatic-critical realism' (2000: 174). Although we can welcome these attempts at combining pragmatism and critical realism, it is probably more helpful to see them as parallel projects. Each of them provides an alternative to both positivism and interpretivism. And they both fully recognise the importance of processes of interpretation and social construction whilst refusing to settle for a post-structuralist or constructivist view of the social and organizational world as 'constituted' by language or discourse.

If one looks across the range of research reports in the sociology of work and in organization studies, there is a clear pattern in which authors tend to identify themselves with one of just two methodological positions: a critical realist position (see Ackroyd and Thompson 2000; Reed 2009) or a non-realist language/text oriented position (see Yanow and Ybema 2009), labelled variously as 'post-structuralist', 'social constructionist', 'interpretivist', 'post-modern' or 'discursive'. Researchers taking the latter stance often relate their position to a so-called 'linguistic turn' (Alvesson and Karreman 2000; Contu and Willmott 2005) starting in the early 1990s. Although it is rarely, if ever, acknowledged, this expression was borrowed from Bergmann, the ideal-language philosopher who, it is interesting to note, argued in his final published work for 'containing the linguistic turn' in philosophy (Bergmann 1992). A clear statement of how this methodological position can be applied to organizations can be seen in the argument of Westwood and Linstead (2001: 4–5) that:

> *organizations exist in the text – there is no structure of boundary or bureaucratic manifestation that can be meaningfully presented as organization … organization has no autonomous, stable or structural status outside the text that constitutes it.*

Critical realism has provided the most powerful reaction to this 'turn to language' and offered a turn (back) to realism (Reed 2005). The starting point for such a way of thinking is that the world that we experience is met by us as already 'structured' and that:

> *this pre-structuring process, and the material conditions and social structures that it reproduces, cannot be collapsed into language or discourse. (Reed 2004: 415)*

The purpose of research rooted in critical realist assumptions is that of 'revealing the mechanisms which connect things and events in causal sequences and requires the elaboration of structures, mechanisms, powers and relations' (Ackroyd and Fleetwood 2000: 15). Such mechanisms are 'real' and have an existence independent of human understandings of them. Although an argument can be made for applying pragmatic thinking to the study of social mechanisms (Gross 2009), I would argue that the representationalism implied by the frequent use in critical realist writing of terms like 'revealing' or 'discovering' is at odds with the pragmatist concern no longer to seek 'a correct 'representation of reality in cognition' (Joas 1993: 21) or to adopt what Dewey called a 'spectator' theory of knowledge in which one stands back from the world as opposed to being actively involved in it. Pragmatism offers a non-representational and action-oriented form of realism. What makes some research accounts better than others is not in terms of how well they represent reality but in terms of how realistic they might be as resources for informing human practices.

To build a bridge over from representationalist notions of social mechanism to a pragmatist non-representational realist alternative, I have increasingly found myself using the notion of 'how the social world – or a part of it – works' when trying to express what I am trying to do in my research. I must stress that I am not implying that organizational research is equivalent to poking about inside a machine to see 'how it works'. I am putting the focus on practices rather than mechanisms. And my experience in ethnographic research has led to my frequent coupling of the notion of 'how the world works' with the nautical metaphor of 'learning the ropes'. I first encountered this metaphor in a social scientific context in the classic ethnographic study *Boys in White* (Becker et al. 1961). The term was used to characterise the processes whereby medical students, through a mixture of formal and informal learning, eventually 'emerged' as doctors capable of practising medicine outside the medical school. It is perhaps not surprising that the 'learning the ropes' metaphor has been meaningful to me for a long time. I started learning about what I would unapologetically call the realities of managerial and organizational work when, as a new graduate, I was simultaneously learning to be an employee relations manager in the engineering industry and learning to be a participant observation researcher and organization theorist as a part-time research student.

One is 'getting to grips with reality' when one learns the ropes of any aspect of social life – be it the world of employees relations in a foundry or the world of academic publishing. But how might we more formally conceptualise just what it is we are learning and writing about when we speak of the 'ropes' of human practices? I suggest that *institutional logics* and the handling of tensions between institutional logics play an important part in this. To explain my thinking here I will give my analysis a more substantive tone than so far by relating this move to my recent work on entrepreneurial action.

Pragmatic Realism and Overcoming Problems in Organization Studies: (3) Institutional Logics, Situated Creativity and Entrepreneurship

To resume briefly the autobiographical theme, I must go back to the mid-1990s when I had completed my ethnography of managerial work in a large organization. I was conscious of the fact that a great deal of my research activity until that time had occurred in large corporations. I had nevertheless been intrigued by what I had seen in some of the smaller enterprises that I had looked at from time to time. But as soon as I turned to the literature on small business in preparation for an ethnographic study of a smaller business, I realised that the field of study had somehow reconstituted itself as the study of 'entrepreneurship'. This, it seemed, was an organization-related activity which was to be distinguished from managerial work – a distinction which I argued, on the basis of the theoretical position which I had taken on managerial work and organizational effectiveness, was unwise (Watson 1995b). I have developed this theoretical position more recently and I am using the concept of institutional logics to argue that when we look at the strategic emergence of business and other enterprises, we should not distinguish between 'managers' and 'entrepreneurs' as two types of person, but, instead, recognise that the initiation and running of organizations involves a mixture of managerial and entrepreneurial *action*. I have argued for the abandoning of the whole notion of 'the entrepreneur' in academic research.

The entrepreneurship literature, rooted in the individualism of psychology and economics, has primarily concerned itself with such matters as the 'traits' of individual entrepreneurs or the 'opportunity recognition' propensities of the same characters. Most of the research has been of a scientistic nature (Hjorth et al. 2008; Watson 2012), operating within the 'spectator' mode rejected by Dewey. It has rarely, therefore, regarded the people involved in entrepreneurial action as *social* actors and its researchers have rarely got 'close to the action' through intensive fieldwork. My own ethnographic efforts in this area have pushed me firmly to the view that many people working to create, develop and maintain enterprises switch back and forth between undertaking entrepreneurial actions and managerial actions. This is where institutional logics (Friedland and Alford 1991; Thornton and Ocasio 2008) come upon the scene. I conceptualise these as *the sets of values, rules, assumptions and practices associated with key institutions of a society (such as family, the market, politics, religion, bureaucratic administration) which have been socially constructed over time and through which patterns of social organization and human activity are shaped and given meaning.* Anyone involved in the running of organizations has to learn the ropes of how to achieve a balance between attention paid to the logic of the competitive market (where, for example, cost-effective deals have to done with suppliers, workers and customers and the like) and the logic of bureaucratic administration in which both efficiency and welfare are sought through application of those principles shown by Max Weber to be central to modern societies.

It might seem, at first, that I am moving away from an obviously pragmatist style of theorising here with this attention to institutional logics. This is far from the case. The logics which all social actors have to come to terms with in their practices are inherent in the basic social institutions of the time and place in which these actors are located. And these institutions, as was stressed in the earlier discussion of the pragmatism and the social construction of reality, are the products of human creativity. They are the means by which the 'unfinished animals' of the human species have struggled to cope with the brute forces of reality pertaining at their point in history and their position in the structure of their society.

Staying with the key pragmatist notion of creativity, it is argued by Joas that all human action (i.e. initiatives that go beyond the habitual) can be understood as *situated creativity*, a concept which can be applied to 'the full spectrum of human action' (1996: 144). This fundamentally pragmatist insight has been invaluable in my attempts to bring a sociological, as opposed to a psychological or economic, perspective to 'entrepreneurship'. I conceptualise entrepreneurship as *entrepreneurial action*. This is action involving creative, adventurous or, imaginative deal-making which can be found – to various degrees at various times – in every emerging or established organization which has a market and a bureaucratic administrative dimension (Watson 2011, 2013a, 2013b). And it is hard to imagine any organization in an industrial capitalist world which does not have these two dimensions. Therefore a concern with entrepreneurial action in organizations not only develops, broadens and enriches entrepreneurship studies as such, it also draws attention to an aspect of organizations which has not had a great deal of attention in organization studies. To move from an emphasis on 'entrepreneurs' as special types of people to one on *entrepreneurial action* as a facet of organizing with which any given 'organiser' may engage to different extents at different times is very much a pragmatist move. It is one that can only strengthen organization studies and, in particular, creative or innovative aspects of the creation and running of organizations.

Conclusion

Pragmatism, at its heart, is an attempt to overcome the dualism between theory and practice, as was noted earlier. This makes it enormously relevant to organization studies. To the pragmatist, this should be an enterprise which not only attempts to make intellectual sense of organizational practices (studying how the organizational aspect of the social world 'works' using, for example, theoretical devices like institutional logics and entrepreneurial action) but is also to be evaluated in terms of the extent to which this intellectual sense-making informs the practices of those who engage with it. A pragmatist conception of social science is one of getting to grips intellectually with the social world so that people can act more successfully in the world. But simply to say this is to beg the question of just who is being informed and to ignore the danger of knowledge being taken up more readily by the privileged groups in society and thus used to assist them in the maintenance of their advantages. I therefore end this chapter by arguing this is an issue for politics and is a responsibility for everyone concerned with the maintenance of a democratic society. The role of the organization researcher is, in a fallibilist manner, to seek the truth about institutions and practices in a society and then to present these understandings to as many citizens of society as possible, in the hope that social and political debates will draw on them in the making of democratic choices.

Pragmatist social science is inherently critical. As a consequence of its philosophical roots in pragmatist anti-foundationalism and non-Cartesian scepticism, it questions all taken-for-granted ideas about the social world, subjecting all knowledge to the test how well it would 'stand up' if we based our actions upon it. If social research is successful in this way, the knowledge which it produces can be utilised by any interest group in society. This is a problem of all realist social science. If we are going to improve our understanding of how various aspects of the social world 'work in practice' we have to face the uncomfortable fact that the 'truths' that we present have potential value to people of whom we may disapprove as well as to those whose purposes we support. If, for example, we write a research report which throws light upon how certain criminal organizations operate we will be offering something valuable to the police, policy-makers and legislators. But that knowledge will have the same potential to inform the practices of people wishing to establish or improve existing criminal enterprises. By the same token, 'good' entrepreneurship research can be of equal value to people starting or running businesses as people wishing to resist the excesses of an entrepreneurially oriented society.

As I have argued elsewhere, with regard to 'critical management studies' (Watson 2001b), 'critical human resource management' (Watson 2004, 2010), the sociology of work (Watson 2009) and ethnographic research (Watson 2011), being 'critical' is not a matter of doing research that 'takes sides' on social and employment issues. The researcher, as a citizen of society, may well 'take sides' in debates and disputes once the research is done by taking their work out of the university or research institute into ongoing democratic debates in society. The pragmatist-sociologist, Mills, and pragmatist philosophers who inspired him (Horowitz 1966) did become socially engaged in various ways. However, pragmatism as such is matter of analysing the world, albeit by engaging in or getting close to social practices. For organizational researchers, it is a superb inspiration and guide to producing practice–oriented social knowledge which has a relevance to anyone in society interested in the way we organise work and other social activities.

References

Ackroyd, S. and Fleetwood, S. 2000. *Realist Perspectives on Management and Organisations*. London: Routledge.

Alvesson, M. and Karreman, D. 2000. Taking the linguistic turn in organizational research, challenges, responses, consequences. *Journal of Applied Behavioral Science*, 36: 136–58.

Becker, H.S., Geer, B., Hughes, E.C. and Strauss, A.L. 1961. *Boys in White*. Chicago, IL: University of Chicago Press.

Bendix, R. 1966. *Max Weber: An Intellectual Portrait*. London: Methuen.

Berger, P. 1969. *The Social Reality of Religion*. Harmondsworth: Penguin.

Berger, P. and Luckmann, T. 1967. The *Social Construction of Reality*. New York: Doubleday Anchor.

Bergmann, G. 1992. *New Foundations of Ontology*. Madison, WI: University of Wisconsin Press.

Bernstein, R.J. 2010. *The Pragmatic Turn*. Cambridge: Polity.

Bhaskar, R.A. 1978. *A Realist Theory of Science*, 2nd edn. Brighton: Harvester.

Blumer, H. 1969. *Symbolic Interactionism: Perspective and Method*. Englewood Cliffs, NJ: Prentice Hall.

Burns, T. 1962. The sociology of industry, in *Society: Problems and Methods of Study*, (ed.) Welford et al. London: Routledge and Kegan Paul.

Contu, A. and Willmott, H. 2005. You spin me around: The realist turn in organisation and management studies. *Journal of Management Studies*, 42(8): 1645–62.

Delanty, G. and Strydom, P. (eds). 2003. *Philosophies of Social Science: The Classic and Contemporary Readings*. Maidenhead: Open University Press.

Eldridge, J., Cressey, P. and MacInnes, J. 1991. *Industrial Sociology and Economic Crisis*. Hemel Hempstead: Harvester Wheatsheaf.

Friedland, R. and Alford, R. 1991. Bringing society back in: Symbols, practices, and institutional contradictions, in *The New Institutionalism in Organizational Analysis*, (ed.) W.W. Powell and P.J DiMaggio. Chicago, IL: University of Chicago Press, 232–63.

Freund, J. 1972. *The Sociology of Max Weber*. Harmondsworth: Penguin.

Gehlen, A. 1940. *Der Mensch. Seine Natur und seine Stellung in der Welt* ('Man, his nature and place in the world'). Berlin: Junker and Dünnhaupt.

Gross, N. 2009. A pragmatist theory of social mechanisms. *American Sociological Review*, 74(30), 358–79.

Haack, S. 1996. 'Pragmatism' in *The Blackwell Companion to Philosophy*, (ed.) N. Bunnin and E.P.Tsui-James. Oxford: Blackwell.

Hennis, W. 2000. *Max Weber's Science of Man*. Newbury: Threshold Press.

Hjorth, D., Jones, C. and Gartner, W. 2008. Introduction to 'Recreating/Recontextualising Entrepreneurship'. *Scandinavian Journal of Management*, 24(2), 81–4.

Horowitz, I.L. 1966. The intellectual genesis of C. Wright Mills, in *Sociology and Pragmatism: The Higher Learning in America*. New York: Oxford University Press.

James, W. 1908. The meaning of the word 'truth'. *Mind*, 17(67), 455–6.

Joas, H. 1993. *Pragmatism and Social Theory*. Chicago, IL: University of Chicago Press.

Joas, H. 1996. *The Creativity of Action*. Cambridge: Polity Press.

Johnson, P. and Duberley, J. 2000. *Understanding Management Research*. London: Sage.

Locke, J. 1689. An essay: Concerning human understanding, in *Of Knowledge and Probability*, Book IV.

Lovejoy, A.O. 1963. *The Thirteen Pragmatisms*. Baltimore: Johns Hopkins University Press.

Luckmann, T. 1983. *Life-World and Social Realities*. London: Heinemann.

McKelvey, B. 2001. From fields to science in *Point/Counterpoint: Central Debates in Organization Theory*, (ed.) R. Westwood and S. Clegg. Oxford: Blackwell.

Mills, C.W. 1959. *The Sociological Imagination*. New York: Oxford University Press.

Mills, C.W. 1966. *Sociology and Pragmatism*. New York: Oxford University Press.

Mills, C.W. 1967/1944. The social role of the intellectual, in *Power, Politics and People: The Collected Essays of C. Wright Mills*, (ed.) I.L. Horowitz. New York: Oxford University Press.Misak, C. 2007. *New Pragmatists*. Oxford: Oxford University Press.

Mounce, H.O. 1997. *The Two Pragmatisms*. London: Routledge.

Popper, K. 1959. *The Logic of Scientific Discovery*. London: Routledge and Kegan Paul.

Popper, K. 1963. *Conjectures and Refutations: The Growth of Scientific Knowledge*. London: Routledge and Kegan Paul.

Putnam, H. 1990. *Realism with a Human Face*, (ed.) J. Conant, Cambridge, MA: Harvard University Press.

Radkau, J. 2009. *Max Weber*. Cambridge: Polity Press.

Reed, M. 2004. Getting real about organizational discourse, in *The Sage Handbook of Organizational Discourse*, (ed.) D. Grant, C. Hardy, C. Oswick and L. Putnam. London: Sage, 413–20.

Reed, M. 2005. Reflections on the realist turn in organisation and management studies. *Journal of Management Studies*, 42(8), 1621–44.

Reed, M. 2009. Critical Realism: Method, or philosophy or philosophy in search of a method?, in *The Sage handbook of Organizational Research Methods*, (ed.) D.A. Buchanan and A. Bryman. London: Sage, 430–48.

Rescher, M. 2003. *Nature and Understanding: The Metaphysics and Method of Science*. New York: Oxford University Press.

Sayer, A. 1992. *Method in Social Science: A Realist Approach*, 2nd edn. London: Routledge.

Schiller, F.C.S. 1907. *Studies in Humanism*. London: Macmillan.

Simpson, B. 2011. Pragmatism, Mead and the practice purn. *Organization Studies*, 30(12), 1329–47.

Thornton, P. and Ocasio W. 2008. Institutional logics, in *The Sage Handbook of Organizational Institutionalism*, (ed.) R. Greenwood, C. Oliver, K. Sahlin and R. Suddaby. London: Sage, 99–129.

Urmson, J.O. 1989. Truth, in *The Concise Encyclopedia of Western Philosophy and Philosophers*, (ed.) J.O. Urmson and J. Rée. London: Routledge.

Van de Ven, A. 2007. *Engaged Scholarship*. Oxford: Oxford University Press.

Watson, T.J. 1995a. Shaping the story: Rhetoric, persuasion and creative writing in organisational ethnography. *Studies in Cultures, Organisations and* Society, 1(2), 301–1.

Watson, T.J. 1995b. Entrepreneurship and professional management: A fatal distinction. *International Small Business Journal*, 13(3), 33–45.

Watson, T.J. 2001a. *In Search of Management*. London: Cengage (originally Routledge, 1994).

Watson, T.J. 2001b. Beyond managism: Negotiated narratives and critical management education in practice. *British Journal of Management*, 12(4), 385–96.

Watson, T.J. 2004. Human resource management and critical social science analysis. *Journal of Management Studies*, 41(3), 447–67.

Watson, T.J. 2008. The social construction of reality, in *Organizing Words: A Critical Thesaurus for Social and Organization Studies*, (ed.) Y. Gabriel. Oxford: Oxford University Press, 7–71.

Watson, T.J. 2009. Work and the sociological imagination: The need for continuity and change in the study of continuity and change. *Sociology* 43(5), 861–77.

Watson, T.J. 2010. Critical social science, pragmatism and the realities of HRM. *International Journal of Human Resource Management*, 21(6), 915–31.

Watson T.J. 2011. Ethnography, reality and truth: The vital need for studies of 'how things work' in organisations and management. *Journal of Management Studies*, 48(1), 202–17.

Watson, T.J. 2012a. *Sociology, Work and Organisation*. London: Routledge.

Watson, T.J. 2012b. Pragmatism, reality and entrepreneurship: Entrepreneurial action and effectuation perspectives, in *Perspectives in Entrepreneurship*, (ed.) K. Mole and M. Ram. Basingstoke: Palgrave Macmillan.

Watson, T.J. 2013a. Entrepreneurial action and the Euro-American social science tradition: Pragmatism, realism and looking beyond 'the entrepreneur'. *Entrepreneurship and Regional Development*, 25(1-2), 16–33.

Watson, T.J. 2013b. Entrepreneurship in action: Studying entrepreneurial action in its personal, organisational and institutional context through ethnographic field research. *Entrepreneurship and Regional Development*, DOI:10.1080/08985626.2012.754645.

Westwood, R. and Linstead, S. (eds). 2001. *The Language of Organization*. London: Sage.

Yanow, D. and Ybema, S. 2009. Interpretivism in organizational research: On elephants and blind researchers, in *The SAGE handbook of Organizational Research Methods*, (ed.) D.A. Buchanan and A. Bryman. London: Sage, 39–60.

5 *Eric Voegelin's Reading of William James: Towards an Understanding of Leading within the Tensions of a Pluralistic Universe*

NATHAN HARTER

Introduction

In 1909, William James published a series of lectures as *A Pluralistic Universe* (1909/1996). His contention that human beings form discontinuous conceptualizations of a paramount reality, that steadily exceeds and violates what we can think of it, injects a healthy dose of skepticism. Humans adopt multiple symbols to represent the same reality, so that we end up with topographical maps, highway maps, weather maps, and jurisdictional maps for the same town, just as organizations are depicted in various abstract ways, such as organizational charts, flow charts, balance sheets, and so forth. Humans are quite prolific at creating these maps. The problem is that each act of conceptualization abstracts to one degree or another from reality and fixes the image in one's mind. James underscored the utility of such concepts, despite their limitations. We do need concepts. Holding our concepts loosely requires being open to contrary evidence and to alternate conceptualizations; or, as James put it, our intelligence 'must at any cost keep on speaking terms with the universe that engendered it' (1909/1996: 207). Failure to be on such 'speaking terms' leads to what came to be known as misplaced concreteness, confusing the map with the territory, and as a result contributes to organizations that become 'obstacles to the very purposes which their founders had in view' (1909/1996: 96). People tend to lock down mentally, closing their minds, and persist in engaging in practices that eventually undermine their interests, because they adhere to concepts that cannot completely correspond to the facts. They rely on their concepts to the exclusion of the reality these concepts were intended to capture.

Dramatizing the problem identified by James, the 2011 feature-length film *Margin Call* (Lionsgate/Roadside Attractions) is based on an overnight panic at an investment firm once management discovers too late that its financial models had been simply erroneous, which in turn had led them unawares to lose more money in a few days than the entire firm was worth. The models on which they were relying proved inadequate. From there, it was a rapid descent into ruin. Their flawed conceptualization of the markets had been driving decisions that ultimately worked against their interests. One can read the more famous lectures on pragmatism by James (1907) as an explanation how to avoid this fate. In other words, it would help those in organizations to accept the argument in the earlier set of lectures in order to profit from the argument in the latter.

An important topic in organization studies is leadership. Leadership exists, in part, to help individuals and organizations achieve their purposes or devise new ones. If James is correct about the pluralistic universe, then one of the tasks of leadership is to encourage a culture of openness and to transcend its long-standing concepts, largely by challenging their ongoing utility. It was this lesson that lay at the center of a popular management handbook titled *Who Moved My Cheese?* by Spencer Johnson (1998/2002). By the same token, of course, leaders need not repeatedly upset the entire conceptual framework being used by people in the organization. That would be needlessly disruptive. Instead, an organization operates in a perpetual tension between continuity and change, familiarity and novelty. Pragmatism promises to help organizations live within that tension and possibly flourish in a pluralistic universe.

After touring the US on a stipend from the Rockefeller Foundation in 1924, a young Viennese scholar by the name of Eric Voegelin tried to make sense of distinctively American contributions to social thought, and he devoted a number of pages in the resulting book-length manuscript to the pragmatism of William James and the importance of his pluralistic worldview (1928/1995). With that, he began a lifelong interest in the tension we have been describing which, in deference to Plato, Voegelin referred to as the *metaxy*, as well as a pursuit of the proper method for living within that tension. This project of Voegelin's culminated in the last work being written on his deathbed: namely, the final volume of the magnum opus *Order and History* (1987).

It is the purpose of this chapter to apply Voegelin's investigations about the *metaxy* to the organizational problems first identified by James, thereby informing prospective leaders what might be done. To the extent organizations operate according to conceptualizations or 'maps' that fail to correspond adequately to the reality on the ground, they will eventually lose opportunities, function in a sub-optimal manner, or even take action contrary to their interests. This is because the maps are not the territory, and leaders especially need to return organizations back to direct encounters with paramount reality in order to appreciate the both/and, pluralistic character of their predicaments.

This chapter will introduce some of the relevant lessons from James's lectures on both pragmatism and pluralism before explaining how Voegelin interpreted them at three stages in his long and distinguished career. First, it summarizes Voegelin's initial findings in the first book he ever wrote, after returning from the US. Second, it describes how these lessons fit into his own mature theoretical statement titled *Anamnesis*. Third, it shows how the scholar was continuing to develop his understanding during the last years of his life. In conclusion, the chapter will set forth implications for leadership today, when so many tensions and 'wicked problems' threaten to overrun our mental models and decision trees. If the evidence suggests we do live in a pluralistic universe, then pragmatism offers to help us function, if not thrive.

William James and Pragmatism

At retirement, William James delivered a series of lectures at the Lowell Institute in Boston in 1906 and 1907. These lectures were subsequently published as a book titled *Pragmatism: A New Name for Some Old Ways of Thinking*. Soon after, in 1908 and 1909, he delivered another series of lectures at Manchester College, Oxford University, and these were subsequently published in 1909 as *A Pluralistic Universe*. In a relatively short span, James delivered two significant lecture series. Early in his presentation of pragmatism, James stated in no uncertain terms that it is a method only (1907: 51). It has no dogma, no substantive doctrine of its own (1907: 54; cf. 1907: 65f.). At the risk of oversimplifying his explanation for how it works, we should be able to ascertain some of the dominant features.

Each of us begins with a stock of existing beliefs that we accept as true. W.V. Quine and J.S. Ullian were to refer to this later as the 'web of belief' (1970/1978). These beliefs became beliefs largely because at some level they worked for us or for those who taught them to others. These beliefs are extremely important, primarily because they have already proven their worth, that is, they have utility, but also because as James pointed out they became increasingly integrated with each other, like many threads pulled together tightly into a whole that is functional. Pragmatism advises great deference to the fabric of one's current beliefs; presumably you hold them for good reason. Periodically, however, experience will cast doubt on one belief or another, introducing new facts to be considered. Existing beliefs do not always account for these facts. What then? At such moments, pragmatism recommends taking the new evidence seriously and formulating an idea that reconciles it best with the prevailing fabric of beliefs. That new idea can be said to 'audition' to become a belief, such that the idea 'counts as "true" just in proportion as it gratifies the individual's desire to assimilate the novel in his experience to his beliefs in stock' (James 1907: 63) To the extent the new idea requires revising or replacing some existing belief, the quandary must be met, both logically and psychologically. James does so by investigating the practical consequences of each alternative (1907: 45). 'In what respects would the world be different if this alternative or that were true?' (1907: 48). Does one belief help us more to thrive in the reality we experience?

Many people fail to follow this method, often because they adhere to existing beliefs despite evidence to the contrary. They regard their own stock of beliefs to be compelling in much the same way that two plus two must equal four. They fail to recognize that their beliefs are instruments toward some end (1907: 53). And that end has to include being on speaking terms with the cosmos, approximating reality like a drapery laid over hard surfaces. New facts – facts that cast existing beliefs into doubt – indicate the extent to which those beliefs might need to be re-examined. When your beliefs prevent you from flourishing, you have a problem. Ronald Heifetz illustrates the predicament when beliefs prevent flourishing, in *Leadership without Easy Answers* (2001), where he describes the fate of Polynesians 1,500 years ago who settled on Easter Island. Without adapting their previous way of life to the new situation, so that as their condition on Easter Island worsened, they turned in desperation to cultic behavior, human sacrifice, cannibalism, and war, before Europeans arrived to subdue them completely (2001: 32–5). It was in response to this kind of predicament that Heifetz teaches what he calls the adaptive work of leadership.

This adherence to existing beliefs can become a problem popularized by management consultant Tim Hurson as 'the elephant's tether'. That is, a tendency to ignore data contrary to familiar ways of thinking. An elephant in captivity gets so used to being tethered that eventually when it matures and possesses the strength to yank itself free, it does not even try (2008: 23–32). Karl Weick and Kathleen Sutcliffe have written about this 'tendency to seek confirmation and shun disconfirmation' – a tendency that prevents organizations from preparing for the unexpected (2001: 35). The human tendency to rely on familiar beliefs is understandable, of course, yet as James wrote elsewhere, 'pragmatism … has to fall back on … a certain willingness to live without assurances or guarantees' (1909/1970: 229).

William James took the position that the process of pragmatism depends upon fostering openness to new facts and new ideas. Existing beliefs have to be subject to change, inasmuch as he stated elsewhere the conviction that '[t]he fundamental fact about our experience is that it is a process of change' (1909/1970: 89). Indeed, he fully understood the ongoing desire to construct a system of beliefs that would be coherent and complete (see 1907: 240). He was not opposed to such a project but the resulting 'system' – whatever it looks like – has to subject itself repeatedly to experience. Otherwise, it tends to block new experiences, especially experiences incompatible with the system. We would, in other words, be prudent to construct an elaborate system of beliefs, so long as that system is always subject to revision. And the way to proceed, as he saw it, is to move back and forth between experience and our conceptualizations of it, in a complementary rhythm (1907: 225). One must occasionally return with the map to inspect the terrain and reconcile discrepancies. In this manner, truth becomes something we approximate over time. Humankind had been doing this as a species, he argued, just as each one of us as individuals has done it over the course of a lifetime. Pragmatism is, as he admitted, our old way of thinking. We can refer to the resulting accumulation of beliefs as common sense (see 1907: 170). But we have to keep in mind how the fabric of our beliefs came to be in the first place, by a process very much like the pragmatic method. Why then should it stop now, as though there is nothing new in the world? If anything, James would advise us to continue reweaving our system of beliefs and, if anything, do it better. Toward the end of his lectures on pragmatism, James put it epigrammatically: 'Previous truth; fresh facts: – and our mind finds a new truth' (1907: 241).

One of the specific ways we neglect the pragmatic method is when we make distinctions in our mind that do not fit reality. We often tend to draw bright lines between two concepts such as black and white, when in reality there may be shades of gray. Common sense often advises us to make such distinctions – night and day, good and bad-as though reality is as neatly divided as our conceptualizations of it. Frequently, then, we hew to our categories and the boundaries we suppose, rather than to a world of indefinite shading (see for example 1907: 177). This is misplaced concreteness all over again. James then asked: can apparent contraries be reconciled? (1907: 269). We should be open to the possibility and sometimes they can be. Or is there perhaps a midpoint between two polar extremes, as James suggested (1907: 295). Pragmatism allows for these both/and, in-between possibilities, as well (1907: 33). In *A Pluralistic Universe*, James will insist on them.

A PLURALISTIC UNIVERSE

Early in this latter series of lectures, William James set forth a distinction between two competing visions or outlooks in philosophy which he named monism and pluralism

(1909/1996: lectures I–II). The specific meaning of these terms is not relevant for our purposes. However, it would be useful to note that James questions the argument that if two things are related, then there is some third thing comprehending them. They can be related in one sense, certainly, he agrees, but unrelated in another sense (1909/1996: 66). There is little reason to infer some kind of third thing between them, some connective tissue, when it could as easily make sense to say their relationship is an interpenetration (1909/1996: 70). James was quite aware that we often unify in our minds distinct things that happen to share something in common, such as the winds, rain, hailstones, lightning, and thunder that constitute in our minds a storm. Logically, each of these distinct phenomena could, upon further examination, be constituted of even smaller things, and so on. The rainwater, for instance, can be understood as two parts hydrogen and one part oxygen. At the other extreme, a storm can actually be part of a larger unity, such as a squall line. This mental operation of unification at various magnitudes of being is not only familiar but useful (1909/1996: 189). We do it all the time. James even went so far as to concede that apparent oppositions can often be seen from a higher synthesis (1909/1996: 99). Nevertheless, whenever we do this unifying in our minds, imagining a composite, we overlook the fact that the unity is also a multiplicity and possibly part of a larger unity. When unifying, we tend to give a label to something such as a soul or a nation state or a river without being entirely sure of its identity. Why? The unity is logically convenient even if it is also artificial. In other words, the unity possesses 'cash-value' of a pragmatic sort. It simply helps in ordinary life to speak in terms of a storm and even give it a name, such as the 2011 hurricane Irene.

James referred to our power to unify conceptually as a sublime prerogative unique to humanity (1909/1996: 217). The problem, of course, is that the unity sometimes fails to account for the reality of experience, and when that happens we should be willing to revise or replace the 'unity' in our minds according to the pragmatic method. Otherwise, our conceptualizations will eventually distort our understanding of reality (1909/1996: 219). We will persist in beliefs that do not accord with the facts.

In the lecture on Henri Bergson (1909/1996: lecture VI), James examined the question of time as a moving thing, as though it were like a movie reel comprised of a series of still images projected so rapidly that viewers infer motion. This explanation of time suggests that we replace one state of being with another. Logically, you could slice linear time into increasingly finer increments, ad infinitum. On the contrary, James wrote about the 'compenetration' of things, their shading into one another (1909/1996: 271). Maybe instead of a space or a time that comes between A and C, A and C participate in each other and we call their compenetration B. Two distinct things might overlap or blend, even when they can be separated conceptually. James even speculated that 'your' consciousness and 'my' consciousness at some point compenetrate (1909/1996: 290). This is not a trivial example, inasmuch as leadership scholars address themselves to shared purpose and other instances of *homonoia* (see for example Carson et al. 2007). As human beings struggle to construct their beliefs, preferably in accordance with experience, they will never arrive at the final, definitive version, partly because the task is just too complex and vast for the human mind,[1] but more importantly because whatever we construct in our minds is not the reality itself. It is only a way of understanding, that is, an abstraction

---

1   Nobel laureate Herbert Simon has written extensively on the principle of bounded rationality and its implications for organizational life (for example Simon 2000).

which necessarily omits or excludes portions of reality. No matter what we witness or think, there is some residue beyond our powers to conceive. 'Something always escapes', James wrote (1909/1996: 321). Abstraction as an activity, by its very nature, requires ignoring something. Because of this, the pragmatic method would advise us periodically to reverse the usual process by which we hypothesize unifications, justify them, use them, and then take them for granted. We can periodically back out of our dogmatic posturing and accept living in a liminal mode, always betwixt and between, attuned to the reality in which we must learn to function. In that way we might hold our beliefs about the world loosely, to the extent they serve our purposes, and remain forever open to revision in the light of experience.

Eric Voegelin

In 1928, a young Austrian scholar by the name of Eric Voegelin published his first book. In it, he presented the results of a trip he took to the US beginning in 1924, some 14 years after William James had passed away and 15 years since the publication of *Pragmatism* and *A Pluralistic Universe*. In that report, Voegelin includes many references to William James in particular, as well as making remarks about pragmatism generally and the influence of John Dewey and Charles Sanders Peirce, among others. Thus, this book is the first account of Voegelin's direct encounter with the pragmatist movement in the US. Voegelin would continue to cite James and pragmatism throughout a long and prolific career as a scholar, even though it cannot be said that Voegelin was himself a pragmatist. The citations can be tracked in his *Collected Works*, published by the University of Missouri Press. Clearly, Voegelin had found uses for the work of pragmatists and said so. This does not include the many occasions when he might have been influenced by the movement without giving explicit citations. In the secondary literature, Arthur Rhydon Jackson wrote: 'James' vision ultimately became an important example for Voegelin of ... 'metaxic' participation ...' (2009: 3f., see Boczek 2009). Voegelin might not have been a pragmatist in the conventional sense, yet he was certainly influenced by James and more specifically by *The Pluralistic Universe*. This much seems probable. Let us briefly consider three of Voegelin's books – from the beginning, middle, and end of his long publishing career – as they describe an arc originating in his exposure to pragmatism.

ON THE FORM OF THE AMERICAN MIND

Voegelin's first book undertakes a study in which the work of William James (and especially *The Pluralistic Universe*) features prominently. What Voegelin as a young scholar detected in the shaping of American thought turned out to have lasting significance, and it begins with the observation that the past survives in the autonomous forms of the present (1928/1995: 14f.). What this means is that scholars cannot completely divorce the present from the past as though the two are distinct in every way but succession. Occasionally, it is the case that we experience one stage or phase in a process and next, another stage or phase that is noticeably different, so that we infer a transition from A to B simply because the two are different, as for example when you return to your hometown and find an elementary school building has been torn down. Each of us is capable of inferring change and motion from a succession of static images. Nevertheless, we can also experience the change itself, directly. Only afterwards do we separate and sort by making conceptual distinctions (1928/1995: 52f.). Experience comes first; conceptualization follows. The sequence here is crucial because the same structure will pertain to other lessons in Voegelin.

Americans in particular, it seems, have resisted conceptual distinctions, especially distinctions that prevent intimacy (1928/1995: 10), distinctions such as between you and me, between us and God, and (in the realm of intellectual life) between my ideas and your ideas (1928/1995: 12) – perhaps this is why both collaboration as well as plagiarism come so easily to American students? We tend to want to close up these apparent distances promiscuously, either as a matter of habit or with some measure of desperation. Distinctions can be said to run against the American ethos. According to Voegelin, William James contributed to the form of the American mind, in part, by articulating a philosophy explaining away these distinctions as mere constructs, inventions of the mind that do not always correspond with the facts. Pure experience, which comes *before* conceptualization, is thoroughly both/and (1928/1995: 52f.). This means that experience is, in the memorable phrasing of James, 'one great blooming, buzzing confusion' until the human mind differentiates it all. Our minds rebel against the compact, undifferentiated hubbub presented to our senses. It means nothing, all interlayered and churning in a bewildering pulp. Making a distinction – like all conceptualization – follows after the fact and immediately tends to obscure the both/and character of experience. We think using differentiation. Regardless how we think, however, we live at points of intersection (1928/1995: 51), where two or more lines can be said to claim the same point in space. Pure experience is for James the moment of intersection: neither of the lines to the exclusion of the other. He urges his reader to become open to the paradox in order to accept the both/and character of experience (1928/1995: 63). And for Americans, so eager to collapse distinctions, openness to the paradox would appear to be an attractive posture (1928/1995: 9 and 63). Where this finding led the young Voegelin was to a conclusion that appears at the very beginning of this, his first book:

The dualism by which we divide being in order to make its structure

> *rationally intelligible does not seem to separate it neatly into two halves. Notwithstanding such divisions, the relations between the two poles remain and the elements that we were careful to separate in fact remain so tightly meshed that it becomes well-nigh impossible to speak of dualism ... [Both poles] transcend into the other to such an extent that it is more accurate to speak of a unity than of a duality. (1928/1995: 23)*

The apparent unity in conceptual dualities interested Voegelin throughout his long career.

ANAMNESIS

At the height of his powers, Eric Voegelin interrupted extensive historical research in order to meditate on the project as a whole. What precisely was the purpose of his extended enterprise? As a result of these meditations, he wrote a book that developed the thoughts and ideas begun with *On the Form of the American Mind* and that, in the words of his editor, stands as 'Voegelin's summary theoretical statement' (2002: 3). This theoretical statement was titled *Anamnesis*. The basic argument of *Anamnesis*, as set forth by his editor David Walsh (2002: 1–27), holds that human beings adopt symbols to represent their experiences, usually by borrowing symbols already at hand in culture, though occasionally by adapting them or creating new ones. Frequently, then, subsequent to this adoption of symbols we tend to literalize the symbols, partly to preserve the experience in memory and share it with others. We cannot convey meaning without something to convey. This process of symbolization is inevitable and even useful for memory and communication. The problem lies in pressing these symbols into service beyond their original purpose. When that happens, the very means for preserving the truth of an experience becomes an obstacle to further experiences of truth. In saying this, Voegelin concurs with James.

To capture Voegelin's purpose, let us begin by examining the very meaning of the word 'anamnesis' that serves as the title of this particular book. *Anamnesis* can be translated from the Greek to mean remembering something that once had been known in the past, bringing it forward after it had been obscured somehow or lost. *Anamnesis* is the third stage after knowing and forgetting. Plato wrote about *anamnesis* as a restoration of knowledge that must have been possessed before we were even born (see for example his *Meno* and *Phaedo*). The tale should not be taken literally. It is not that *anamnesis* is a return to a previous state or condition of knowing that has become the past. Rather, we might more profitably regard it as the restoration of a state or condition that is, always present, the *metaxy* of James's pure experience. Symbolization that results in words, schemas, and dogma carries forward the past, like casting it in amber, whereas *anamnesis* would put the individual back into the mode that led to the symbols in the first place. Symbols are in one sense like ladles of water taken from a mountain spring and carried around for subsequent use, despite the increasing risk that the water will become stale or contaminated. According to this metaphor, it pays frequently to revisit the spring for fresh water. *Anamnesis* is the process that permits this. It is a recovery of the *present* and not of the past (2002: 17). *Anamnesis* restores the primordial.

A.E. Taylor makes the same basic point with regard to Plato's dialog *Meno*. Socrates was trying to overcome 'habituation in conformity to a tradition' and 'loyalty to an established tradition' by driving himself and his interlocutor to the personal effort of thinking (1963: 129–45). In this regard, see also Hans-Georg Gadamer (1968/1980: ch. 6) who writes:

> *Like all knowing, philosophical knowing is identification of something as what it is and has the structure of recognition, or 'knowing again'. ... [I]t is always reconstituted anew, and that occurs only when one tries to think it through for oneself.*

This experience of *anamnesis* confronts us with the *metaxy*, the structure of reality, for that is the purpose of *anamnesis*. It puts us back into the both/and structure known as *metalepsis*. In fact, the dominant image in Voegelin's text is the *metaxy* itself, finding oneself between two poles, at an intersection, a bend in the river without being able to see where it comes from or where it goes. Voegelin examined the *metaxy* in theories of consciousness, autobiographical reminiscence, historiogenesis, philosophy (including a philosophy of science), before he even began recounting the empirical studies on which this book was based. Over and over, one sees evidence of the same image, finding oneself between, in a state or condition of tension, trying to make sense of the predicament, unable to get a fix on the object of investigation. The sensitive person feels pulled in opposite directions, unable to turn completely one way or the other. How people together respond to the *metaxy* will ultimately influence their social order. We might say that, for Voegelin, the *metaxy* exquisitely depicts the human condition qua human. In concrete situations, then, in the flux of perplexing circumstances, we deliberate about what to do (2002: 152f.). How do we respond to the paradoxical structures of reality? Whatever we choose to do, there must be some goal or purpose, for this is why we take action (2002: 353). The problem is that we cannot ever discern the final goal; all we have is a general direction. Making matters worse, many of our fellow human beings resist taking action at all or they distort the goal. Probably the most pernicious distortion of all is believing you can discern the final goal, that for which reality (and humanity) exists. Yet is that not the purpose of *phronesis*, that is, to arrive at such a vision? By no means; instead, the goal in any situation appears to be to preserve the tension and, toward that end, to cultivate the permeability or openness of humankind toward the whole complex (2002: 154). Like James, Voegelin recommends openness. How this 'openness' has been understood has changed throughout the ages, and this is why Voegelin undertook his empirical studies.

These empirical studies examine (among other things) the effort to understand the leader as one who rises above fortune and makes things happen in the world, so that we might learn to imitate them (2002: ch. 8). The purpose of these studies was not so much to understand history as to understand a way of being in history, a way of being exemplified by the one we are calling a leader (2002: 203). The leader moves somewhere between being a mere mortal, subject to fortune, and being God. We should reasonably want to learn: how exactly does one actively participate in making history? Leaders can be said to participate in the creative work of the divine:

> In participation there is first a relation of identity because [the poles] must have something in common. A sort of area of overlapping; the same relation also does not hold true because they are not identical; when you get these relations and nonrelations of identity you can call the whole thing together: participation [emphasis applied]. (Voegelin, 2004: 252)

Voegelin's study of the Mongol Orders of Submission (2002: ch. 9) reveals the temptation of relying predominantly on symbols of authority, especially pronouncements, as though this alone will bring the rest of the world to subordination. The Mongol leaders believed their purposes to be practically indistinguishable from God's, such that making an utterance of their authority was supposed to convince others. It didn't. They confused the map with the territory.

Voegelin's brief examination of John Stuart Mill's treatment of 'discussion' (2002: ch. 11) considers the same question from within a more democratic ethos in which mere utterances by those in authority have lost their power. Societies that reject leadership based on godlike authority have adopted other political practices, not least of which is the practice of conversation and debate, which has the merit of subjecting participants to new points of view, new facts, new ideas. Discussion returns participants to that uncertainty about what to believe and what to do that is, characteristic of the *metaxy*. There is, in other words, an 'open' character to genuine dialog, congruent with the teachings of both James and Voegelin. Even here, however, things can go wrong. Discussion can be closed off by derailment into irrelevancies, back stair psychologizing, simplistic classifications, an overreliance on the assertion of values as dogma, as well as the dismissal of all talk of values altogether. What lessons, therefore, does Voegelin draw, especially for political life? The attempt to avoid or escape the inherent tension of existence will only result in falsehood and misery. What is to be done?

IN SEARCH OF ORDER

On his deathbed, Voegelin struggled to complete the masterwork titled *Order and History*. Once he realized it would be impossible to finish the fifth and final volume, he made sure to destroy any portions that he himself had not conclusively edited. By that point, the concept of the *metaxy* had become thoroughly integrated into his vision of the structure of reality (Rhodes 2003), finding a place of importance in both his very first and his last books. Notably, Voegelin said as much in a letter to Ellis Sandoz in 1971 (quoted in Sandoz 1987: 12). Once again, in this last book, Voegelin emphasized that one must not hypostatize either pole in a given tension, for without the one you cannot fully understand the other. But then, as he noted, one must not hypostatize the tension itself as an autonomous object, 'for that would fragmentize the paradoxic complex' by neglecting each of the poles (1987: 28). The whole belongs together. Voegelin then re-stated this principle when he asserted that 'they would lose their meaning if the complexes were fragmented and their parts hypostatized into intentionalist entities' (1987: 92). What is required, therefore, is (in echoes of James) openness to the paradox (1987: 47), 'a balanced state of existence, formed in reflective distance to the process of meditative wandering through the paradoxic manifold of tensions' (1987: 100).

There is then such a manifold of tensions that Voegelin wrote of 'the metaxic structure of the Cosmos' (1987: 89). Reality itself appears to be governed by these tensions which are, in his words, 'persuasively mediated by the process of the psychic reality "between" ...' (1987: 89). It is, in other words, we human beings who recognize the relationships comprehending apparent opposition, the unity behind the duality, holding the respective poles both apart and together in our minds. It is we who apprehend and confront the 'paradoxic' structure of reality. For this reason, humans enjoy the opportunity to witness and perhaps even participate in the 'creative fertility' of this structure as the symbol of becoming (1987: 105). Here I think is the best place to introduce a few of the more important implications of *The Pluralistic Universe*, *anamnesis*, and the *metaxy* for leadership studies.

Conclusion

Reality appears to be structured as a *metaxy* or tension that humans profitably symbolize, according to conceptual schemas that serve as abstractions for practical purposes, like maps. On occasion, however, those with a stake in human organizations rely on these abstractions at the cost of experiencing the more complete reality, in all its confusion known variously as both/and thinking, participation, metalepsis, mixture, compenetration, and so forth. By backing out of familiar abstractions in order to recover pure experience, they might encounter lessons for getting by in the world – lessons that serve their mutual purposes even better. To do all of that, of course, they must temporarily doubt what they have come to believe, and this doubt will likely feel threatening and uncomfortable. It rarely seems prudent when lost to throw away the map.

This disturbing in-between state or condition can be referred to as the *metaxy*, a liminal phase during which we let go of the past before arriving at some new understanding. Put differently, it is a troubling uncertainty that promises new knowledge. In anthropology, liminality refers to the creative potential in ritual before an outcome can be known, when the future is still in question and yet to be established. Presumably during ritual one encounters the mystical substructure, the truest moment, out of which the participant derives some sort of meaning and direction, perhaps with a new name and vocation (van Gennep 2004; Turner 1995). In short, liminality casts identity into doubt, raising those existential questions about who I am and what I am meant to be doing.

William James presented a method for navigating these dark waters, such that it will seem less intimidating beforehand and more useful as a consequence. Eric Voegelin investigated the role of the leader as one who not only enters this state or condition in search of a way forward, but who also induces others to undergo the same experience to reach the other side. In democratic cultures, this would be accomplished by dialog, as well as efforts to create and protect times and places for these liminal experiences, such that the dialogs recur continually, for only in that way can human beings act collectively in closest approximation to the order of reality wherein we hope to flourish. Those who would lead by relying on these lessons must first be open to alternative versions of the reality they occupy.

Gareth Morgan (1986), for example, set forth a variety of images of organizations to demonstrate there is more than one way to see the same thing. But it is more than making the hackneyed 'paradigm shift' from one version of reality to another, as though you could lay one down and pick up one that is better, even if a learning organization were dedicated to doing this over and over. Studies about transitions from one way of seeing to another, which Peter Senge called *metanoia* (1990: 13f.), appear many places already in the literature on the change process. Pragmatism, especially as interpreted by the likes of Eric Voegelin, goes further than saying leaders must be open to change and must bring followers through the change process from point A to point B. Voegelin invited leaders to hold multiple versions simultaneously, even if they appear to clash against each other, so long as there is evidence for each. One is not advised to replace versions of reality so much as add them together, interweaving them in the fashion advocated by Quine and Ullian (1970/1978). Roger Martin (2007) refers to the capacity for doing this as 'an opposable mind'. We can find writers making the case for fuzzy and paradoxical thinking and for polarity management to guide leaders through the stress and confusion of these blurry conditions. What it comes down to is something Peter Drucker advocated that schools teach more intentionally, namely a greater emphasis on simple, direct perception (1989: 255–64). What exactly is the case? Subsequent writers might call it 'mindfulness' or 'presence', but really it is a return to an encounter with the paramount world in which we hope to operate. Plato's *anamnetic* experience was about restoring one's attention to the evidence, the encounter. F. Byron Nahser, in his 1997 book subtitled *Reclaiming Pragmatism for Business*, concluded with a chapter urging the leader to focus more on 'What's really going on?' What we find is that reality is messier than our constructs probably led us to believe. Charles Handy put it succinctly: 'We have to find ways to make sense of the paradoxes, to use them to shape a better destiny' (1994: xi). What we will find are not just the so-called 'tame' problems susceptible to linear conceptualizations but also the "wicked" problems of complex, intersecting systems for which no simple, elegant solution presents itself (see Grint 2010, citing Rittell and Webber

1973) In those situations, a pragmatic response would have to hold the complexity as a tension, an inescapable tension, which begins with the leader who has the openness to see it for what it is and be comfortable with that.

References

Boczek, M. 2009. William James' pure experience and the creative potential of the metaxy. [Online: APSA 2009 Toronto Meeting Paper]. Available at: http://ssrn.com/abstract=1449463 [accessed: 4 October 2011].

Carson, J., Tesluk, P. and J. Marrone. 2007. Shared leadership in teams: An investigation of antecedent conditions and performance. *Academy of Management Journal*, 50(5) 1217–34.

Drucker, P. 1989. *The New Realities*. New York: Harper and Row.

Gadamer, H. 1968/1980. Plato's unwritten dialectic, in Gadamer, H. *Dialogue and Dialectic: Eight Hermeneutical Studies on Plato*. New Haven, CT: Yale University Press, ch. 6.

Gennep, A. van 2004. *The Rites of Passage* (Routledge library editions: Anthropology and ethnography). London: Routledge.

Grint, K. 2010. *Leadership: A Very Short Introduction*. New York: Oxford University Press.

Handy, C. 1994. *The Age of Paradox*. Boston, MA: Harvard Business School Press.

Heifetz, R. 2001. *Leadership without Easy Answers*. Cambridge, MA: Belknap Press.

Hurson, T. 2008. *Think Better: An Innovator's Guide to Productive Thinking*. New York: McGraw-Hill.

Jackson, A.R. 2009. Science and paradox: Peirce and Voegelin on the practice of language amid God, man, world, and society. [Online: APSA 2009 Toronto Meeting Paper]. Available at: http://ssrn.com/abstract=1449472 [accessed: 4 October 2011].

James, W. 1907. *Pragmatism: A New Name for Some Old Ways of Thinking*. New York: Longman, Green, and Co.

James, W. 1909/1950. *The Meaning of Truth*. Ann Arbor, MI: The University of Michigan Press.

James, W. 1909/1996. *A Pluralistic Universe*. Lincoln, NE: University of Nebraska Press.

Johnson, S. 1998/2002. *Who Moved My Cheese?* New York: G.P. Putnam's Sons.

Margin Call. 2011. Lionsgate/Roadside Attractions.

Martin, R. 2007. *The Opposable Mind: How Successful Leaders Win through Integrative Thinking*. Boston, MA: Harvard Business School Press.

Morgan, G. 1986. *Images of Organizations*. Newbury Park: Sage.

Nahser, F.B. 1997. *Learning to Read the Signs: Reclaiming Pragmatism for Business*. Boston, MA: Butterworth-Heinemann.

Quine, W.V. and Ullian, J.S. 1970/1978. *The Web of Belief*, 2nd edn. New York: McGraw-Hill.

Rhodes, J. 2003. What is metaxy? Diotima and Voegelin. [Online: Annual Meeting of the American Political Science Association]. Available at: http://www.lsu.edu/artsci/groups/voegelin/society/2003%20Papers/Rhodes.shtml [accessed: 15 September 2011].

Sandoz, E. 1987. Introduction, in *In Search of Order*, (ed.) E. Voegelin. Baton Rouge, LA: Louisiana State University Press, 1–12.

Senge, P. 1990. *The Fifth Discipline: The Art and Practice of the Learning Organization*. New York: Doubleday Currency.

Simon, H. 2000. Bounded rationality in social science: Today and tomorrow. *Mind and Society*, 1, 25–39.

Taylor, A.E. 1963. *Plato: The Man and His Work*. Cleveland: World Publishing Co., 129–45.

Turner, V. 1995. *The Ritual Process: Structure and Anti-Structure* (Lewis Henry Morgan Lectures). Piscataway, NJ: Aldine Transaction.

Voegelin, E. 1987. *In Search of Order*. Baton Rouge, LA: Louisiana State University Press.

Voegelin, E. 1928/1995. *The Collected Works* (vol. 1) (R. Hein, trans.), (ed.) J. Gebhardt and B. Cooper. Baton Rouge, LA: Louisiana State University Press.

Voegelin, E. 2002. *The Collected Works* (vol. 6) (G. Niemeyer and M.J. Hanak, trans.), (ed.) D. Walsh. Columbia, MO: University of Missouri Press.

Voegelin, E. 2004. *The Collected Works* (vol. 33), (ed.) W. Petropulos and G. Weiss. Columbia, MO: University of Missouri Press.

Weick, K. and K. Sutcliffe. 2001. *Managing the Unexpected: Assuring High Performance in an Age of Complexity*. San Francisco, CA: Jossey-Bass.

6 Pragmatism, Social Reconstruction, and Organizational Theory

DAVID C. JACOBS

Introduction

Philosophical pragmatism, especially as advanced by the American scholar John Dewey, has much to contribute to organizational theory. Deweyan pragmatism subjects existing institutions and practices to a thorough examination through the consideration of social consequences. Neither market nor hierarchy benefits from any a priori preference. Instead, individuals and groups practice an experimental method which treats customs and practices as subject to evidence-based revision. Truths are necessarily contextual, contingent, and verified by experience. Dewey (1925) writes, 'Every thinker puts some portion of an apparently stable world in peril and no one can wholly predict what will emerge in its place', by which he meant that inquiry may undo habits and upend existing organizations. Deweyan pragmatism focuses on problem-solving, which is a common preoccupation of managers, but Dewey's perspective transcends the traditional managerial framework. At the root of many of the deficits of business practice and organizational theory is a narrow and bounded practicality that sharply contradicts Deweyan pragmatism. Dewey's philosophy acknowledges a world of organizations that are highly imperfect, rife with institutionalized inequality that limits human development, and yet susceptible to pressure for democratization.

In this chapter I explore Dewey's contribution to organizational theory through the consideration of his written works and his activism. First, I will introduce the concept of the 'public', which necessarily exists in tension with formal organizations. I will explore the democratic core of pragmatist organizational theory as well as the emphasis on experimentation. I will contrast Deweyan pragmatism with organizational behavior contingency theories which superficially resemble pragmatism. I will then turn to two forms of pragmatism in action: a brief history of activist groups Dewey helped form in pursuit of pragmatist social change and an analysis of the related notions of social invention and social entrepreneurship. In these last two sections I will place Dewey in the context of important debates with such individuals as Leon Trotsky and Edward Filene, in order to illuminate pragmatism in action. My argument here relies, in part, on my earlier thoughts published in *Collective Bargaining as an Instrument of Social Change* (Jacobs 1994).

Dewey's Publics

Dewey regarded organizations as provisional instruments of social action, as temporary embodiments of the shared knowledge and capacity of social groups. Existing organizational practices are subject to challenge by concerned communities arising to remedy problems that beset members. This is Dewey's public: a group of people who recognize a problem and mobilize in order to address it.

Contrary to the notion of perpetual life for the corporation or any form of inherited privilege, Deweyan pragmatism demands that organizations serve the living and embody the problem-solving capacity of all of their members. For Dewey, the individual, group, and 'public' are the fundamental overlapping units of social life to which organizations should be responsible. The concept of 'public' is barely distinguishable from the notion of community. However, community ordinarily has a geographical context; a public may not. Publics are scalable. They are framed by a shared consciousness and shared problem that defines boundaries which are themselves contingent on the presentation of consequences in need of remedy. Indeed, Dewey is at pains to avoid the reification of the concept, to foreclose the rigid categories of vulgar Marxism or orthodoxies of Hegelianism. Dewey explained:

> Indirect, extensive, enduring and serious consequences of conjoined and interacting behavior call a public into existence having a common interest in controlling these consequences. (Dewey 1927: 126)

He found in the public and the community it constituted:

> conjoint activity whose consequences are appreciated as good by all singular persons who take part in it. (Dewey 1927: 149)

Publics constitute a protean foundation on which to anchor organizational theory. They are unstable and evolving. Most strands of organizational theory assign a greater priority to the claims of existing organizations and to institutional inertia. Consider, for example, the centrality of the concept of equilibrium to the sociology of Emile Durkheim and Talcott Parsons and the new institutionalism of DiMaggio and Powell (1983). Dewey did not deny that habit, power relations, and mimetic forces constrained the choices of individuals and groups. In fact, Dewey's *The Public and Its Problems* examined the perils posed by media manipulation and concentrated power to the formation of publics. However, Dewey saw few limits to the potential of creative experimentation.

Scholars like Herrigel (2010), Piore and Sabel (1984), and Zeitlin and Trubek (2003), among others, have applied Deweyan pragmatism to contemporary organizational life and have found a world of choices for the construction of alternative political economies. In his *Manufacturing Possibilities*, Herrigel (2010: cli) identified a role for the public: 'one surveys the terrain of action with an eye for promising experiments'. Elsewhere, Manicas (1982) makes an interesting claim about pragmatism considering this constructivist dimension. He writes that Dewey's ideas have much in common with anarchist theory. The pragmatist vision of a non-authoritarian society emerging from a decentralized constellation of alternative institutions (brought into being by publics) is consistent with many formulations of anarchism. Of course, Dewey did not associate his philosophy with any potentially limiting 'isms'. Still, his formulation of pragmatism is closely intertwined with the concept of democracy.

Democracy and Social Intelligence

Dewey explained democracy as a process (as *praxis*):

> *Democracy is much broader than a special political form, a method of conducting government, of making laws and carrying out governmental administration by means of popular suffrage and elected officers. It is that, of course. But it is something broader and deeper than that ... It is ... a way of life, social and individual. The keynote of democracy as a way of life may be expressed ... as the necessity for the participation of every mature being in formation of the values that regulate the living of men together ... . (Dewey 1939: 400)*

Democracy so defined is not satisfied by existing governmental or corporate structures. Dewey advanced this democratic standard: 'all those who are affected by social institutions have a share in producing and managing them' (Dewey 1939: 400). Thus, arbitrary power in corporations and other 'private' forms is no more legitimate than undemocratic government. Dewey proposed no specific model for democracy in industry, but it is clear from his practical work with the League of Industrial Democracy and his support for trade unions that he regarded collective bargaining as a means to democratization. Dewey was rarely specific about the details of institutional development and yet his embrace of thoroughgoing democratization was unequivocal. Clearly, experimentation in democratic forms is appropriate.

Dewey's defense of democracy makes both its protective and participatory dimensions clear: '[Democracy rests] upon the idea that no man or limited set of men is wise enough or good enough to rule others without their consent'. Exclusion from participation deeply harms the excluded. They suffer because they are habitually denied the opportunity to develop their own powers and knowledge. Society suffers because it is much poorer. Limited popular participation leaves legitimate interests without representation. The 'submerged mass' know better than the elites 'where the shoe pinches' (Dewey 1939: 401). Dewey was explicit about the radical character of his democratic approach:

> *The end of democracy is a radical end for it is an end that has not been adequately realized in any country at any time. It is radical because it requires great change in existing social institutions, economic, legal and cultural. (Dewey 1937a)*

In *Liberalism and Social Action*, Dewey (1935) disputed elitist philosophies and affirmed his conception of a social intelligence:

> *Again, it is said that the average citizen is not endowed with the degree of intelligence that the use if it as a method demands. This objection, supported by alleged scientific findings about heredity and by impressive statistics concerning the intelligence quotients of the average citizen, rests wholly upon the old notion that intelligence is a ready-made possession of individuals. This last stand of oligarchical and anti-social seclusion is perpetuation of this purely individualistic notion of intelligence ... native capacity is sufficient to enable the average individual to respond*

and to use the knowledge and skill that are embodied in the social conditions in which he lives ... There does not now exist the kind of social organization that even permits the average human being to share the potentially available social intelligence ... . (1935: 52–4)

Dewey rejected the notion of intelligence as a ready-made possession of individuals. In his mind, all human discovery was the outcome of a social process, of social intelligence in action, rather than of individual achievement. The scientific method required democracy so that the social intelligence was not inhibited by the privileges of an elite, and so that all members of an organization participated in decision-making. One consequence of his conception of social intelligence is that extraordinary achievements in invention and discovery are understood as the accumulation of multiple contributions by a network of thinkers, all of whose ideas become widely accessible to the masses. Note, for instance, how the Internet facilitates the diffusion of ideas and therefore accelerates the development of social intelligence (Jacobs and Yudken 2003).

None the less, one might question Dewey's embrace of radically democratic principles on at least two grounds. First, his frequent reference to the scientific method and his own career at several distinguished universities demonstrates that he belonged to a scientific and educated elite. Can a member of this elite renounce the privileges pertaining to membership without hypocrisy? Much of Dewey's writing is verbose and opaque. Unlike his colleague at the League for Industrial Democracy, Harry Laidler, Dewey seldom wrote for a wide audience. Perhaps there is an irreconcilable tension here between the democratic project and academic practice, but it does not necessarily inhere in pragmatism. Secondly, Dewey's democratic stance may appear to constitute a rigid principle. Is it doctrinaire in a way that contradicts the spirit of pragmatism? Dewey's concept of social intelligence places individuals and groups at the center of action. Authoritarian practices are necessarily rejected because they do not benefit from the participation of the many and probably will diminish their concerns. Many forms of democratic action remain available. Flexibility and innovation are not constrained by democratic and developmental strategies.

Inquiry and Human Capacity

Dewey was a prominent psychologist as well as a philosopher. He had a long-standing interest in the nature of human consciousness. He collaborated closely with Myrtle McGraw in her studies of child development. McGraw's work contributed to Dewey's understanding of the process of inquiry in which an individual identifies a problem and poses solutions, whether about locomotion or obstacles on the job. According to Dewey, biological structures and chemical processes are the foundation of inquiry. Intelligence arises from the interaction of mind and body responding to varied challenges. Finding a sense of balance and walking erect is a prelude to inquiry of all sorts. As a result, every individual has sufficient experience with inquiry to permit the consideration of social and physical problems of apparently greater complexity, especially since the individual has access to the accumulated wisdom of others (Dalton 2002). Arguably, Dewey would probably have agreed with paleontologist Stephen Jay Gould (1981), who chronicled the historical development of pernicious theories of differences in 'native intelligence' in *The Mismeasure of Man*.

Contingency Theories: Pragmatism Honored in the Breach

It is important to emphasize that Dewey's contributions to organizational theory challenge much of organizational behavior and management theory. Organizational behavior and 'human relations' as a discipline were shaped by the Hawthorne studies at Western Electric and were intrinsically connected to management's drive for more sophisticated forms of control (see Sheppard 1950). Elton Mayo' s research was intended to demonstrate the worth of the Harvard Business School to business and academia, and was informed by Mayo's condescension toward the working class and close identification with the managerial elite. In contrast, Dewey was never focused on the improvement of management per se, but examined the conditions for the fuller development of human capacity and broader sharing of knowledge.

Early twentieth century scholar Mary Parker Follett, among many others, made explicit the relevance of a form of pragmatism to her work. She insisted that managers be guided by the lessons of experience rather than by any a priori principles. She asserted that both superiors and subordinates should identify the 'law of the situation' and thus take whatever actions are indicated by the organizational reality. She believed that managing was a practical task whose success depended on the successful integration of the diverse concerns of members of the organization. Whatever policies led to this integration were the correct ones (Feldheim 2004). Over Follett's career her relative commitments to democracy and management interests evolved. Her *New State* (Follett 1920) was a stirring endorsement of a radical democracy informed by Deweyan pragmatism and her experience in community organizing. Later her fundamental concern became the reform of management rather than the perfection of democracy.

So-called 'contingency theories', very popular in organizational behavior and other business disciplines, seem to exhibit a kind of pragmatism. They are based on the assumption that no universal truths govern organizational life, but that specific circumstances and situations determine employee and manager behavior. Douglas McGregor's Theory X/Y (1960) represents a familiar contingency theory (although, as I argue elsewhere [2004], McGregor tended to question the value of directive management) and Burns and Stalker (1961) introduced the concepts of mechanistic and organic structures, matching predictable and volatile environments, respectively. Contingency theories may lack the ethical dimension of Follett's approach because they do not assign the priority Follett did to the integration of interests. They also lack the democratic anchor of Deweyan pragmatism. They appear to ask of managers that they make the proper contextual judgments with regard to the design of work and organizations, but no substantive justice or other standards are imposed. Implicit within the apparently pragmatic calculus of contingency theories is a powerful managerial bias that constrains problem-solving. Indeed, C. Wright Mills provided a critique of organizational behavior that retains validity today:

Management's purpose or interest, as revealed in (the human relations) literature,

is often stated as a technical one; it is the engineer's perspective of producing and distributing goods; or management's purpose is generalized for the whole of those involved in industry … When the problems, set by these purposes are concrete, they always seem to be stated from the managerial standpoint, from the top … . (1948: 209)

Despite the frequent instances of popularity of various forms of participative management, the emphasis upon 'contingency' in business scholarship ensures that the limitations of a managerial bias remain. In other words, allowance for employee input is subject to reversal based on managers' unilateral judgment.

'Stakeholder management' in the Business and Society literature tends to share this weakness. Business ethics scholar R.E. Freeman (1984), an early prophet of stakeholder management, curiously sought to bind his argument for voluntaristic management initiatives for stakeholders to pragmatism (ultimately, to Richard Rorty's formulation). By no means did Dewey reserve pragmatism for managers or bureaucrats. In his assessment of social consequences, managers have no special priority. Their privileges are subject to examination and challenge. Organizations benefit from the scientific method, which does not mean that scientific managers should rule, but that the 'social intelligence', the accumulated wisdom of all organizational members, should be liberated to judge choices by social consequences (Dewey 1939). Dewey's approach was indeed a contingency theory, but within it democracy, rather than managerial flexibility, represents the anchor. He did not argue from the perspective of a manager who seeks to maximize influence from mere sensitivity to worker concerns. Democracy in the workplace would accord workers more power, not influence contingent upon managerial indulgence. Increased commitment to the firm is not a primary goal, nor is a less adversarial worker-manager relationship. Dewey endorsed neither cooperation nor conflict in the workplace as an overall rule or appropriate route to democracy. Workers, unions, and citizens must determine the best means to advance democracy and the free exercise of social intelligence; this is Dewey's contingency model (Dykhuizen 1973).

Many historic and contemporary business practitioners claim that they will choose whatever strategy 'works' in sustaining the enterprise and improving profits. They appear to disdain theory. Rather than pragmatism, it is a profit-maximizing opportunism that they embrace. Countless politicians and organizational leaders have called their modest administrative steps 'pragmatic' while failing to consider the actual impact on people's lives. Deweyan pragmatism has often been honored in the breach by those who have taken it to mean expediency in the maintenance of the status quo. The many varieties of contingency theory and opportunism lack the radically democratic character of Dewey's philosophy. Not only is democracy central to Dewey's prescriptions, it is a democracy focused on developmental and educative processes, rather than administration alone.

Organizational Interventions

In keeping with Dewey's notion of the provisionality of organizations and the role of publics in remedying negative social consequences, it is valuable to consider the wide array of organizations in which Dewey played a founding role. These organizations may be regarded as experimental interventions. Unlike many contemporary institutional theorists, Dewey believed that there were many openings for profound social change that would unsettle existing institutions.

Dewey examined the persistent unemployment and poverty of the American economy and attributed these social ills to fundamental deficits in the performance of capitalist institutions. He participated in a variety of reform movements, helping to found the American Federation of Teachers, leading the League for Industrial Democracy, the League for Independent Political Action, the People's Lobby, and sponsoring third party initiatives. The common theme in these activities was the expansion of democracy so that ordinary people were able to apply their experience to the remedy of harm visited upon them by powerful organizations. Also, all of these political projects were informed by a radical liberalism linking reformers in the Democratic and Republican parties with militant farm, labor, and progressive groups.

Dewey lent specific support to the defense of persecuted radicals like the anarchists Sacco and Vanzetti, philosopher Bertrand Russell (when he was denied a position at the City University of New York for his controversial views), and exiled Bolshevik Leon Trotsky. His activism and scholarly work touched the New Left through at least two routes. The 1960s group Students for a Democratic Society emerged from the Student League for Industrial Democracy. Founder Tom Hayden's conception of participatory democracy was inspired by Dewey's democratic philosophy mediated by University of Michigan philosopher Arnold Kaufman. Dewey embraced a creative process of social invention, of continuous experimentation, and inspired several generations of social reformers. Of course, Dewey was denounced simultaneously from right and left for radicalism and moderation. Note then that Dewey's pragmatism led to his association with a variety of problem-specific, time-delimited, provisional organizations, coordinating activism by multiple constituencies or 'publics'.

Their Morals and Ours

The relevance of Deweyan pragmatism to organizational theory receives further illumination through a focus on Dewey's spirited debate with exiled Bolshevik Leon Trotsky in the late 1930s. Dewey chaired a commission created to investigate Joseph Stalin's charges against Trotsky in the so-called Soviet show trials. The commission was, in fact, a manifestation of a global public aroused to challenge Soviet policy. Dewey's intervention in the struggle between Stalin and Trotsky revealed nuances of his pragmatist perspective. He placed himself in physical danger in order to investigate the charges against Trotsky. Dewey had been impressed by the Soviet educational system in his visit in 1928. However, he distinguished these practical programs from the rigid orthodoxies of Soviet ideology and maintained a relatively open mind about specific developments on the ground.

At the age of 78, Dewey traveled to Mexico City where Trotsky was in exile. In doing so he subjected himself to intense criticism from pro-Soviet intellectuals and won himself no support from American conservatives. In works published later by pro-Soviet philosophers, Dewey was characterized as the principal philosopher of American imperialism. It is likely that Dewey's courageous defense and criticism of Trotsky contributed substantially to the controversies surrounding pragmatism, limiting its appeal within disparate communities, right and left. After the commission exonerated Trotsky, Trotsky and Dewey published a series of letters in the 'Trotskyist' *New International Review* outlining their starkly different conceptions of organizational justice. Trotsky impugned pragmatism as bourgeois liberalism as against his revolutionary morality and scientific Marxism. Trotsky specifically aligned Dewey with the petty bourgeoisie. Convinced of the infallibility of his class analysis, Trotsky did not seek to demonstrate the objective consequences of any philosophical stance. He inferred the material foundations of pragmatism through deduction, dismissed it, and predicted its descent into reaction (Trotsky et al. 1973). Indeed, Trotsky correctly anticipated the trajectory of the pragmatist Sidney Hook, who moved from anti-Communism to right-wing politics. However, Trotsky's rigid interpretation of the exigencies of class struggle and embrace of proletarian dictatorship preserved the peril of authoritarianism, as both Dewey and Rosa Luxembourg argued.

Dewey placed democratic struggle at the heart of social change, not because it is a law of history, but because it is a likely outcome of the conflict between the human capacity for self-governance and the coalescence of property interests. The development of human consciousness is bound up with the processes of measurement and comparison; solidarity and greed emerge organically, Dewey might argue (Dalton 2002). Trotsky accused Dewey of bourgeois confusion in the face of the imperatives of class struggle. However, Dewey was consistent in his emphasis on social consequences as the measure of action. He was ready to embrace, with Trotsky, the liberation of humanity as a goal to be achieved and measure of progress, but he rejected Trotsky's insistence on a vision of class struggle in which ideas were denied by a mysterious assessment of their class paternity (Trotsky et al. 1975). The crux of the debate between Dewey and Trotsky was the relationship between means and ends. Trotsky believed that the historic law of class struggle justified proletarian dictatorship. Dewey denied that any such historic law could inform the choice of means and tactics. He argued that there was no ultimate end but only proximate ends (or 'ends-in-view') and that ends and means were interdependent (Trotsky et al. 1975).

After his tangle with Trotsky, Dewey observed:

> *The great lesson for all American radicals and for all sympathizers with the USSR is that they must go back and reconsider the whole question of the means of bringing about social changes and of truly democratic methods of approach to social progress … The dictatorship of the proletariat had led to and, I am convinced, always must lead to a dictatorship over the proletariat and the party. I see no reason to believe that something similar would not happen in every country in which an attempt is made to establish a Communist government. (Dewey 1937b)*

The Dewey–Trotsky debate about means and ends qualifies as an exchange of world-historic importance. Trotsky's comments confirm his reputation for polemical argument. His voluminous historical knowledge is evident. His implicit claim to the knowledge of the law of class struggle and to the ability to discern the proper way to prosecute class struggle reveals an arrogant misconception that distinguishes democratic philosophy from authoritarianism.

Dewey probably puzzled about the relationship between conflict and democracy. His early formulation of democracy, influenced by his boyhood experiences in Vermont and the doctrines of the Congregational Church, held out the potential of a harmonious society. His witness of the Pullman strike and the trials of the Depression may have acquainted him with the persistence and necessity of conflict. Did Dewey truly have the audacity to demand change in a moment of crisis? Lincoln Steffens famously left it to his sons to seek revolution (Bernstein 2010).

Trotsky was not wrong to question 'bourgeois liberalism'. Certainly conservative employers routinely appeal to abstract universal values in order to disguise crass economic interests. Dewey also found tremendous coercion implicit within the reality of 'free markets' in his *Liberalism and Social Action*. It remains an open question what means are effective in order to combat reactionary employer interests when they are hostile to democracy. Consider the contemporary Republican Party in the US. Republican politicians often practice something Mark Tushnet (2003) has called 'constitutional hardball', according to which party leaders exploit their position in the nodes of power of the federal system at the expense of political pluralism. An example is the unprecedented use of the filibuster by Senate Republicans to frustrate Democratic majorities or the Supreme Court's intervention in the recount of the Florida vote, awarding the presidency to George W. Bush in 2000. This is a dilemma for democrats like Dewey. How does one confront authoritarian power when the democratic process is breached? How does one determine the means that truly liberate the masses from authoritarian control? Are there moments when 'extreme measures' are necessary, and what measures will enhance democracy rather than deny it? Dewey argued for the potency of the 'method of intelligence', which may sound inadequate to the job.

Dewey addressed some of these issues in *Liberalism and Social Action*. He was explicit about the veiled violence under existing social arrangements:

> *It is not surprising in view of our standing dependence upon the use of coercive force that at every time of crisis coercion breaks out into open violence. (Dewey 1935: 64)*

He went on to say:

> *... the issue is not whether some amount of violence will accompany the effectuation of radical change of institutions. The question is whether force or intelligence is to be the method upon which we consistently rely and to whose promotion we devote our energies. (1935: 78)*

Here, the method of intelligence includes open deliberations, problem-solving, organizational democratization, movement building, and direct challenges by the majority to the privileges of economic and political elites. Perhaps in the modern vernacular some of this is captured by the idea of social entrepreneurship, especially if we stipulate a form that incorporates struggle for systemic change.

I will now consider the organizational experimentation of business leaders who were inspired by Dewey's experimental method or whose practice is consistent with it. In *Liberalism and Social Action* Dewey considers the trajectory of such reformers.

Social Entrepreneurship and Social Reconstruction

Social entrepreneurship is ordinarily defined as the mobilization of business to solve a social problem. Porter and Kramer (2011) provide a current formulation: the 'shared value' strategy, according to which managers discover the positive sum advantages of environmental investment and reducing outsourcing. Social entrepreneurship in the Deweyan mold (he would have called it 'social invention' on the way to 'social reconstruction') would not constitute a minor adjustment of traditional business models to permit gestures to social relevance. For example, the concept of shared value explicitly excludes significant wealth redistribution. Solving vexing problems of social inclusion, inequality, and power imbalances are beyond the capacity of existing corporations. Note that Dees' (1998) definition of social entrepreneurship has elements that coincide with Dewey's notion of bold and persistent experimentation: a search for new opportunities to create social value, continuous innovation, and aggressive action without regard for resource limitations. There are several instructive historic examples of individuals and groups who have designed organizations designed to resist social injustice and implement social reform. Robert Owen, William Morris, and Edward Filene represent a group of business reformers who excelled at institution-building and problem-solving. The 'Owen–Morris–Filene' tradition of organizational experimentation and social action constitutes an important example of social invention consistent with Deweyan pragmatism. Yet much received theory in economics and the business disciplines encourages disregard of the reformers in business leadership. In a capitalist political economy, it is assumed that the market is the guarantor of equal opportunity. Managers and owners reap unequal rewards, but this very inequality is the engine that creates greater wealth for all. The capitalist is inclined to regard poverty as the outcome of personal deficiencies, the solution to which is greater effort in the marketplace. The capitalist owes nothing to the worker and consumer other than the active and honest pursuit of his self-interest.

From a Marxist perspective, the capitalist acts in accord with fixed class interests. Managerial practices are merely instruments to these class interests. Worker exploitation is inherent in capitalist practice and will not end without the end of private property in the means of production and a revolution in class relations. However, there are several business leaders who have been led by their experience or fundamental values to depart from business norms and to support experiments or practices that contradict the self-interest of capitalist virtue or the class interest of the Marxist calculus. These cases fall in two categories: the Engels and Owen options. Engels was a capitalist who challenged capitalism not so much in his own enterprise but in his collaboration with Karl Marx in the writing of *The Communist Manifesto* (Marx and Engels 1964) and other works, and in his financial support for Marx. On the other hand, Robert Owen was an experimenter, within his Scottish cotton mill and in his 'utopian', New Harmony project in Indiana. Thus, I distinguish between Engels' focus on political agitation and Owen's institutional experimentation (Laidler 1968; Quarter 2000).

Radically dissenting views within the business community are likely the product of a consciousness of consequences. Class standing or managerial status does not necessarily blind one to the consequences of one's actions or of the practices of powerful institutions. Robert Owen found evidence in the circumstances of industrialization that caused him to identify with the grievances of the working class. He saw poverty as a result of capitalist exploitation rather than as a reflection or moral deficiency. He visualized an alternative economic system and even an alternative human nature, despite the privileged position he held as a capitalist. His working class origins, his period of apprenticeship in a craft, his multiple partnerships with leading industrialists, and his purchase of the New Lanark plant may have allowed him to conceive of business as a changing array of roles rather than as a fixed hierarchy of functions (Quarter 2000). As an experimenter, Owen showed himself to be an exponent of a consequentialist philosophy anticipating the pragmatism of John Dewey. That is, he judged institutions and practices by their social consequences and sought to identify better institutions through experimentation. Owen was a friend and disciple of Bentham. However, he severed utilitarianism from Bentham's classical economics and placed emphasis on the social conditions for happiness (Dewey 1935: 1–27).

William Morris, the nineteenth-century British designer, artist, author, and activist, was successful in the business of home arts and crafts. However, he viewed himself as craftsman more than entrepreneur. He favored democratic enterprises controlled by the workers themselves, practicing art and craft in production following a socialist revolution. In the interim, Morris sought to practice business in a manner that was consistent with the moderately reformist ideas of John Ruskin. Ruskin called for socially responsible business honoring craft and avoiding the perils of greed and traditional industrialism. Harvey and Press write that the pace of work in Morris' firm was humane, wages were somewhat above the norm, and that Morris himself joined the craftsmen in production (Harvey and Press 1995). In *William Morris: Romantic to Revolutionary* (1976: 99), E.P. Thompson stressed Morris' fidelity to Ruskin's vision of craft production in the former's business. Morris refused to convert his business to a workers' cooperative or even to practice profit-sharing. Moreover, his employees lacked much influence over the production process, at least partly to give him direct control over quality. In *Beyond the Bottom Line: Socially Innovative Business Owners*, Jack Quarter goes so far as to group Morris with Engels as socialists who 'separated their contribution to society from their business role ...' (2000: xi). I agree that Morris awaited revolution for the implementation of his most rigorous demands but believe that he did apply a measure of reformism in his business practices. Ironically, as he turned toward Marxian or 'scientific socialism', his interest in social experimentation diminished. The Marxist conceit that there is a law of history is a disincentive to the creative improvization practiced by Owen.

Edward Filene, a founder of Filene's Department Store, was similarly an experimenter and innovator in progressive business practices. Henry Wallace, publisher, farmer, and New Dealer, may also have met this description. Filene pioneered mass retailing, recognizing that his department store would be well served by low margins and high volume sales. Like Henry Ford, he argued that higher wages were a prerequisite for mass retailing. He went much further than Ford in his advocacy of government activism as well as private generosity to boost purchasing power. Filene earned the enmity of his business partners by his institution of a form of employee representative government in the department store. Management could be overruled by two-thirds vote of the council and Filene's colleagues were not pleased. He was ultimately ousted from the company. Filene grew increasingly close to organized labor and worked particularly effectively with Amalgamated Clothing Workers and CIO leader Sidney Hillman in the advocacy of progressive social policy (Fraser 1991: 208–9). Filene aptly explained his dissenting approach to business practice in this way:

> *I do not know of a better word [other than business liberal] for describing the sort of business man who, broadly speaking, is the opposite of the reactionary, the sort of business man who faces fresh problems with a fresh mind, who is more interested in creating a better order of things than in defending the existing order of things, who realizes that a private business is a public trust, and who has greater reverence for scientific method than for the traditions and majority opinion of his class. (1924: 284)*

Note in the above the invocation of the scientific method in the pursuit of a 'better order of things'. Filene and Dewey were almost certainly in dialog about opportunities for pragmatist social reform.

Robert Owen and Edward Filene would qualify as 'utopians', according to Marxists, due to their insistence on choice and agency (rather than the law of class struggle) in social change. However, they were acutely interested in questions of strategy. By no means did they assume that the example of one factory or community would be sufficient to propel social change. Owen's support for factory legislation, for trade unions, and cooperatives; Filene's advocacy of credit unions, civic clubs for rich and poor alike, and founding of an enduring progressive think tank, the Twentieth Century Fund, demonstrate their consideration of multiple strategies for justice. What is most valuable about the Owen/Morris/Filene/Wallace tradition of progressive business is the underlying idea of mobilizing intelligence in the solution of social problems. Their experience gave them varied models for business practice which they sought to refine in a world of manifold injustice. While their businesses do not survive today, at least as monuments to their progressive ideals, other institutions they founded continue to exercise influence. Dewey obviously could not take credit for their social inventions, but their experimentation was consistent with his 'method of intelligence'.

The relevance of Deweyan pragmatism to social entrepreneurship is demonstrated through these significant precedents in creative, even utopian, problem-solving. The multiple roles and achievements of utopian socialist and manufacturer Robert Owen, socialist advocate of arts and crafts William Morris, and business reformer Edward Filene, as well as the contemporary exponents of worker cooperation in the Mondragon industries in Spain and within the United Steelworkers of America suggest the radical potential of social entrepreneurship (see the work of Marcus Raskin [1971] for a relatively recent application of pragmatism to social reconstruction). As mentioned above, social entrepreneurship ordinarily means the application of for-profit business practices to social purposes (or the enhancement of social value in business projects). Alternatively, and maybe more importantly, radical social entrepreneurship may effectively describe the improvizational, precedent-challenging character of the best social innovations. Pragmatism points in the latter direction.

Conclusion

John Dewey's works and organizational activities reflect his advocacy of a rigorous democratization of existing institutions. His conception of human capacity, his understanding of social intelligence, and his assessment of the role of publics constitute the basis for an organizational theory of democratic reform and experimentation. Despite superficial similarities between pragmatism and contingency theories in management, Deweyan pragmatism locates agency in individuals and groups and not managers. Of course, Dewey was sufficiently engaged in the public sphere to understand the myriad hierarchies and authoritarian systems that constrained democratic reform. He demonstrated courage in his willingness to confront Soviet apologists and Trotsky's own orthodoxies in his stewardship of the Trotsky Commission. However, he was by means alone in his democratic project. One can identify a string of social entrepreneurs whose innovative interventions have much in common with Dewey's pragmatist perspective.

Here lie some apparent contradictions. Dewey is remembered for his prodigious contribution to American philosophy, for his careful development of the concept of social intelligence. And yet, within the framework of the social intelligence, he is one mind among many, important, but not indispensable. The significance of his contribution curiously reflects deficits in the implementation of ideas like his in a world still shaped by concentrated power and hierarchies. One may legitimately question whether Dewey's method of intelligence is sufficient to advance the radical vision he embraced. Publics may not have the capacity to challenge powerful structures. Dewey's own language is often inaccessible, remote, and susceptible to misunderstanding. Arguably, Dewey's insights would benefit from a more concise presentation.

Perhaps one can summarize much of Dewey's thinking by describing an experientially derived skepticism that challenges the multiple ways in which privilege and invidious distinctions assert themselves in organizations. The extraordinary knowledge and achievements of any one individual are at least as much tribute to the collected wisdom of the many as they are reflections of personal qualities. Recent discoveries in neuroscience only reinforce Dewey's arguments about the flexibility and capacity of the brain. Despite the apparent dominance of hierarchical systems, everywhere we find critical minds questioning authority.

References

Asen, R. 2003. The Multiple Mr. Dewey: Multiple publics and permeable borders in John Dewey's theory of the public sphere. *Argumentation and Advocacy*, 39(3), 174–88.

Berkley, G.E. 1998. *The Filenes*. Boston, MA: International Pocket Library.

Bernstein, R. 2010. Dewey's vision of radical democracy, in *The Cambridge Companion to Dewey*, (ed.) M. Cochran. New York: Cambridge University Press, 288–308.

Burns, T. and Stalker, G.M. 1961. *The Management of Innovation*. London: Tavistock.

Dalton, T.C. 2002. *Becoming John Dewey*. Bloomington, IN: Indiana University Press, 230–51.

Dees, J.G. (1998). *The Meaning of Social Entrepreneurship*. Palo Alto, CA: Stanford University Graduate School of Business.

Dewey, J. 1925. *Experience and Nature*. Chicago, IL: Open Court Publishing.

Dewey, J. 1927. *Public and its Problems*. New York: Holt.

Dewey, J. 1935. *Liberalism and Social Action*. New York: G.P. Putnam.

Dewey, J. 1937a. Democracy is radical. *Common Sense*, 6, 10–11.

Dewey, J. 1937b. Significance of the Trotsky inquiry: Interview with Agnes Meyer in *Washington Post* [online], December 19. Available at: http://books.google.com/books?id=pb0N4SgQGLQC&pg=PA330&dq=significance+of+the+trotsky+inquiry&hl=en&ei=WDmwTu9YpODRAcOh8KkB&sa=X&oi=book_result&ct=result&resnum=1&ved=0CC4Q6AEwAA#v=onepage&q=significance%20of%20the%20trotsky%20inquiry&f=false [accessed 1 November 2011].

Dewey, J. 1939. Democracy and educational administration, *in Intelligence in the Modern World*, (ed.) J. Ratner and E.A. Post. New York: Random House, 400–404.

Dykhuizen, G. 1973. *The Life and Mind of John Dewey*. Carbondale, IL: Southern Illinois University Press.

DiMaggio, P.J. and Powell, W.W. 1983. The iron cage revisited: Institutional isomorphism and rationality in organizational fields. *American Sociological Review*, 48(2), 147–60.

Feldheim, M. 2004. Mary Parker Follett lost and found – again, and again, and again. *International Journal of Organization Theory and Behavior*, Fall, 341–62

Filene, E.A. 1924. *The Way Out: A Forecast of Coming Changes in American Business and Industry*. Garden City, NY: Doubleday, Page, and Company.

Follett, M.P. 1920. *The New State*. London: Longmans, Green, and Company.

Fraser, S. 1991. *Labor Will Rule: Sidney Hillman and the Rise of American Labor*. New York: The Free Press.

Freeman, R.E. 1984. *Strategic Management: A Stakeholder Approach*. Boston, MA: Pitman.

Gould, S.J. 1981. *The Mismeasure of Man*. New York: Norton.

Harvey, C. and J. Press. 1995. John Ruskin and the ethical foundations of Morris and Company 1861–1896. *Journal of Business Ethics*, 14(3), 181–94.

Herrigel, G. 2010. *Manufacturing Possibilities: Creative Action and Industrial Recomposition in the U.S., Germany, and Japan*. New York: Oxford University Press.

Jacobs, D. 1994. *Collective Bargaining as an Instrument of Social Change*. Westport, CT: Quorum.

Jacobs, D. 2004. A pragmatist approach to integrity in business ethics. *Journal of Management Inquiry*, 13(3), 215–23.

Jacobs, D. 2004. Douglas McGregor: Human side of enterprise in peril. *Academy of Management Review*, 29(2), 293–311.

Jacobs, D. and Yudken, J. 2003. *The Internet, Organizational Change, and Labor: The Challenge of Virtualization*. London: Routledge.

Laidler, H.W. 1968. *History of Socialism: A Comparative Survey of Socialism, Communism, Trade Unionism, Cooperation, Utopianism, and Other Systems of Reform and Reconstruction*. New York: Crowell.

Manicas, P.T. 1982. John Dewey, anarchism, and the political state. *Transactions of the Charles S. Peirce Society*, 18(2), 133–58.

Marx, K. and F. Engels. 1964. *The Communist Manifesto*. New York: Monthly Review Press.

McGregor, D. 1960. *The Human Side of Enterprise*. New York: McGraw-Hill.

McQuaid, K. 1976. An American Owenite: Edward A. Filene and the parameters of industrial reform 1890–1937. *The American Journal of Economics and Sociology*, 35(1), 77–94.

Mills, C.W. 1948. *The Contribution of Sociology to Studies of Industrial Relations: Proceedings of the First Annual Meeting* (Champaign, IL: Industrial Relations Research Association), 199–222.

Piore, M.J. and Sabel, C.F. 1984. *The Second Industrial Divide: Possibilities for Prosperity*. New York: Basic Books.

Porter, M.E. and Kramer, M.R. 2011. The big idea: Creating shared value. *Harvard Business Review* [online], January. Available at: http://hbr.org/2011/01/the-big-idea-creating-shared-value/ar/1 [accessed 13 August 2011].

Quarter, J. 2000. *Beyond the Bottom Line: Socially Innovative Business Owners*. Westport, CT: Quorum Books.

Raskin, M. 1971. *Being and Doing*. New York: Random House.

Thompson, E.P. 1976. *William Morris: Romantic to Revolutionary*. New York: Pantheon.

Sheppard, H.L. 1950. The social and historical philosophy of Elton Mayo. *Antioch Review*, 10(3), 396–405.

Trotsky, L., Dewey, J. and Novack, G. 1973. *Their Morals and Ours: Marxist vs. Liberal Views on Morality*. New York: Pathfinder Press.

Tushman, M.L. and Nadler, D.A. 1978. Information processing as an integrating framework in organization design. *Academy of Management Review*, 3, 613–21.

Tushnet, M. 2003. *Constitutional Hardball* [online]. Available at: http://papers.ssrn.com/sol3/papers.cfm?abstract_id=451960 [accessed 1 November 2011].

Zeitlin. J. and Trubek, D. (eds). 2003. *Governing Work and Welfare in a New Economy: European and American Experiments*. New York: Oxford University Press.

7 *American Pragmatism and Critical Management Studies*

IAN EVANS

Pragmatism, according to Mr James, is a temper of mind, an attitude; it is also a theory of the nature of ideas and truth; and, finally, it is a theory about reality. It is pragmatism as method which is emphasised, I take it, in the subtitle, 'a new name for some old ways of thinking'. It is this aspect which I suppose to be uppermost in Mr James's own mind; one frequently gets the impression that he conceives the discussion of the other two points to be illustrative material, more or less hypothetical, of the method. The briefest and at the same time the most comprehensive formula for the method is: 'The attitude of looking away from first things, principles, "categories", supposed necessities; and of looking towards last things, fruits, consequences, facts' ... But pragmatism is 'used in a still wider sense, as meaning also a certain theory of truth'; it is 'a genetic theory of what is meant by truth' (Dewey 2007/1907: 156).

Introduction

In his path-breaking study *The American Evasion of Philosophy*, US philosopher Cornel West defines American pragmatism as 'a diverse and heterogeneous tradition' of thought with one common denominator: 'a future-oriented instrumentalism that tries to deploy thought as a weapon to enable more effective action' (West 1989: 5). Its 'basic impulse', he argues, 'is a plebeian radicalism that fuels an antipatrician rebelliousness for the moral aim of enriching individuals and expanding democracy' (West 1989: 5); an instinct which, at least on the surface, seems to bear much in common with the critical animus at the heart of Critical Management Studies Scholarship. CMS, as it is known to its practitioners, seeks to critique organizational (and more specifically managerialist) orthodoxy in the business world and beyond by cutting to the heart of the discourses that underwrite capitalism and its by-products – wealth inequality, environmental degradation, oppressive, unsafe and unfair working conditions and so on. Since its inception, a variety of critical 'approaches', including postmodernism, poststructuralism, classical Marxism, Critical Theory, and different kinds of feminism have been employed in doing so.

This chapter seeks to evaluate the potential utility of American pragmatism to Critical Management Studies, specifically in regard to internecine debates about its ability to influence public policy and real-world management practices. These disputes continue to rage and have included voices from 'within' and 'without' the CMS 'movement' for well over a decade, the latest example being Ahu Tatli's 'On the Power and Poverty of Critical (Self) Reflection in Critical Management Studies' (2011).[1] If CMS remains a 'glass-bead game played by the cognoscenti' in which serious discussion of progressive alternatives to organizational orthodoxy is fixed 'within the cloistered boundaries of academic work', as Martin Parker (2002: 116) suggests, does pragmatism (as both critical *method* and, in a sense, *a way of operating* within and beyond institutional contexts, an *approach* to them) offer a viable means by which CMS scholars might overcome the institutionalization of the movement which many, such as Bridgman and Stephens (2008), see as debilitating?

If we assume – playing devil's advocate for a moment – that CMS privileges intellectual complexity and abstraction at the expense of meaningful engagement with the real world; if it is constantly 'retreating into a private and self-referential world of specialist publications and arcane debates' (Bridgman and Stevens 2008: 262) when it intends to make a concrete impact, what can pragmatism bring to the debate that prior scholarship in the field has failed to account for? Do the tenets of philosophical pragmatism – anti-foundationalism, provisionality and contingency – validate or correspond with views about the radical implications of CMS, or simply stand to refute them? Filtered through the lens of pragmatism, can CMS 'transcend the circumstances of its own constitution' (Tinker 2002: 420) and make a real difference to managerialist practices?

While it may be reductive – and perhaps even 'unfair and untrue' – to reduce CMS 'to some obscure intellectualism refusing to engage in anything other than hermetic exchanges with itself' (Fournier and Grey 2000: 22), questions still linger about its ability, in lieu of any 'unitary 'critical' position' (Fournier and Grey 2000: 16), to mount a successful assault on the absolutism of prevailing organizational structures and the ideologies they embody. Should this absolutism be met with more pluralism in the shape of pragmatism (and indeed, would this mean a different kind of pluralism to the broadly left-leaning disciplinary ecumenism that currently characterises CMS)? Or should it be met with more 'absolutism', this time of a defiantly ideological left-wing stripe, which might point us towards more effective modes of transmitting ideas, which move us beyond the hand-wringing compromises and gradualist reforms that usually ensue when pragmatism is taken seriously, into the public arena?

In this chapter I err tentatively towards the latter, partly out of personal conviction and partly based on reservations – to which I aim to give some color here – about pragmatism's ability to challenge the hegemony of right-wing ideas at anything other

---

1   It is worth expanding a little on Tatli's piece here, because she is very critical of CMS and identifies as a non-member of the 'movement'. On the one hand, it is difficult to swallow her claim that 'in reality CMS has been institutionalized as a representative of postmodern and poststructuralist approaches to organizational research' because 'This theoretical closure alienates critical researchers who commit themselves to ontologies and theoretical perspectives that CMS is not subscribed to' (Tatli 2011: 7). Tatli's argument seems to bear little correspondence to reality, such is the broadness of the CMS church, and certainly offers no usable way forward beyond her critique. But the point remains salient that much of the *language* employed by CMS practitioners of postmodernist and poststructuralist critique has perhaps had the negative effect of rendering the work inaccessible to many outside the academy as well as inside. This is surely a first stumbling block to the body of work having any concrete impact. See also Grey and Sinclair (2006), who do identify as CMS scholars, on this issue. As Grey comments in this piece, 'If someone who has been involved in this stuff for two decades doesn't get it, then could there be something wrong with the way it is expressed? And even if that isn't true, then what might be the point of writing something which only a handful of people can understand?'(Grey and Sinclair 2006: 447–8).

than an epistemological level, particularly in the midst of an entirely ideological climate of global 'austerity'. This is not to renounce pluralism, or to suggest that the worst problem with CMS is its catholicism, its openness. Conversely, *diversity within unity* is an admirable, important and usable characteristic, and one which is compatible with both pragmatism and other kinds of critique much further to the left. Despite this, however, it seems that the plurality of critical approaches CMS scholars adopt, rather like the variety of standpoints that characterise the organized left in the UK, either do not or cannot cohere effectively enough to challenge the hegemony of right-wing ideas (the right, whilst diverse, rarely seems to suffer this kind of internal strife, possibly because it generally holds the upper hand). Nor can it presently find a way to break out of the institutional 'trap' in which it operates. And, in light of the 'approach' culture that characterises the movement, is pragmatism really the best place to turn to help us break out of this 'trap', or is it just another 'approach' to add to the already burgeoning grab-bag of critical tools CMS makes use of?

Pragmatism and the Rejection of Epistemology-Centered Philosophy

Ever since philosophical pragmatism was conceived by American thinkers Charles Sanders Peirce and William James in the 1890s, most pragmatist thought has been characterized by a moral and ethical concern with affecting democratic change. In going about this, as Cornel West suggests, pragmatists are interested in the practical application of ideas. A pragmatist thinker, whether a classical one such as James or a neo-pragmatist like Richard Rorty, might ask, 'What are the consequences of an idea? Can we be sure of its practicality without first putting it into practice?' As such, a radical empiricist bent is a major facet of the pragmatist outlook, while practice, often of an open-minded and experimental nature, is integral to the approach. The usefulness of revising assumptions in the light of new evidence – admitting we could be wrong – is equally important.

Underpinning this, more profoundly, is an anti-foundationalist rejection of epistemology-centered philosophy. Marked by 'disenchantment with transcendental conceptions of philosophy', pragmatism rejects all claims to empirical truth (West 1989: 3). Ideas are only 'true' insofar as their practical usefulness can be demonstrated, and as with other expressions of anti-foundationalist thought, the contingency of truth is of vital importance to pragmatists. During the 1980s neo-pragmatists like Rorty (1989) made implicit connections between this aspect of pragmatist thinking and emerging currents of postmodernist critique, building on the insights of anti-foundationalist thinkers such as Thomas Kuhn (1962), whose hugely popular book *The Structure of Scientific Revolutions* posed a serious challenge to the objectivity of scientific ideas. They were, for Kuhn, merely contingent on whatever historical paradigm held sway at a given moment (Kuhn: 1962). Logical positivism was off the table. Of course, 'a rejection of positivism is not automatically a move towards critique' as Fournier and Grey (2000: 13) suggest – even Rorty (1986) criticised Michel Foucault's commitment to anti-positivism on the grounds that he simply substituted older systems for equally frustrating new ones, for example. Nonetheless:

there is some linkage ... At the very least, a recognition of the socially constructed nature of
social arrangements points to their contingency and the possibility of their reconstruction along
different lines. (Fournier and Grey 2000: 13–14)

Pragmatism, Political Efficacy and CMS

CMS scholars have made ample use of these insights, so in a sense pragmatism seems like a reasonable place for its practitioners to go next – a kind of retrograde delving back into a philosophy that influenced more familiar modes of critique. W.V.O Quine (1951) is perhaps worth mentioning here as one of the key pragmatist thinkers to critique positivism during the 1950s in his influential paper 'Two Dogmas of Empiricism', which helped to pave the way for the welter of postmodernist approaches that would soon follow. But how useful is this rejection of positivism at the current moment? Andrew Wicks and R. Edward Freeman (1998) argued that anti-positivism 'held promise' for overcoming a perceived 'hostility towards ethics' within organization studies, ethics being particularly pertinent to pragmatism and, in one sense, crucial to modern capitalism; such is the stock capitalists place in reputation (Wicks and Freeman 1998: 123).[2] Ultimately, however, they judge anti-positivism to have retained 'some of the destructive elements of positivism that create[d] new and equally troubling difficulties'. Pragmatism, they argued, although also anti-positivist in its sentiments, offered a different way through the mire, allowing scholars to 'develop research that is focused on serving human purposes – i.e., both morally rich and useful to organizations and the communities in which they operate' (Wicks and Freeman 1998: 123). In hindsight these reservations about the limits of anti-positivism seem prescient. Given the social, political and economic turmoil we are currently experiencing it would be difficult to argue that the critique of positivism integral to Anthony Giddens's 'Third Way', say – so central to former UK Prime minister Tony Blair's peculiar version of neoliberalism, so pervasive at the time and so lasting in impact – had any positive effect whatsoever.

So is pragmatism any different from the forms of critique CMS is more likely to draw on? What does it offer that is distinctive, or less problematic given the extant criticisms of CMS? According to Maxim Voronov (2008), practitioners of CMS, who often think of themselves as political radicals, 'enact the mainstream habitus by replicating the traditional theory-practice split and privileging the academic over the non-academic' (Voronov 2008: 940), thereby rendering their work epistemologically radical but not politically so. In one sense, then, pragmatist thought seems to bolster this thesis – if an idea is not applied practically it cannot be considered radical as there is no empirical proof of its socio-political efficacy. But in another sense, pragmatism poses another question that could help overcome the theory-practice distinction entirely. If there is no epistemological basis for political claims in the first place, what does it actually mean to accuse someone of being an epistemological radical rather than a concretely political

---

2   Global capitalism prides itself on presenting a diversity-conscious façade, for example, ostensibly to appear benign but more obviously so as not to limit its potential labor, services or product market to a particular group. Parker (2002: 93), quite correctly I think, calls business ethics 'the managerial colonization of emancipatory projects'. For instance, businesses often adopt anti-racist principles as part of their employment policy so as to appear non-threatening to potential consumers – in one sense the only color the free market cares about is green.

one? Holding that it means very little, the debate for pragmatists then becomes one about the positioning of intellectuals in relation to the actual machinery of power.

Intellectuals in Power: From the 'Brains Trust' to Barack Obama

At this point, then, it is useful to briefly discuss an example of pragmatism in action – a case from the storybook of American history when pragmatist intellectuals had the opportunity to put their ideas into practice in the political arena. As per my earlier reservations, the impact this had, whilst not without merit or gain, was fatally limited. My example concerns the 'Brains Trust' founded by President Franklin D. Roosevelt during the Great Depression and is, I think, apposite in the current moment, such are the parallels between the events of 1929 and today. As the American economy plummeted in the aftermath of the catastrophic Stock Market crash of 1929, a group of liberal intellectuals were invited to join Roosevelt's infant administration. They were charged – unprecedentedly – with tackling the crushing social problems brought about by the Great Depression. With unemployment at a high of 23.6 percent,[3] the American establishment might have retreated inside itself. Indeed, outgoing Republican President Herbert Hoover's response to the crisis had been tepid and non-committal, hampered by a diffidence which precipitated his departure from office. At least ostensibly (and certainly in the public imagination) Roosevelt was a different breed of politician, committed to social democracy, and perhaps most pressingly given the circumstances, willing to try *anything* to remedy the crisis of laissez-faire capitalism that had dragged the nation to its knees.[4] 'It is common sense to take a method and try it', he argued in his address at Oglethorpe University on 22 May 1932. 'If it fails, admit it frankly and try another. But above all, try something' (Lloyd 2006: 75).

His response was to establish the Brains Trust. Comprising Ivy League law professors Adolph Berle and Raymond Moley, left-wing economist Rexford Tugwell and the prominent financial adviser James Warburg, the Brains Trust gave policy advice in their respective areas of expertise and, in Tugwell's case, took up important positions within the first New Deal administration. The New Yorker became Assistant Secretary of the United States Department of Agriculture in 1933, and later took office as Governor of Puerto Rico. The significance of the Brains Trust was twofold. Its success represented a coup for the intellectual community – for the first time in America, excepting Johns Hopkins graduate Woodrow Wilson, top-class thinkers previously confined to the ivory towers and gilded halls of the Ivy League were having a major say in the running of concrete politics. The Agricultural Adjustment Act of 1933, The Resettlement Administration (RA) (1935–36) and other such inventions of the first New Deal – some successful and some, including the RA, denounced for being too radical – were contrived under their watch.

Perhaps more importantly, however, the Trust generally believed in an untested approach to politics. Echoing Roosevelt at Oglethorpe, to varying degrees they promoted pragmatic experimentalism as the solution to the economic problems that had brought about the Depression. Tugwell in particular was a devotee of experimental economics

---

3   This would peak at 25 percent in 1933.

4   For more on Roosevelt's pragmatic bent see Richard Hofstadter, 1948, *The American Political Tradition and the Men Who Made It*, 315–52.

and, significantly, he had been taught by the great pragmatist philosopher John Dewey at Columbia, whose espousal of the untried and the tentative (of 'bold, persistent experimentation', as Tugwell puts it) greatly influenced the future Governor (Tugwell 1968: 93).

If Roosevelt had tried something unprecedented by charging the intellectuals with this level of responsibility, the group themselves would explore new political possibilities –chiefly, a form of collectivism, albeit heavily diluted by the influence of Raymond Moley and others, which even the President would baulk at (Tugwell 1968: xxiv–xxv),[5] in their effort to rejuvenate the US economy and bring relief to those afflicted by the economic downturn, thrusting pragmatic principles into the political spotlight. At the far-left of the Trust's ideological spectrum, Tugwell had substantive reservations about the extent and effectiveness of the New Deal reforms (Tugwell 1968: xii).[6] But, as a temporary salve – presiding over a period when the left got to moonlight as America's most influential economic and political actors, thereafter returning to theoretical opposition – that aided the wartime production that kick-started the American economy, they worked. But it was World War II and the consequent burgeoning of production more than anything else that ultimately saved the American economy, putting millions back to work. And we should take heed of what followed. Not the collectivist turn Tugwell had envisaged and wanted, but a period of unprecedented success for consumer capitalism which established US primacy on the world stage. This era also heralded a shift in the political arena to 'Cold War Liberalism' – a hard-line anti-Communism (and virulently pro-capitalist) version of liberalism bolstered by a disingenuous sense that ideology itself (except capitalist ideology, of course) had ceased to explain the world. In this worldview, the clash of extreme ideologies embodied by the conflict between Nazi Germany and Stalin's Russia served to discredit for all time any political perspective too far from the center ground.[7]

While the UK today faces an almost rabidly ideological assault from the conservative right – we are not even allowed the social 'liberalism' embodied by the likes of John F. Kennedy in the post-war period – parallels between the present political environment and events in post-war America are also clear, even if economically the situation is very different. Today left-wing alternatives are likewise dismissed and 'discredited' and 'reformers' such as David Miliband, the fresh face of New Labour always on the look-out for a compromise to benefit the 'squeezed middle', look to be dead in the water. To a certain extent, further parallels might be drawn between this and the current state of CMS, if not academia in general. Seemingly endless 'debates' rage between those slightly left of the center with very little tangible result. See, for instance, Tatli's (2012) unproductive and misdirected sniping at other management scholars she sees as dyed-in-the-wool postmodernists. Why does it matter? Shouldn't 'progressive' scholars attempt to

5   Moley was arguably the most conservative member of the Brains Trust. Roosevelt, while more progressive than Moley, was likewise certainly no collectivist (Tugwell 1968: xxiv–xxv).

6   Recollecting the events of 1932 years later, Tugwell went so far as to suggest that in actual fact Roosevelt shared an 'amazing resemblance' to Herbert Hoover, who had wanted to implement some of the reforms that eventually became the New Deal but lacked the conviction to push them through Congress and beyond the traditionalist wing of the Republican Party. As such, according to Tugwell, the reforms Roosevelt allowed represented 'a carrying on, not a reconstruction'. This is significant because it reveals the limited extent to which the intellectuals were able to influence policy (Tugwell 1968: xii). Richard Hofstadter concurs, naming his chapter on the president 'Patrician as Opportunist'. As noted previously, many identify an *anti*-patrician sensibility within pragmatism (Hofstadter 1948: 315).

7   See, for example, Daniel Bell, 1960, *The End of Ideology: On the Exhaustion of Political Ideas in the Fifties*.

band together rather than revel in disunity, while the orthodoxies they critique remain aloof and untouched.

To labor the point, David Miliband, whose 'pragmatism', if indeed that is what it is, is only vulgar, does not even countenance the idea that he might actually mount a sustained and *meaningful* ('political' in its proper sense rather than the bluster we have come to associate with term) critique of *conservatism* in the Commons; instead, discussing David Cameron's decision to 'veto' a recent EU treaty designed to repair the Eurozone's ailing economy, he suggested that:

> *a veto is supposed to stop something happening. It is not a veto when the thing you wanted to stop goes ahead without you. That is called losing, that is called letting Britain down. (Watt 2011)*

This is not critique, as such, but it *is* pragmatic in the way it implicitly tries to maintain the center ground by sniping at the errant Cameron and appealing to the 'national interest'. And needless to say, the troublingly monikered 'Red Ed'(current UK Labour Leader Ed Miliband) spends large parts of the rest of his time sowing disunity amongst the nominal left by criticising the unions that secured him the party leadership. Both 'pragmatic' appeals to the middle ground *and* meaningless infighting, then, are not particularly helpful in terms of advancing a genuinely progressive politics, either in parliament or via the medium of CMS scholarship.

Nonetheless, if American pragmatism is to be brought to bear on debates within CMS about its political implications, or its political efficacy, or its 'radicalism', we need to be clear about its practical application, limitations and relative successes in the past. The example of the Brains Trust demonstrates two things. In the first instance, there is a distinction to be drawn between what is meant by pragmatism in its common usage (usually compromise of some sort) and philosophical pragmatism. In his recent book on Barack Obama, James Kloppenberg (2011), who sees the current President as a pragmatist *par excellence* not altogether dissimilar to Roosevelt, distinguishes between these two varieties of pragmatism:

> *America's principal contribution to the Western philosophical tradition, the philosophy of pragmatism that originated over a century ago in the writings of William James and John Dewey, has provided a sturdy base for Obama's sensibility. It has become [a] cliché to characterize Obama as a pragmatist, by which most commentators mean only that he has a talent for compromise – or an unprincipled politician's weakness for the path of least resistance. But there is a decisive difference between such vulgar pragmatism, which is merely an instinctive hankering for what is possible in the short term, and philosophical pragmatism, which challenges the claims of absolutists – whether their dogmas are rooted in science or religion – and instead embraces uncertainty, provisionality, and the continuous testing of hypotheses through experimentation. (Kloppenberg 2011: xi–xii)*

Challenging the claims of absolutists, then, is a key facet of philosophical pragmatism as distinct from vulgar pragmatism, and this is certainly something that applied to the Brains Trust, concerned as they were to rebut the laissez-faire assumptions of their age. Indeed, for Kloppenberg 'the philosophical pragmatism of James and Dewey and their descendants has played an important part in shaping progressive politics since the early twentieth century' (Kloppenberg 2011: xii), from the Trust through JFK and LBJ to Obama. In this the Brains Trust perhaps also differed from Roosevelt, whose progressive pragmatism, at least according to Rex Tugwell, was tempered by his well-heeled background.

Breaking out of the 'Glass-Bead Game'

The question of how much influence left-leaning intellectuals can wield in the political arena – or indeed in the world of corporate management and what has been described as the New Public Management – has been and continues to be a vexed one. When we speak, who is listening? The 'ivory-towerness' of CMS, encompassing a lack of accessibility at the level of discourse and a physical inability (or perhaps in some cases even unwillingness) to break out of institutional boundaries, surely contributes to this malaise. Even philosophical pragmatism, which seems to offer a progressive alternative to the partisanship of left and right may be 'particularly ill-suited to our own cultural moment' (Kloppenberg 2011: xii). As Kloppenberg suggests:

> when partisans left and right vie to proclaim rival versions of certainty with greater self-righteousness, the pragmatists' critique of absolutism and embrace of open-ended experimentation seems off-key, unsatisfying, perhaps even cowardly. (Kloppenberg 2011: xii)

Indeed, these reservations about pragmatism – or perhaps more accurately, about pragmatists – are nothing new. At the beginning of this chapter it was noted that one of pragmatism's foremost concerns is with the expansion of democracy. What is interesting about this is the way that the rhetoric of 'democracy' continues to be hijacked by the right for its own ends. George W. Bush's references to 'democracy' and 'freedom' in many of his 'War on Terror' speeches are a good example of this – 'they' hate our 'democracy' and resent our 'freedom', therefore we must impose it upon them. Disappointingly, some pragmatist intellectuals have adopted positions vis-à-vis the expansion of democracy which, whilst ostensibly progressive, play into and perhaps even inform such damaging attitudes about America's role in the world. In 1917 the essayist and intellectual Randolph Bourne published 'Twilight of Idols', a pointed critique of his mentor John Dewey. Dewey (1917) had consistently argued that America should enter the First World War in order to preserve and promote democratic principles. This sort of compromising with political power, or the mainstream of political opinion – power which most likely had very different motives to Dewey's, whose belief in the integrity of American democracy was blind – did not sit well with Bourne, who tragically died just a year after the piece was published in *The Seven Arts* magazine, a victim of the post-war influenza pandemic at just 32.

Still, pragmatism retained a progressive potential for the left-leaning Bourne in its original conception. 'If William James were alive would he be accepting the war situation so easily and complacently?' he countered:

> I think of James now because the recent articles of John Dewey's on the war suggest a slackening in his thought for our guidance and stir, and the inadequacy of his pragmatism as a philosophy of life in this emergency. Whether James would have given us just that note of spiritual

adventure which would make the national enterprise seem creative for an American future – this we can never know. But surely that philosophy of Dewey's which we had been following so uncritically for so long, breaks down almost noisily when it is used to grind out interpretation for the present crisis. These articles on 'Conscience and Compulsion', 'The Future of Pacifism', 'What America Will Fight For', 'Conscription of Thought', which The New Republic has been printing, seem to me to be a little off-color. A philosopher who senses so little the sinister forces of war, who is so much more concerned over the excesses of the pacifists than over the excesses of military policy, who can feel only amusement at the idea that any one should try to conscript thought, who assumes that the war technique can be used without trailing along with it the mob-fanaticisms, the injustices and hatreds, that are organically bound up with it, is speaking to another element of the younger intelligentsia than that to which I belong. Evidently the attitudes which war calls out are fiercer and more incalculable than Professor Dewey is accustomed to take into his hopeful and intelligent imagination, and the pragmatist mind, in trying to adjust itself to them, gives the air of grappling, like the pioneer who challenges the arid plains, with a power too big for it. It is not an arena of creative intelligence our country's mind is now, but of mobpsychology. (Bourne 1917/1999: 53–4)

Bourne's point lends some shading to my argument about the potentially fatal contradictions within pragmatist thought and its lack of utility for CMS. Simply put, pragmatism and what Bourne calls the 'mobpsychology' of a pro-American mindset may be, however paradoxically, compatible – or, at the very least, pragmatism cannot break this mentality down very easily. If we liken the psychology, which encompasses a blind faith in the veracity of American democracy, a penchant for bullishness – even jingoism – to some of the absolutisms that CMS scholars like to critique, it is plain that 'creative intelligence' of the pragmatist mindset, as Bourne puts it, can only tinker, in an ultimately unproductive way, with powers 'too big', too ingrained, too attractive, for it to overcome (Bourne 1917/1999: 53–4). Why compromise with this power, Bourne seems to be saying, when, if the mind has the potential to be creative, surely a more penetrating, more forceful mode of critique is possible; one closer to James's 'old ways of thinking' perhaps, or perhaps something different, something more sure of itself in regard to epistemology? To relate this to the present chapter, the question might be put this way: why would CMS scholars put faith in a critical approach that can be put to disingenuous purposes just as much as it can be used to pursue progressive ideals? Why adopt another cerebral 'approach' that bears so much potential for confusion and disenchantment?

Philosophically speaking, if pragmatism constitutes a 'genetic theory of what is meant by truth' (Dewey 2007: 156), and that means something unstable and contingent upon circumstance – a 'temper of mind' not given to critical realism – then it certainly bears comparison to epistemologically relativist currents within CMS. In one sense, too, in its will to constantly experiment, to undermine 'accepted' truths, pragmatism corresponds with the impulse towards forms of denaturalization and reflexivity Fournier and Grey (2000: 7) see at the heart of much CMS scholarship. But is 'denaturalization', or simply exposing problems in existing structures with the aim of questioning their validity, without ever really offering a solution beyond the 'provisional', enough? Ultimately, the answer depends upon what we consider to be a meaningful political act.

Conclusion

Throughout this chapter I have tried to demonstrate how pragmatist ideas, even at the level of epistemology, may be of little use to CMS, assuming its practitioners truly do wish to break out of the institutional trap of self-referentiality and pre-packaged 'approach' culture that seems to have prevailed. Pragmatism may be concerned with 'last things' or 'facts' (Dewey 2007: 156), but not their 'stability', or *the usefulness of assuming their stability*. And while this facet of pragmatism poses a theoretical challenge to absolutism, so do many other approaches, or 'methods', to employ Dewey's terminology, adopted by CMS scholars. William James called pragmatism a 'new name for some old ways of thinking', and we might just as easily describe the prospect of its use today as a new (at least to CMS) way of making the same points, over and over again. Admitting the fallibility of one's ideas will always be a 'reasonable' gesture, but, faced with people and institutions whose conviction in the veracity of their own ideas is indomitable, it will not always be a progressive or useful one.

References

Bell, D. 1960. *The End of Ideology: On the Exhaustion of Political Ideas in the Fifties*. Glencoe, IL: Free Press.

Bourne, R. 1999. Twilight of idols, in *War and the Intellectuals: Collected Essays 1915–1919*, (ed.) Carl Resek. Indianapolis, IN: Hackett.

Bridgman, T. and Stevens, M. 2008. Institutionalizing critique: A problem of critical management studies. *Ephemera*, 8(3), 258–70.

Dewey, J. 1917. What America will fight for. *New Republic*, 12, 68–9.

Dewey, J. 2007. What pragmatism means by practical, in *Essays in Experimental Logic*, (ed.) D. Micah Hester and R.B. Talisse. Carbondale, IL: Southern Illinois University Press, 303–29.

Fournier, V. and Grey, C. 2000. At the critical moment: Conditions and prospects for critical management studies. *Human Relations*, 53(1), 7–32.

Grey, C. and Sinclair, A. 2006. Writing differently. *Organization*, 13(3), 443–53.

Hofstadter, R. 1948. *The American Political Tradition and the Men Who Made It*. New York: Knopf.

Kloppenberg, J.T. 2011. *Reading Obama: Dreams, Hope, and the American Political Tradition*. Princeton, NJ: Princeton University Press.

Kuhn, T. 1962. *The Structure of Scientific Revolutions*. Chicago, IL: University of Chicago Press.

Lloyd, G. (ed.) 2006. *The Two Faces of Liberalism: How the Hoover–Roosevelt Debate Shapes the 21st Century*. Salem, MA: M&M Scrivener Press.

Parker, M. 2002. *Against Management: Organization in the Age of Managerialism*. Cambridge: Polity.

Quine, W.V.O. 1951. Two Dogmas of Empiricism. *The Philosophical Review*, 60, 20–43.

Rorty, R. 1986. Foucault and epistemology, in *Foucault: A Critical Reader*, (ed.) D.C. Hoy. Oxford: Blackwell, 41–50.

Rorty, R. 1989. *Contingency, Irony and Solidarity*. Cambridge: Cambridge University Press.

Tatli, A. 2012. On the power and poverty of critical (self) reflection in critical management studies: A comment on Ford, Harding and Learmonth. *British Journal of Management*, 23(1), 22–30.

Tinker, T. 2002. Disciplinary spin. *Organization*, 9(3), 419–27.

Tugwell, R.G. 1968. *The Brains Trust*. New York: Viking.

Voronov, M. 2008. Speaking out: Towards engaged critical management studies. *Organization*, 15(6), 939–45.

Watt, N. 2011. EU Veto a 'diplomatic disaster', claims Miliband. *The Guardian* [Online]. Available at: http://www.guardian.co.uk/politics/2011/dec/12/eu-veto-diplomatic-disaster-miliband [accessed: 12 December 2011].

West, C. 1989. *The American Evasion of Philosophy: A Genealogy of Pragmatism.* Madison, WI: The University of Wisconsin Press.

Wicks, A.C. and Freeman, R.E. 1998. Organisation studies and the new pragmatism: Positivism, anti-positivism, and the search for ethics. *Organization Science*, 9(2), 123–40.

2 *American Pragmatism Applied*

8 *Pragmatism and Public Administration: Looking Back, Looking Forward*

PATRICIA M. SHIELDS, TRAVIS A. WHETSELL AND EMILY KAY HANKS

Introduction

The eminently practical science of administration. (Woodrow Wilson 1887)

Public administrators are charged with translating law into public policy. They are responsible for making policy *work*. A key insight based on this practical fact led to the development of 'Pragmatism: Exploring Public Administration's Policy Imprint' (*Imprint*) (Shields 1996). In this article, the cubist painting metaphor illustrated the multifaceted way various disciplines and professional groups use conceptual lenses that leave distinct imprints on public policy. For example, the economist's imprint is efficiency, while the politician's is power.

Public administrators are judged by whether the social security check arrives on time, the traffic lights work, the meat supply is healthy, and the streets are safe, etc. Public administration (PA) is concerned with the practical problem of making policy work. Unlike economics or political science, PA seems to lack an overarching intellectual identity. Classical American pragmatism provides an imprint for PA, and its concept *the community of inquiry* furnishes an 'organizing principle'. Classical pragmatism also provides PA with an intellectually sustaining philosophy that focuses on practitioner experience while incorporating social ethics, participatory democracy, and a flexible research tradition that integrates theory and practice.

In 1996 the literature of public administration contained few references to classical pragmatism. The first explicit call to actively cultivate classical pragmatism as a source of theoretical identity came from the *Imprint* article (Shields 1996). Subsequently, a coherent and diverse literature emerged, demonstrating the promise of pragmatism for PA. This chapter examines that literature and discusses five interconnected themes:

1. the practice perspective;
2. the rediscovered historical connection;
3. the ideas of Jane Addams as a feminist/pragmatist/public administrator;
4. the debate between varieties of pragmatism in PA;
5. the role of pragmatic inquiry in research methods.

Practitioner Perspective

> *A philosophy that is so firmly planted in the nexus of theory and practice is a natural resource for the public administrator who has an office at that nexus. (Brom and Shields 2006: 312)*

One of public administration's most persistent concerns has been how to integrate theory and practice. In classical pragmatism, theory has immediate relevance to practitioners because its focus on problematic situations treats theory as a useful tool, not an ideological position. Unfortunately, the complexity of pragmatism made it difficult to communicate to PA practitioners. In *Healing Psychiatry* (2006), David Brendel captured the essence of pragmatism in a way that was both understandable and accessible. Brendel distilled pragmatism down to four Ps: practical, pluralistic, participatory, and provisional. The applicability of the four Ps was first recognized and adapted to PA in 'Rediscovering the Taproot' (Shields 2008). Thus, the four Ps provided a memorable heuristic useful for PA practitioners. The four Ps also serve as a running theme throughout this chapter.

Pragmatism provides a practical approach because it focuses on the value of 'practical outcomes for people in ordinary life' (Brendel 2006: 29). The routine problems of public administration prompt administrators to seek practical outcomes. This orientation connects inquiry to problematic situations (how to make programs work) as an opportunity to generate potential solutions that can be tested in practice. Since most problematic situations derive from the world of experience, this perspective puts the practitioner in the driver's seat.

Pragmatism's pluralistic perspective takes into account that the scope of problematic situations generally impacts on a variety of persons and groups. Further, problems can be approached using multiple theoretical approaches. The decision to build a road, for example, may call forth neighborhood interest, environmental groups, and business alliances. Each of these groups brings to the table their own theoretical perspectives and policy agendas. Though occasionally these perspectives may seem harmonious, they are often in conflict. A pluralistic orientation encourages the city manager charged with building the road to recognize and evaluate competing perspectives.

Pragmatism's participatory character gives voice to myriad groups with interests in resolving problematic situations. A critical insight of pragmatism is that participation by the community enables a deeper and fuller understanding of the problematic situation. In other words, effective inquiry has a social dimension and promotes a democratic spirit. Participatory democracy is perhaps the most profound component of classical pragmatism (Dewey 1938b). The term 'democracy' is usually associated with representative or procedural democracy, voting, and the rule of law, however, the participatory, social democracy of Addams and Dewey is more visible at the agency level (Ansell 2011) where, for example, notice and comment requires agencies to solicit the participation of the community.

Public administrators must also be able to tolerate ambiguity and unintended consequences in an environment ridden by partisan politics. Hence, practitioners should maintain a provisional orientation. The practical nature of pragmatism implies that program implementation cannot be endlessly deliberative. Actions are called for. These actions, however, should not be based on unquestioned, rigid doctrine; rather, in pragmatism, truth becomes a provisional working hypothesis. The provisional orientation contrasts with an all-knowing expert who has the one best solution (another prominent model in PA). Classical pragmatism does not deny expertise but admits that even highly qualified experts can be wrong. The greater error is in persisting in strategy that experience renders un-useful and rationalizing preconceived commitments with arbitrary dogma. Every expert can be incorrect and every community of inquiry can produce error. Hence, pragmatic truth is provisional. Clearly, pragmatism has much to offer public administration.

Historical Roots

> Because pragmatism and public were never properly wed, PA was deprived of a nourishing theoretical base. (Brom and Shields 2006: 310)

Public administration in the United States traces its origin as a self-aware field to the 1880s when future president Woodrow Wilson gave his famous speech *The Study of Administration* (1886) at the American Political Science Association. In this speech, Wilson distinguished administration as separate from politics: 'Administration is the most obvious part of government; it is government in action; it is the executive, the operative, the most visible side of government'. Just nine year earlier, Charles S. Peirce (the founder of pragmatism) published the 'Fixation of Belief' (1877). In retrospective, Wilson's 'eminently practical science' of public administration seemed to have been drawn from the popular and influential ideas of Peirce, James and Dewey (Mahoney 2004). But in 1996, by the time of the *Imprint* article, the historical connection was seemingly severed. In 2000, Keith Snider explored the mystery of PA's apparent disappearance from the PA literature; and, in 2008, Shields contributed a different perspective.

Snider argued that Dewey and James had never influenced the founding of PA. Snider noted that the pragmatic dissolution of dualisms was incompatible with the politics-administration dichotomy. In addition, a vulgarized conception of pragmatism in the popular media wrongly conflated it with unprincipled, short-term expediency. The leaders of PA found it necessary to distance themselves from these corrupt ideas. Finally, the new practice oriented field just didn't seem all that interested in philosophy (Snider 2000a, 2000b).

From another perspective, Shields (2008) claimed that pragmatism was indeed present at PA's founding, but was implicit and embedded in the spirit of progressivism. For example, the early PA literature made a practical distinction between politics and administration, consistent with Dewey's approach to non-invidious dichotomies; reform movements of the period encouraging civil service were centrally concerned with enhancing democracy (not just efficiency); and the movement towards the merit system emphasized concepts of expertise and qualification that were more egalitarian than those of the patronage system.

As a major American philosophy, classical pragmatism played a key role in PA but was obscured by numerous social factors. Unfortunately, the progressive American spirit that fostered pragmatism was crushed by its experience with two world wars, leading PA to focus excessively on efficiency, expertise, and scientific certainty (Waldo 1948). Thus, PA abandoned progressive era pragmatism in favor of logical positivism, which dominated the PA literature until the end of the twentieth century. Finally, one of classical pragmatism's principal advocates, Jane Addams, remained in obscurity as prominent twentieth-century philosophers and PA theorists failed to note the contribution of women. Subsequently, Jane Addams has been recognized as a founder of both public administration (Stivers 2000) and classical pragmatism (Seigfried 1996). The next section explores that connection.

Jane Addams: The First Practicing Pragmatist

We judge [a living institution] not by its creed … but by its blundering efforts to apply its principles to living affairs. (Jane Addams)

Despite being one of the most famous women of her time, Jane Addams's place in the scholarly record was by no means assured. When Shields wrote the *Imprint* article in 1996, the influence of Jane Addams on both pragmatism and public administration was hidden – it was what Stivers labels a 'buried heritage' (2000: 33). Indeed, the remarkable achievements of Addams were often overlooked, criticized, or dismissed as 'old-fashioned do-goodism fired by the charitable impulses of a "lady" who wound up fashioning an over-personalized approach to social problems' (Elshtain 1997: 105). Many early biographers found her writing plagued by 'lacunae in her thinking' as well as paradoxes and tensions. These early interpretations reveal a fundamental misunderstanding, attributable in part to the failure to place her work within the context of pragmatism, feminism, and public administration (Siegfried 2009).

Since that time, a fundamental rethinking of pragmatism by (pro) feminist philosophers has revived interest in Jane Addams (Seigfried 1996, 2001, 2001; Elshtain 1997, 2002; Rumens and Kelemen 2010). These thinkers cast Addams in a renewed light – as an intellect in her own right and constructed a critical link between feminism and pragmatism (Shields 2006). Classical pragmatism provided Addams with the philosophical underpinnings necessary to construct a social world in which women were able to participate in the public sphere. In other words, pragmatism provided a way around the rigid and prevailing dichotomy between masculine and feminine. Moreover, Addams's own social ethics provided pragmatism with a rich normative framework, constituting an original contribution to American philosophy.

While feminist philosophers restored Addams to her rightful place as a founder of pragmatism, another group of scholars pursued a different, less traveled path, exploring her contributions as an administrator (Shields 2003, 2005b, 2006a, 2011; Stivers 2000, 2005, 2009). PA researchers note Addams's service as the first woman Sanitary Inspector in Cook County's nineteenth ward. She was also the leader of Hull House, a large nonprofit institution for poor Chicago immigrants. Jane Addams was, in practice, a public administrator. Although Addams's philosophy of public administration was unique and profound, until the work of Stivers and Shields, it remained one of the least recognized aspects of her work. This literature illustrates the promise of pragmatism as a source of intellectual identity for American public administration by (re) incorporating the view of Jane Addams and the women of Hull House. From this perspective, the life, work, and writing of Jane Addams can be interpreted as the first fully realized portrait of a 'practicing pragmatist' in public administration. Unlike many of her pragmatist contemporaries, however, Jane Addams lived and worked among the immigrant poor. Addams literally and symbolically resided at the nexus of feminism, pragmatism, and public administration.

From this unique position, she was able to envision her work as integrating the theory of pragmatism with the everyday practices at Hull House (Siegfried 2009).

The close-knit community at Hull House was a deliberate experiment in resolving the practical problems of the day warranted by the philosophy of pragmatism (Seigfried 2009). Indeed, the Settlement women of Hull House saw their work not as philanthropy, but as public service. Here we see the embodiment of Dewey's call for social science to bring 'a desired state of society into existence' (1931/1939: 951). Dewey himself remarked upon the significance of Addams's work at Hull House, saying:

> *my indebtedness to you for giving me insight into matters there is great ... Every day I stayed*
> *there only added to my conviction that you had taken the right way. (954)*

Given the source of the compliment, it seems appropriate to consider: 'What might Addams have gotten so "right" at Hull House?' The literature reviewed here uncovers several key theoretical tenets of Addams's work that inform the contemporary theory and practice of PA. During her tenure at Hull House, Addams realized an alternate vision of PA, one that emphasized social democracy, free association, experience, and inquiry. As noted earlier, Addams's extended the social claim of women beyond the threshold of private, domestic affairs into the public sphere. However, she was concerned with more than cultural feminism. Addams advocated a way of seeing all human beings as interconnected:

> *In a crowded city quarter, however, if the street is not cleaned by the city authorities, no amount*
> *of private sweeping will keep the tenement free from grime; if the garbage is not properly*
> *collected and destroyed a tenement house mother may see her children sicken and die of*
> *diseases from which she alone is powerless to shield them ... In short, if woman would keep*
> *on with her old business of caring for her house and rearing her children she will have to have*
> *some conscience in regard to public affairs ... individual conscience and devotion are no longer*
> *effective. (Addams 1910b: 21)*

No longer, argued Addams, may citizens remain at the periphery of public affairs; the private interests of every citizen are connected in the public sphere (Stivers 2009). Participation, then, is not a luxury but a necessity (Seigfried 2009). Moreover, public administration provides the connective tissue – the mechanism for attachment – between citizens and government, which is perhaps even more so today (Evans 2010; Stivers 2005).

Referring to Dewey, 'a democracy is more than a form of government; it is primarily a mode of associated living, of conjoint communicated experience' (1916: 87). The practice of public service, then, should involve an attempt to identify, or participate in a shared understanding of the 'other'. As Shields (2006) points out, a sympathetic understanding is the difference between being good *to* people, or good *with* them (432). To do so requires regard for pluralism, or the dignity of all citizens' lived experience. Seigfried suggests:

> *one of [Addams's] major contributions to pragmatist theory ... is her recognition and*
> *demonstration of the concrete diversity of such experience, with all this implies. (2009: 49)*

For the women of Hull House, the implications of diversity of experience meant first-hand knowledge of social problems such as disease, inadequate child labor laws, and poverty. Here Addams's approach to working with the public showed considerable sensitivity to both scientific findings and historical-cultural patterns. Thus, Addams experimented with multiple perspectives and methods when addressing public problems (Shields 2006a; Seigfried 2009). For instance, consider the striking contrast between the scientific, methodological rigor of *The Hull House Maps and Papers* and the narrative logic of, as Elshtain (2002) calls it, 'The Story of the Self-Sacrificing Mother's Spotless House, All in Vain' (167). The former is a paragon of social science. *The Hull House Maps and Papers*, as directed by Addams and Kelley, contained cutting-edge cartography, demographic data on nationality, wages, occupation, as well as detailed descriptions documenting deplorable working conditions (Shields 2003; Deegan 1990). In contrast, the latter is a particularistic parable telling the story of a mother who, despite her best intentions inside of her own home, cannot protect her daughters from typhoid. Rather than make her case with charts and figures, the narrative ends with a moral:

> *The entire disaster affords, perhaps, a fair illustration of the futility of the individual conscience which would isolate a family from the rest of the community. (1910a)*

These examples indicate that, for Addams, knowledge was provisional; there could be no 'one best way' to explain human experience.

According to Stivers (2009), Addams was critical of public administrators who lost sight of the human impact in their attempts to investigate and remedy social problems. 'Such a state of mind', Addams lamented, 'affords one more example of the dangers of administrating any human situation upon theory uncorrected by constant experience' (1935: 70–71). To avoid this potential pitfall, Shields (2003) urges administrators to apply the following formula:

> *the problematic situation in public administration should be vetted through a wide audience, it should be investigated using reasoned arguments, and it should be data driven. (434)*

To that list, one might add that administrators pay close attention to how they communicate policy decisions to the public – making every effort, as Addams did, to align the message and the medium with the audience.

The promise of pragmatism as a source of intellectual identity in PA is epitomized by Addams's metaphor of the 'civic household'. Strictly interpreted, the city-as-home approach shifts the primary concern of public administration from the duty to protect citizens from external attack (the city as citadel) to a more domestic agenda. The city is understood as a literal 'home' for citizens; and the role of municipal government, such as sanitation and health, is equivalent to the nineteenth-century woman's household chores. The metaphor of the civic household is also a powerful alternative to the city-as-a-business metaphor. Interpreted in this way, municipal housekeeping is a model of public service derived from household values and the spirit of the family. Caring, immediacy, and interconnectedness animate public service. Rooted in this renewed metaphor of the civic household is the untapped (but not unrecognized) potential for Addams to provide a compelling, modern identity for PA. In both theory and practice, identification with the civic household mitigates the rigid dualisms between public and private, individual and community, and procedure and substance, all of which have long been assumed to be inherent in PA. These dichotomies, however, are only rigid when the 'norms of administrative practice ... remain much closer to business management than housekeeping or motherhood' (Stivers 2000: 101). In fact, a growing body of research on emotional labor (Guy et al. 2008), nonprofit management, and feminist democratic organization (Nickel and Eikenberry 2006) hints that a major restructuring of the current identity of PA may already be afoot. Such studies demonstrate that the image of the civic household can serve as a 'source domain' in PA. This recapitulation could produce an alternative perspective equipped to counter the dominant image of bureaucratic efficiency and professionalized expertise.

Jane Addams's vision of civic affairs as fundamentally consubstantial with the values of the home and family stresses the organic and essential 'belongingness' of citizens (Stivers 2005). Democratic citizenship, like family membership, is a centripetal force; no matter how hard one might try to escape civic duty (individualism), democracy will always exert a connective pull (communalism). 'Belonging' to an extended, democratic family also mitigates the dichotomy between the public and the private by reconfiguring how public servants relate to citizens. Public interaction would be governed in part by the private, subjective, and familial obligations of kindness, care, and cooperation. The practice of public administration envisioned through this identity is undoubtedly an ideal type. True to Addams's pragmatic spirit, this image is also grounded in the 'real' because families, although idealized, are rarely ideal. The family is a 'real' institution; it is fallible because it is human. In the words of Leo Tolstoy, who Addams greatly admired: 'All happy families resemble each other, each unhappy family is unhappy in its own way' (1887/1995: 1). Elshtain (2002) regards the civic household metaphor as the culmination of Addams's logic, 'the rock-bottom ground of her civic philosophy and her social feminism' (158). By (re)reading and (re)claiming the values embedded in this metaphor, a new identity for modern public administrators (re)emerges. Whether this frame offers PA a coherent modern identity, or a fractured, postmodern self is a matter of some debate, as we discuss below.

Varieties of Pragmatism

A universe of experience is a precondition for a universe of discourse. (Dewey 1939: 74)

In 2003, Shields identified *The Community of Inquiry* as PA's organizing principle. This article marked the practical starting point for a new thread in the ongoing theoretical debate between competing philosophical traditions in PA, which occurred between classical and neo-pragmatists. *The Community of Inquiry* included three principle areas of focus: problematic situation, scientific attitude, and participatory democracy. The problematic situation serves as the practical focus for social inquiry; scientific attitude provides those involved with an empirical, experimental, and provisional approach; and emphasis on participatory democracy engages all interested parties in a pluralistic way. While classical and neo-pragmatists mostly agreed on problematic situation and participatory democracy, the scientific attitude presented the basis for a renewed philosophical debate centering on questions of epistemology and legitimacy.

In 2004, Hugh Miller countered *The Community of Inquiry* arguing that reliance on scientific attitude revealed ignorance of the postmodern reaction to *scientism*. Thus, advocates of 'old' pragmatism did not heed the 'postmodern assault on foundations' (244), which left language un-tethered to an objective reality. Confronted by the challenge of postmodernism, new pragmatists tied language to itself in an ironically circular fashion, while classical pragmatism tied language to experience in a contextual fashion. As Miller argued, 'new' pragmatism rejects experience as a foundational concept, emphasizing analysis of language. Problems in PA can thus be deconstructed, revealing language games in which public figures assert their legitimacy through claims at foundational knowledge. Thus, deconstructing language and the legitimacy of authority becomes the focus of PA as an academic discipline under neo-pragmatism.

While it may seem that experience is particularly important in the decision-making process of the administrator, the validity of experience is called into questioned under neo-pragmatism. Thus, Miller argued, 'experience is a concept about reality. It is no more real than any other concept ... experience is a word shaped object' (2004: 244). Hence, concepts are not real and do not correspond to objective truths in an external reality, and the administrator's experience is no more reliable in the construction of knowledge than language since they are both conceived as mere concepts. Classical pragmatism's practical emphasis on problematic situations, however, fixes the relevance of experience to the resolution of contextual problems, not to the construction of universal truths. While experience may not have a foundational correspondence to a fixed reality, it nevertheless remains the object of much inquiry throughout life. Accordingly, classical pragmatism abides the postmodern assault on foundationalism, embracing uncertainty by rejecting quests for absolute truth in favor of a limited, contextual, provisional truth. In response to Miller's suggestion that PA embrace Richard Rorty, Shields argued that neo-pragmatism's epistemic position makes it 'unabashedly non-empirical' and therefore useless to administrators: 'From the perspective of the practitioner, Rorty's linguistic pragmatism is aloof and abstract in the "bad sense"'(2004: 358). Rather, a moderate scientific attitude, residing somewhere between the extremes of reductive foundationalism and circular coherentism, qualifies classical pragmatism as a more suitable philosophy for public administration.

Experience is an essential tool of the administrator. Practitioners use experiential knowledge to navigate indeterminate situations and assess potential consequences associated with public problems. These existential constraints promote experience as the subject of inquiry in the face of problematic situations. Thus, PA practitioners entered the debate between Shields and Miller, contesting Miller's dismissal of experience. For example, in 2004, Gregory Stolcis advanced 'A View From The Trenches', providing a practitioner's response:

> Miller assured us that, in the newer, improved version of pragmatism 'public administration would work better' ... Imagine my disappointment upon learning a little about new pragmatism and in discovering my experiential knowledge is vastly overrated and, according to Miller, not to be entirely trusted in the practice of daily government. (Stolcis 2004: 362)

James Webb entered the debate shortly thereafter, arguing neo-pragmatism 'does not accept the naïve view of the purpose of public administration as a practice', which explains its disregard for practitioner experience and hence its fear of experiential confidence (2004: 480). Rather than being an 'upgrade', neo-pragmatism's rejection of experience makes it particularly unsuitable to PA by threatening to undermine the link between theory and practice that classical pragmatists carefully constructed and defended. Webb

(2004) noted, in response to Miller, 'the imputation of epistemological foundationalism to classical pragmatism suggests a failure to grasp the nature of experience (in Dewey's rich, deep, and nuanced sense) and the nature of discourse and the relation between the two in classical pragmatism' (481). Larry Hickman added to the debate, by supporting Webb's response, noting that Dewey's pragmatism 'rejected the notion that there is some foundation of certainty on which we can take a stand. That was, in fact, the main point of his book *The Quest for Certainty*' (2004: 498). David Hildebrand (2005) later suggested that it appeared as if neo-pragmatists simply had not bothered to read the works of classical pragmatists, which explains why they largely fail to reference Dewey. Indeed, Karen Evans notes, 'it would be better for postmodern thinkers to acknowledge their debt to Dewey than to dismiss him as archaic' (2005: 252). After the inclusion of these arguments in the debate, Miller (2005) clarified his original position, arguing 'residues of foundationalism' present in classical pragmatism serve to perpetuate illegitimate power structures under the guidance of the 'man of reason', who advances favored norms of social control. The 'man of reason' uses science to legitimate his otherwise arbitrary administrative authority.

Miller and other neo-pragmatists such as O.C. McSwite, however, seem excessively concerned with problems of epistemic certainty, rejecting experiential knowledge in one fell swoop as dangerously over-confident. As McSwite argued, 'what seems to be behind evil most often is certainty' (1997: 273). Thus, epistemic certainty exercised in the name of science by the 'man of reason' constitutes a liability, generating illegitimate assertions of authority based on claims to objective truth; but, while American politics is replete with unquestioned dogma, the debunking of objectivism only goes so far in enhancing the practice of governance. In fact, this criticism of classical pragmatism is much like Bertrand Russell's, though interestingly enough it emanated from the opposite end of the epistemic spectrum. British empiricist Bertrand Russell criticized John Dewey for evaluating truth in terms of consequences, noting that leaders who define the consequences can manipulate historical truths to serve arbitrary assertions of power. Russell thought pragmatism a 'power philosophy' rooted in the American experience with the industrial revolution; though he acknowledged that in pragmatism 'it is the power of the community that is felt to be valuable' (1946: 827). Given the widely disparate epistemologies of Russell and Miller, and the similarity of their conclusions, it would seem that legitimacy could be argued from either epistemic vantage. While the legitimate exercise of authority remains an important political science issue, legitimacy is less so in postmodern bureaucracy. Agencies rarely engage in what Stolcis (2004) termed 'tangential discourse', though they often question their own policies in an attempt to generate new ideas through participatory policy formulation groups. A pragmatic spirit can aid in this process by encouraging participation from a variety of interested groups or persons within the community.

In classical pragmatism the legitimate exercise of authority is intimately connected to its community-based ethics of democracy. As Dewey reasoned in *Logic: The Theory of Inquiry*, systems of logic and the scientific method are far more contingent upon social processes such as cooperation, debate, and consensus than previous thinkers had realized (1938a). Charles Hoch contributed to the debate by attempting to reconcile Dewey and Rorty, pointing out that Rorty simply recapitulated the social contingency of scientific belief in a more zealously anti-foundational manner. Hoch argued, 'what matters in science are the liberal social virtues that encourage participants to conduct critical and tolerant inquiry' (391). Both varieties of pragmatism argue that knowledge is intimately connected to the community and its norms of legitimacy in a rich and interdependent way.

The contemporary debate between varieties of pragmatism in public administration has clear implications for how it chooses to view its role in the practice of American governance. As a uniquely American contribution to the history of Western philosophy, pragmatism offers an alternative to the ubiquitous influence of logical positivism. The legacy of positivism in PA amounted to little more than a method for conducting quantitative analysis and enhancing the efficiency of policy implementation, but avoided the subjective complexity of social interaction and eschewed the subject of ethics entirely. As a result, PA under this school of thought often appeared rudderless, lacking an organizing principle to provide it with a normative mission that could elevate its stature as a mature discipline. Evans (2010) reoriented the debate away from the epistemic discourse between competing varieties of pragmatism towards the fundamental issue: the problematic conceptualization of PA solely around implementation and efficiency. Snider (2011) responded to Evan's call for pragmatism, reiterating his prior observation that Dewey's philosophy had never been adopted by PA, adding a sense of grim determinism about the incommensurability of pragmatism with PA's dominant paradigm. Concluding this period of the debate for now, Whetsell and Shields (2011) assert that qualifying PA as a 'paradigmatic' discipline generates an unrealistic image of positivism as monolithic; rather, PA seems to be made up many communities of academics and practitioners, some of whom appear to be embracing different varieties of pragmatism.

Pragmatism in Research Methods

There is the same sort of advantage in having conceptual frameworks manufactured and on hand in advance of ... their use, as there is in having tools ready instead of improvising. (Dewey 1938a: 136)

While the philosophical debate continued in the pages of the journal *Administration & Society*, pragmatism made inroads into public administration research methods, a landscape dominated by scholars schooled in logical positivism. As a philosophy of science, pragmatism influenced the PA literature through a very unlikely avenue – research design in master's level student scholarship. In the early 1990s, an accrediting team identified problems with Texas State University Master of Public Administration (MPA) capstone research papers (weak literature reviews and conceptual incoherence). This led to the creation of a preparatory class on research design, which significantly improved student capstone papers. In this class, John Dewey's *Logic: The Theory of Inquiry* (1938a) was used as the basis for the development of the course.

Like many applied fields, public administration has engaged in an ongoing debate about the role of theory in practice and the connection between theory and methodology. Dewey's inquiry integrates theory and practice by transforming theory into a tool of inquiry. Theory is judged by its usefulness in resolving problematic situations. When theory is a tool, it at once becomes practical, provisional and pluralistic. Tools are practical because they solve problems, provisional because they can be replaced by better ones, and pluralistic because they can be used in tandem with others. James's (1907) hotel corridor metaphor illustrates the tool-like properties of theory. We enter the hotel corridor with a problematic situation. The rooms along the corridor represent theories that may be useful to resolve the problematic situation, various theories are tried and, if they help to resolve the problem, are put into use. Pragmatism's philosophy of science provided a way to address the problem of weak conceptual frameworks in student papers. Conceptual frameworks are a kind of intermediate theory, which organize inquiry by clarifying the connection between research purpose, theory and method. These connections are often a challenge for practitioner oriented student scholars. Thus, a taxonomy was developed to resolve the problem by linking conceptual frameworks to the particular research purposes and typical methods of data collection (Shields 1998) (see Table 8.1).

Table 8.1   Conceptual framework and research purpose taxonomy*

Research purpose	Conceptual framework	Typical Method/Statistics*
Exploration	Working hypotheses	Case study, anything goes
Description	Descriptive categories	Survey, content analysis, descriptive statistics ...
Gauging	Practical ideal type	Case study, survey, descriptive statistics
Decision-making	Models of operations research	Linear programming, cost benefit analysis, cost effectiveness analysis ...
Explanation	Formal hypotheses	Survey, existing data analysis, time series, experimental design, multivariate statistics ...

Note: See Shields and Tajalli (2006: 318) for complete table.

The system of purpose and framework informed the way an empirical research problem is approached. If, for example, a student wanted to find out what bicyclists in Austin Texas thought about the quality of their biking experience, the research purpose would be descriptive and the conceptual framework would be categories. On the other hand, if a student wished to know the effect of a snack tax on obesity rates their explanatory purpose would lead them to develop formal hypotheses. The framework/purpose pairing also provides a larger coherence because they link to modes of data collection, measurement, statistics and analysis (Shields and Tajalli 2006).

Dewey (1938) noted that inquiry occurs when an indeterminate situation (writing a research paper) is transformed into 'a unified whole' (complete paper). The transformations begin as doubt emerges to replace an accepted belief system. When students write papers, one would expect that in the process of doing a literature review, they would be confronted with surprises that produce this unsettled doubt filled situation. Unfortunately, students often find the route from belief to doubt to a unified whole unsettling and anxiety provoking. They often do not have the organizational tools to successfully navigate the transformation. Using this insight and a pragmatic theory of inquiry, *Step by Step: Building a Research Paper* was developed to help students transform writing a paper into managing a project. With a process and a way to organize themselves, students were better able to conduct inquiry. This tool combined ways to stay organized with Dewey's theory of inquiry (Shields 2006b), providing students with an organizational tool that facilitated the reflective thought necessary for satisfying, fruitful scholarship. This process is manifest through the explicit connection between the literature and conceptual frameworks. These insights reached the larger PA audience through the success of student papers. All capstone papers are available in Texas State's electronic repository and have been downloaded over 300,000 times in the last five years (15 percent from outside the USA) (see https://digital. library.txstate.edu/handle/10877/105). The World Health Organization and international scientific journals have also cited them, for example. Moreover, five of the papers have won first place in national competition (Shields et al. 2012). Practitioner-students author these Applied Research Projects. The papers generally deal with practical problems of state and local government. Their widespread use and acclaim suggest the appeal of the practitioner perspective. Their quality attests to pragmatism's capacity to bridge theory and practice.

Conclusion

Since its inception public administration, like many social sciences, has tentatively embraced an array of organizing principles. In 1996, the literature of public administration turned towards pragmatism as a way to reconcile theory and practice. The early history of PA was marked by the spirit of progressivism that permeated American life; the middle years were dominated by the new empiricism in the post-World War era, logical positivism; and recently PA has experienced a revival of interest in pragmatism, exemplified by debates between classical and neo-pragmatists and coterminous with a new and fruitful application of Jane Addams's ideas. Moreover, renewed interest in pragmatism has led to the development of successful new methods of public administration research.

Public administration's search for an organizing principle has been confounded to some extent by its distinct roles in academia and government. This chapter has argued that classical pragmatism provides PA with an identity that suits its dual role as an academic discipline and as the steward of American democracy. Pragmatism's emphasis on problematic situations grounds public problems in their existential context and history; its emphasis on experience provides the discipline with a method of inquiry that avoids the dogmas of empiricism and the circularity of rationalism; its emphasis on the community collapses the dichotomy between the individual and society, substituting in its place a theory of governance grounded in principles of democracy; in this respect, pragmatism asserts and establishes a normative framework of ethics particularly suitable to American public administration as an extension of participatory government.

References

Addams, J. 1910. *Twenty Years at Hull House*. Mineola, NY: Dover Publications.
Addams, J. 1910. Why Women Should Vote. *Ladies' Home Journal*, 27(January), 21–2. Available at: http://www.fordham.edu/halsall/mod/1915janeadams-vote.asp [accessed: 12 March 2013].
Addams, J. 1935. *My Friend Julia Lathrop*. New York, NY: Penguin Books.
Ansell, C. 2011. *Pragmatist Democracy: Evolutionary Learning as Public Philosophy*. Oxford: Oxford University Press.

Brendel, D.H. 2006. *Healing Psychiatry: Bridging the Science/Humanism Divide*. Cambridge, MA: MIT Press.

Brom D. and Shields P. 2006. Classical Pragmatism, the American Experiment and Public Administration, in *Handbook of Organization Theory and Management: The Philosophical Approach*, 2nd edn, (ed.) T. Lynch and P. Cruise. Boca Raton, FL: Taylor and Francis, 301–22.

Deegan, M.J. 1990. *Jane Addams and the Men of the Chicago School*. New Brunswick, NJ: Transaction Books.

Dewey, J.H. 1916. *Democracy and Education: An Introduction to the Philosophy of Education*. New York, NY: Free Press.

Dewey, J. 1938a. *Logic: The Theory of Inquiry*. New York, NY: Holt, Rinehart, and Winston.

Dewey, J. 1938b. Creative Democracy: The Task before Us, in *The Essential Dewey: Vol. 1: Pragmatism, Education, Democracy*, (ed.) L. Hickman and T. Alexander. Bloomington: Indiana University Press, 340–44.

Dewey, J.H. 1931/1939. Social Science and Social Control, in *Intelligence in the Modern World*, (ed.) L.J. Ratner. New York, NY: Modern Library.

Elshtain, J.B. 1997. A Return to Hull House: Reflections on Jane Addams. *Feminist Issues*, 15(1–2), 105–13.

Elshtain, J.B. 2002. *Jane Addams and the Dream of American Democracy*. New York, NY: Basic Books.

Evans, K.G. 2005. Upgrade or Different Animal All Together? Why Old Pragmatism Better Informs Public Management and New Pragmatism Misses the Point. *Administration and Society*, 37(2), 248–55.

Evans, K.G. 2010. Into the Woods: A Cautionary Tale for Governance. *Administration and Society*, 42(7), 859–83.

Guy, M.E., Newman, M.A. and Mastracci, S.H. 2008. *Emotional Labor: Putting the Service in Public Service*. Armonk, NY: M.E. Sharpe.

Hickman, L.A. 2004. On Hugh T. Miller on 'Why Old Pragmatism Needs an Upgrade'. *Administration and Society*, 36(4), 496–9.

Hildebrand, D.L. 2005. Pragmatism, Neopragmatism, and Public Administration. *Administration and Society*, 37(3), 345–59.

Hoch, C. 2006. What Can Rorty Teach an Old Pragmatist Doing Public Administration or planning? *Administration and Society*, 38(3), 389–98.

James, W. 1907. *Pragmatism: A New Name for Some Old Ways of Thinking*. Cambridge, MA: The Riverside Press.

McSwite, O.C. 1997. *Legitimacy in Public Administration: A Discourse Analysis*. Thousand Oaks, CA: SAGE.

Mahoney, D. 2004. *Politics and Progress: the Emergence of American Political Science*. MD, Lanham: Lexington books.

Miller, H.T. 2004. Why Old Pragmatism Needs an Upgrade. *Administration and Society*, 36(2), 243–9.

Miller, H.T. 2005. Residues of Foundationalism in Classical Pragmatism. *Administration and Society*, 37(3), 360–74.

Nickel, P.M. and Eikenberry, A.M. 2006. Beyond Public vs. Private: The Transformative Potential of Democratic Feminist Management. *Administrative Theory and Praxis*, 28(3), 359–80.

Peirce, C.S. 1877. The Fixation of Belief. *Popular Science*, 12(1–15).

Rumens, N. and Kelemen, M. 2010. American Pragmatism and Feminism: Fresh Opportunities for Sociological Inquiry. *Contemporary Pragmatism*, 7(1), 129–48.

Russell, B. 1946. *A History of Western Philosophy*. London: George Allen & Unwin Ltd.

Seigfried, C.H. 1996. *Pragmatism and Feminism: Reweaving the Social Fabric*. Chicago, IL: University of Chicago Press.

Seigfried, C.H. 2001. *Feminist Interpretations of John Dewey*. University Park, PA: Pennsylvania State University Press.

Seigfried, C.H. 2009. The Courage of One's Convictions or the Conviction of One's Courage? Jane Addams's Principled Compromises, in *Jane Addams and the Practice of Democracy*, (ed.) M. Fischer, C. Nackenoff and W. Chmielewski. Chicago, IL: University of Illinois Press, 40–62.

Shields, P. 1996. Pragmatism: Exploring Public Administration's Policy Imprint. *Administration and Society*, 28(3), 390–411.

Shields, P. 1998. Pragmatism as Philosophy of Science: A Tool for Public Administration. *Research in Public Administration*, 4, 195–225.

Shields, P. 2003. The Community of Inquiry: Classical Pragmatism and Public Administration. *Administration and Society*, 35(5), 510–38.

Shields, P. 2004. Classical Pragmatism: Engaging Practitioner Experience. *Administration and Society*, 36(3), 351–61.

Shields, P. 2005a. Classical Pragmatism Does Not Need an Upgrade: Lessons for Public Administration. *Administration and Society*, 37(4), 504–18.

Shields, P. 2005b. Classical Pragmatism: Roots and Promise for a PA Feminist Theory. *Administrative Theory and Praxis*, 27(2), 370–75.

Shields, P. 2006a. Democracy and the Social Feminist Ethics of Jane Addams: A Vision for Public Administration. *Administrative Theory and Praxis*, 28(3), 418–43.

Shields, P. 2006b. *Step-by-Step: Building a Research Project*, 3rd edn. Stillwater OK: New Forums Press.

Shields, P. and Tajalli, H. 2006. Intermediate theory: The missing link in successful student scholarship. *Journal of Public Affairs Education*, 12(3): 313–34.

Shields, P. 2008. Rediscovering the Taproot: Is Classical Pragmatism the Route to Renew Public Administration? *Public Administration Review*, 68(2), 205–21.

Shields, P., Rangarjan, N. and Stewart, L. (2012). Open Access Digital Repository: Sharing Student Research with the World. *Journal of Public Affairs Education*, 18(1): 157–82.

Snider, K.F. 2000a. Expertise or Experimenting? Pragmatism and American Public Administration 1920–50. *Administration and Society*, 32(3), 329–54.

Snider, K.F. 2000b. Rethinking Public Administration's Roots in Pragmatism: The Case of Charles A. Beard. *The Review of Public Administration*, 30(2), 123–45.

Snider, K.F. 2005. Rortyan Pragmatism: "Where's the Beef" for Public Administration? *Administration and Society*, 37(2), 243–7.

Snider, K.F. 2011. On the Problem of Adopting Pragmatism in Public Administration. *Administration and Society*, 43(1), 133–41.

Stivers, C. 2000. *Bureau Men, Settlement women: Constructing Public Administration in the Progressive Era*. Lawrence, KS: University of Kansas Press.

Stivers, C. 2005. A Place Like Home: Care and Action in Public Administration. *American Review of Public Administration*, 35(1), 26–41.

Stivers, C. 2009. A Civic Machinery for Democratic Expression: Jane Addams on Public Administration, in *Jane Addams and the Practice of Democracy*, (ed.) M. Fischer et al. Chicago, IL: University of Illinois Press, 87–97.

Stolcis, G.B. 2004. A View From the Trenches: Comment on Miller's "Why Old Pragmatism Needs an Upgrade." *Administration and Society*, 36(3), 362–9.

Tolstoy, L. 1887/1995. *Anna Karenina*, trans. Maude and Maude. New York, NY: Oxford University Press.

Waldo, D. 1948. *The Administrative State*. New York: Ronald Press Co.

Webb, J.L. 2004. Comment on Hugh T. Miller's "Why Old Pragmatism Needs an Upgrade". *Administration and Society*, 36(4), 479–95.

Whetsell, T. and Shields, P. 2011. Reconciling the Varieties of Pragmatism in Public Administration. *Administration and Society*, 43(4), 473–83.

Wilson, W. 1887. The Study of Administration. *Political Science Quarterly*, 2(2), 187–222.

9 Understanding Organizational Creativity: Insights from Pragmatism

DIANE-LAURE ARJALIÈS, PHILIPPE LORINO AND BARBARA SIMPSON

I am told I am creative – I don't know what that means … I just keep on plodding …

Peter Drucker, quoted in Csikszentmihalyi (1996: 14)

Introduction

Creativity is arguably one of the most crucial features of organization as it infuses and influences all epistemic practices (Cook and Brown 1999). From an evolutionary perspective, creativity may be understood as the source of novelty in key organizational change processes such as product and process innovations, strategic renewals, restructurings, identity reconstruals, and market reorientations. Thus interest in creativity is by no means limited to the so-called creative industries since every organization is inevitably at some time faced with imperatives to change. However, creativity remains significantly under-researched (Joas 1996; Sternberg and Lubart 1999; Hennessey and Amabile 2010), leaving many unanswered questions about its antecedents, the conditions in which it flourishes or is inhibited, and the social processes by means of which it emerges.

In this chapter we propose that American pragmatism, especially the works of Charles Sanders Peirce, John Dewey and George Herbert Mead, offers a potentially fruitful way of understanding creative practice as a dynamic social process. From this viewpoint, creativity *is* the human condition (Joas 1996) that exists as a potential in even the most mundane, everyday plodding actions of social practice (Kilpinen 1998). It begs a dynamic, real-time theorization that can address *how* questions by accommodating the temporal aspects of social practice (Tsoukas and Chia 2002). We develop our argument by drawing on an empirical example that demonstrates the temporal emergence of creative practice in a small financial services company. We show that creativity cannot be explained simply in terms of the application of planned techniques and formulae (Bohm 1996). Rather, it arises as a response to uncertain and unanticipated situations that call out changeful actions.

Researching Creativity

Existing research on creativity is characterized by a huge diversity of disciplinary interests in design and performance, spanning the entirety of the arts and sciences. Of particular relevance to organizational scholars, creativity has been explored in both the psychological and sociological literatures. On one hand, critics of developments in the psychology literature point to the somewhat fragmented state of creativity research (Simonton 2003; Hennessey and Amabile 2010), and call for an integrative mechanism to draw the creative person, the creative product, and the creative process together in a contextualized and dynamic theoretical frame. On the other hand, in a comprehensive review of the classical writers in sociology, Joas (1996) concluded that none of these has succeeded in smoothly integrating a theory of creativity into their thinking, thus condemning creativity to remain ever an externality in social theory.

Attempts to overcome these problems have drawn on systemic, or ecological, understandings of human activity. For instance, Csikszentmihalyi (1996) argued that creativity arises in the interaction between individuals and their sociocultural contexts, in what Woodman, Sawyer and Griffin (1993) independently characterized as an interactionist view of creativity. However, these models do not explain *how* contexts influence behaviors, nor *how* creative behaviors at an individual level can be joined together to comprise group or organization level creativity. Hargadon and Bechky (2006) challenged the dualistic separation between individual and collective levels of analysis, adopting instead a relational perspective that focuses on interpersonal interactions and their potential to produce 'moments of collective creativity' (2006: 484). They proposed a model that used collective mind (Weick and Roberts 1993) to describe the triggering of collective creativity through interpersonal interactions. Their interest in mind and cognition, however, creates an inappropriately individualistic focus that leaves much of the communicative potential of interpersonal interactions unexamined.

The pragmatists were trenchant in their opposition to the dualistic distinctions evident in much of this work on creativity. Dewey in particular railed against the separation of mind and body (thinking and feeling), arguing that although these are two different aspects of the process of living, by separating them into discrete conceptual categories, we effectively cut across the very practices that we seek to understand (Simpson 2009). In contrast to more rationalistic philosophies, the pragmatists understood human experience and conduct in practical, everyday terms wherein we are all active participants, rather than mere spectators, in the construction of social meanings (Bernstein 1972). From their perspective, the key to creativity is abduction, a process that generates creative insight by forming hypotheses to explain problematic situations (Peirce 1965). Abduction broadens the scope of experience mobilised in any given situation from habitual to less habitual forms of action, integrating emotional and rational judgments to overcome the classical dichotomy between 'creative thinking' and 'rational thinking'.

However, a comprehensive understanding of creative action in organizations requires more than abduction alone. Drawing on the wider pragmatist canon, we argue firstly that abduction arises when habits of action are disrupted by unanticipated events, prompting a process of inquiry that seeks to transform experience and reinstate action (Dewey 1938 (1986)). Secondly, this creative process is inherently social and conversational (Mead 1934). To avoid possible confusion with 'interactionist' theories such as those mentioned above, we follow Dewey and Bentley (1949 (1991)) who made a distinction between interactions and transactions. They saw these as two different levels of inquiry: an interaction is something that happens between actors who are physically and mentally independent, while a transaction happens across actors who are aspects of a relationally integrated whole; whereas meanings are transmitted between actors in an interaction, the actors are the continuously emerging meaning in a transaction. Both selves and situations are continuously reconstructed in transactional processes (Elkjaer and Simpson 2011). Further, this process of transactional meaning-making is semiotically mediated by signs that facilitate the sharing of meanings (Mead 1934; Peirce 1965).

In our view, these pragmatist themes of abduction, habit, inquiry, transactional meaning-making and semiotic mediation are all necessary components of a theory of organizational creativity that is both social and dynamic. In the empirical example that now follows, we will elaborate these themes and demonstrate the interplay between them as the managers of a troubled company seek creative ways of regaining competitiveness in an increasingly challenging market. We hope, in this way, to offer a more complex and subtle understanding of the creativity inherent in everyday organizational practices.

Innovation in a Financial Services Company

This example concerns X Corporation,[1] a small French asset management company that specialises in socially responsible investment (SRI) equities, managing funds amounting to €2 billion. An SRI equity portfolio usually comprises 40 to 50 companies, often the three to five best companies – in terms of both financial and SRI performance – in a variety of activity sectors (e.g. utilities, banking and insurance). There may be up to 20 different sectors represented in any portfolio. For promoters of socially responsible investment, better financial performance is achieved in the long term by minimizing the costs that result from below-average performance in social, environmental and governmental domains. However, asset management companies find it difficult to achieve optimal financial and SRI performance. It was in this context that X Corporation's senior managers recognised an urgent need to develop creative new ways of designing their SRI portfolios.

Prior to 2007, the SRI equity funds of X Corporation were invested among the Eurostoxx, an index representing the 300 largest capitalizations of 12 Euro zone countries. A quarterly SRI ranking of the companies in each sector was calculated by X Corporation's SRI analysts to inform investment decisions made by its asset managers. The method of calculating this SRI ranking was very simple, and had not changed since 1998: an external social rating agency would provide company scores based on more than 100 different criteria, such as carbon emissions, board independence, mix of energy sources, human resource management practices, and so on; these were then used by X Corporation's SRI analysts to assign a weighted average SRI grade between 0 and 100 for each company. Asset managers then followed the so-called 'best-in-class' approach: in each sector, they favored companies with the best SRI grade relative to their peers. To maintain good financial performance, assets needed to be invested in different sectors so that if one particular sector suffered, other sectors could compensate for the loss. A monthly SRI grade was given to each portfolio – this consisted of assessing the weighted average SRI grades of companies present in the portfolio. Within X Corporation, it was

---

1   X Corporation is a pseudonym.

mandatory for each portfolio to achieve an average SRI score greater than 50/100. In the event that this requisite grade was not achieved, the portfolio manager would be required to change the content of his/her portfolio for the following month. In practice, though, no such requirement was ever exercised.

The data for this example are drawn from a three-year ethnographic study that combined participant observation, semi-structured interviews (conducted with all the members one year after the systems redesign) and documentary evidence. One of the authors was present in the company for the year during which the investment decision systems were redesigned, and participated in all the meetings of the working group as an SRI analyst. Being full-time inside the company, she also attended informal discussions between the different members. Hundreds of pages of notes were taken on a daily basis to record the different events occurring at X Corporation. Emails, minutes of meetings and responses to invitations to tender were also analyzed. Consistent with the pragmatist orientation of this chapter, we have adopted a non-representational approach to data analysis (Lorino et al. 2011) that focuses on the processual and narrative unfolding of an emergent system for evaluating investment choices within X Corporation. The following narrative of creative action plays out over five phases throughout which, we have explicitly woven pragmatist themes as an explanatory commentary.

PHASE 1: NORMAL PRACTICE IS DISRUPTED

The challenge for SRI funds is twofold: (1) to perform well financially; and (2) to be perceived as very innovative in terms of SRI. Yet, the most socially responsible companies are not always the most attractive financially speaking, which raises many problems in constructing balanced investment portfolios. In August 2007, X Corporation's SRI funds were judged to be no longer competitive by external consultants who act as intermediaries between institutional clients and asset management companies. They are paid by clients to select the best asset management companies to be invited to tender for shares. Therefore, if an asset management company is not chosen by consultants, it has almost no chance of receiving invitations to tender. The concerns the consultants raised about X Corporation's SRI funds were firstly, the form of the SRI constraint (a monthly score in excess of 50/100), which was insufficiently discriminating as a predictor of performance. Indeed, by combining very good and very bad companies in the same portfolio, this grade could mask consistently poor performing stocks. Secondly, the integration of SRI criteria in the company selection process was deemed too superficial: according to consultants, more companies had to be excluded for SRI reasons only, a criterion known as 'SRI selectivity'. Contrary to the company's existing SRI grading system, SRI selectivity forces asset managers to exclude a minimum percentage of the SRI laggards from the portfolios: in other words, SRI leaders cannot be used to compensate for SRI laggards. Thirdly, the company's SRI criteria lacked innovation compared to competitors. As a result, X Corporation was no longer able to meet the SRI demands of clients, consultants and competitors in the current market. Consequently, its survival was threatened.

To address this problem, the CEO of X Corporation decided to redesign the company's SRI equity funds. According to him, X Corporation had become a laggard due to its lack of innovation, so he established a cross-disciplinary working group comprising representatives of the Marketing Department (two sales representatives, responsible for selling the funds), the Asset Management Department (two asset managers, responsible for the investment decisions) and the SRI Department (three SRI analysts who were responsible for the SRI analysis inside the company. Based on the social rating agencies' information, they advised asset managers where to invest and controlled the SRI compliance of portfolios).

> *Post-mortem assessments were no longer useful [...] We had to think up new attractive products, which meant performance and originality in the presentation. The working group was launched for two reasons: we're cleverer when we work as a group and employees needed to appropriate the process. [...] It had to be a communal project. That's how it works best. (CEO)*

The working group planned to meet face-to-face once a week; full-attendance at each meeting was compulsory. The agenda was to be set one week in advance so that each member would have time to prepare his/her input for the following meeting. Since they were responsible for responding to invitations to tender, it was the sales representatives who took the lead in shaping the working group activities. They believed that they could explain to SRI analysts and asset managers what was lacking in the existing funds and help them to achieve a compromise between SRI and financial concerns.

> *I tried to reconcile each party's interests, which were evidently different: SRI purists, asset managers without regret, and the Director of Marketing & SRI who really wanted to show that the process was, in fact, simple, robust and immutable. (Sales Representative)*

Pragmatist Commentary – Prior to this first phase of change at X Corporation, the company appeared to be dwelling in a cosy state of complacency regarding its market competitiveness. In pragmatist terms, this state equates to 'habit'. For Peirce (1965: 5.388–410),[2] habit refers to a learned predisposition to undertake a standard course of action in response to specific circumstances, or to attribute a standard meaning to specific events. Dewey further elaborated this notion as follows:

> *[Habit is] that kind of human activity which is influenced by prior activity and in that sense acquired; which contains within itself a certain ordering or systematization of minor elements of action; which is projective, dynamic in quality, ready for overt manifestation; and which is operative in some subdued subordinate form even when not obviously dominating activity. (Dewey 1922 (1957): 31)*

It is habit that allows us to reliably anticipate both our own and others' conduct in given situations by making the future seem predictable. However, although habits express social norms of conduct, they are neither rigidly fixed for all time, nor are they 'Pavlovian' reflexes. Rather, they are dynamically emergent practices that admit the possibilities of mutability and change over time through social transactions. The continuing accomplishment of habits depends upon the situated interpretation of circumstances. If nothing specific draws actors' attention in a given situation, then habit will prevail as the normal way of doing things. However, when the anticipations afforded by habit prove inadequate or inappropriate for the situation, then actors may choose to transform their course of action. The interruption of habitual action is a key point in pragmatist thinking

---

2   Citations to Peirce refer to the Collected Papers, Volume Number, Paragraph and Number(s).

as it is this that initiates the cycle of inquiry by means of which social practices mutate over time.

In the case of X Corporation, habitual ways of evaluating SRI investment portfolios are interrupted in this first phase by external consultants who argue that the company's products are no longer competitive in the changing marketplace. It is this disruption to habitual practice that propels the company into the extended process of inquiry, which plays out over the ensuing phases of this change story. We see that the CEO's first action is to establish a working group that offers a context for transactional conversations to tackle the seemingly intractable problem of restoring competitiveness to the company's products.

PHASE 2: MAKING OUR EXPERTISE MORE VISIBLE

The first meeting of the working group took place in September 2007. Group members did not have any shared views about how to tackle the situation, but they did have a shared purpose to reinstate the company's competitiveness. The sales representatives saw the problem as a communication gap: X Corporation only needed to prove its expertise; tacit knowledge needed to be formally represented and made visible to clients. For this purpose, they asked the SRI and Asset Management Departments to design 'company factsheets', which would summarise the SRI and financial profile of each company in their investment portfolios. In this, they were following what they perceived to be a market trend where increasing numbers of competitors were providing such factsheets. After one and half months, the working group reached a deadlock: SRI analysts and asset managers were unable to design usable factsheets. Among several problems, there were not enough SRI analysts and asset managers to regularly update the information provided by the factsheets. Since they were always obsolete, factsheets could not be used by asset managers and SRI analysts in their own day-to-day practices.

> *The company factsheets were merely for commercial purpose [...] We completely disagreed. Sales managers really needed them as a commercial tool. Whereas, for us [asset managers and SRI analysts], it was rather the opposite. It wasn't a tool, it was pure reporting. And, I must say, reporting with very little added-value [...] It was completely of secondary importance. (Asset Manager)*

> *It was the worst thing we could have done! It was putting the cart before the horse. It was not triggered by the redesign of the process but by the external motivation to demonstrate that we had a process which did not exist! (SRI Analyst)*

> *Even today, working on the company factsheets is not easy. Frankly, these company factsheets have been a failure. (Director of Marketing &SRI)*

Pragmatist Commentary – In this phase we see the working group's initial response to the change imperative. The sales representatives have offered what seems, on the face of it, a plausible account of the problem (tacit knowledge needs to be made visible to clients) and its potential resolution (provision of factsheets). The other members of the working group appear, at least initially, to accept this position without debate, thus limiting the transactional potential that might otherwise have been afforded by working together.

The process of conjectural thinking that was employed by the sales representatives reflects Peirce's notion of abduction, which he proposed as a third type of inferential reasoning (alongside deduction and induction):

> *[Abduction] is the only logical operation which introduces any new idea; for induction does nothing but determine a value, and deduction merely evolves the necessary consequences of a pure hypothesis. Deduction proves that something must be; Induction shows that something actually is operative; Abduction merely suggests that something may be. (Peirce 1965: 5.171)*

He explained abduction as the process of inventing a hypothesis as a plausible explanation for surprising or unexpected events that arise in the social interplay of experience. Peirce defined the syllogistic form of abduction as follows:

> *The surprising fact, C, is observed;*

> *But if A were true, C would be a matter of course,*

> *Hence there is reason to suspect that A is true. (Peirce 1965: 5.189)*

For example, if a witness looks away during cross-examination (C), we might observe that people look away if they feel guilty (A), and therefore conjecture that this witness is guilty. Continuing the analogy with criminal justice, Corrington suggested that detective work is more about abduction than deduction 'because it must create a total picture of the crime and read the conjectural picture backwards onto the clues assembled' (1992: 85). Similarly, Czarniawska (1999: 21) maintained that the social sciences 'owe their insights mostly to abduction' and indeed, abduction may be seen threading through all living experience, giving meaning and value to all social actions. In the case of X Corporation, this initial abduction proved inadequate as the asset managers and SRI analysts became increasingly aware of the limitations of factsheets. This outcome represents a second interruption to practice, which triggers a second phase of abduction.

PHASE 3: REDESIGNING THE INVESTMENT PROCESS

In October 2007, the working group members realised they were on the wrong track. There were more substantive issues than 'making things explicit'; they realised that they should probably provide something else to clients. In other words, they needed to innovate. For this purpose, they decided to redesign the investment process for the SRI funds (i.e. the various stages through which companies are selected for the portfolio) by working together on a graphic representation. This collaboration evolved during the meetings but also between the meetings in an informal way. Members discussed the different problems during coffee breaks, exchanged emails, and shared their ideas with each other on a daily basis.

They came up with a new process comprising three steps (Figure 9.1):

> Step (1): SRI analysts define an 'investment universe' comprising all companies in which asset managers may invest, and an SRI typology that encompasses the different strategies of companies regarding non-financial aspects.

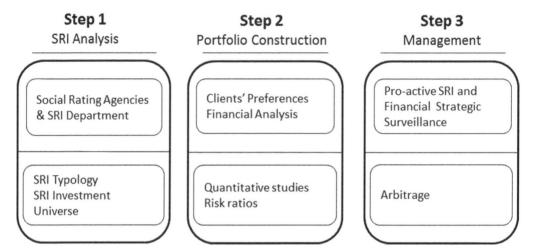

Figure 9.1   Investment process (October 2007)

Step (2) portfolios are constructed according to the risk ratios chosen by clients.

Step (3) asset managers select companies based on classical financial quantitative studies and controlled for the good performance of funds, including 'arbitrage' (taking advantage of a price difference between two or more markets).

Comparison of this investment process with competitors' processes and clients' and consultants' demands revealed two further problems to be remedied: the asset managers had insufficient freedom when investing, and too few companies were excluded for SRI reasons.

Pragmatist Commentary – In this phase, we see abduction, deduction and induction working together in the meaning-making process that the pragmatists called 'inquiry'. This process is central to their understandings of human, social and organizational change. The concept was originally proposed by Peirce (1965: 5.358–387) in his model of doubt and belief, in which he saw inquiry as a struggle in the face of doubt to attain a state of belief that is consistent with experience. In his view, inquiry is undertaken for the exclusive purpose of eliminating doubt and attaining belief. Thus any learning, or any new meaning, results from an active process of inquiry that is grounded in experience in a given context. It is neither the context nor the organism that is intrinsically and positively doubtful. Doubt and belief characterise the relationship between the organism, viewed as the locus of habits, and its context. Thus belief is an existential state of fitness between habits and context, whereas doubt is a state of unfitness. Inquiry must therefore be understood as an existential, rather than merely cognitive, concept.

Dewey later developed this notion by adding the idea of 'a situation':

> *Inquiry is the controlled or directed transformation of an indeterminate situation into one that is so determinate in its constituent distinctions and relations as to convert the elements of the original situation into a unified whole. (Dewey 1938 (1986): 108)*

For him, a situation is not a single object or event, nor a set of events (Dewey 1938 (1986): 72), but the entirety of all conditions under which, and within which, an organism functions at a given time. A situation is problematic or indeterminate when it is not intelligible because its constituent factors are in disarray. For Dewey then, the aim of inquiry is not the discovery of an antecedent fact, but rather the creation, or construction, of a new situation, bringing into being a new object of knowledge that did not exist prior to the act of inquiry. There are various identifiable phases in an inquiry process, though these do not necessarily follow in any prescribed, linear sequence. Still, inquiry is always triggered by existential unease associated with an unanticipated situation, which challenges ongoing habits of practice. This disruption is not yet a problem: it 'becomes problematic in the very process of being subjected to inquiry' (Dewey 1938 (1986): 111). Here, we have seen triggers to inquiry in both Phase 2 and Phase 3 of the X Corporation story, both of which were then constituted by the working group as problems; firstly, 'our products are competitive, but customers do not know it', and secondly, 'our products are no longer competitive'. In each case the working group then abductively proposed a plausible scenario that could explain events (the lack of factsheets; products that are insufficiently discriminating).

With a hypothesis in place, inquiry then moves to testing by means of the deductive reasoning of experimentation. Whereas Phase 2 negated the hypothesis that factsheets are the correct solution, Phase 3 demonstrates a more inclusive and more comprehensive effort to develop testable hypotheses that address the interests of all the working group members. The practical testing that then ensues reflects an inductive form of reasoning. Through this process, the members of the working group have themselves changed by coming to a greater awareness of the issues and concerns of colleagues in different departments, and their practices change accordingly. However, the conclusion of inquiry is always tentative and fallible, so we see there are still unsolved problems at the end of Phase 3, which trigger yet another cycle of inquiry.

The epistemology of inquiry contrasts with more familiar epistemologies of observation and correspondence. In the latter 'knowing' means observing a situation from outside in order to represent it as accurately as possible, so that it can then guide further action. With pragmatist inquiry, however, knowledge *is* intelligent action, intelligent action *is* knowledge, and the synthesis of knowledge and active experience is the inquiry. Learning then is the embodied and situated construction of meaningful experience rather than the production of 'true' representations in suspended time. Thus the concept of inquiry is a key tool in transcending dualistic separations between knowledge and action, decision and execution, design and utilization.

PHASE 4: INTERACTING TO TRANSFORM PRACTICE

The main challenge for the working group was to meet the objectives of all three departments. However, SRI criteria and financial performance often contradicted each other, and asset managers and SRI analysts did not always understand business demands. To help them work through these challenges, they set up a white board for each member to physically transform the representation of the investment process shown in Figure 9.1. Over the course of a few weeks, the working group attempted to develop the three stages of the investment process. Arrows were added, new stages appeared, others disappeared, names changed and so on. Each actor reacted to the proposed changes from his/her

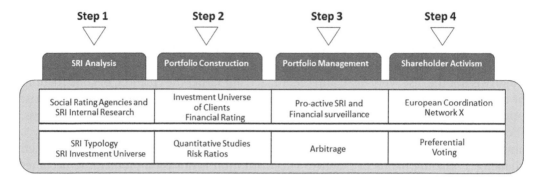

Figure 9.2   Investment process (November 2007)

perspective. By November 2007, they had come up with a new diagram upon which they all agreed (Figure 9.2).

The main change in this revised investment process was the addition of a fourth step concerning shareholder activism (i.e. the use of equity stakes at a European level in collaboration with other asset managers to put public pressure on the company's management – referred to in Step 4 of Figure 9.2 as 'preferential voting'). However, this new investment process still did not solve the problems. Indeed, the first three steps had hardly changed. Further work was required and the working group decided to continue transforming the process. Throughout, there was a constant iteration between reasoning and experimenting, as one of the sales representatives explained:

> *The problem was that we needed to sell the funds as we created them. This led to many tensions in the working group, notably in terms of timing. We submitted the presentation to a prospect one day, and the following day, we had to redesign the process [...] Each time I came back with new questions we needed to answer. (Sales Manager)*

Working group members started to become discouraged by these additional demands and by the lack of closure in their project.

> *There came a moment when I felt worried because I could sense lassitude; this happened at the end of the first term of 2008. I saw that guys were dragging their feet, that some of them no longer wanted to attend meetings. We no longer knew what to do: one day, we did one thing, the next day, another [...] To my mind, we were steering off course, although we did finally get back on track. (Director of Sales & SRI)*

However, the global financial crisis which had started just a few months earlier, perhaps surprisingly, provided a good incentive to continue the redesign process: the working group members found themselves with more time available for this task. Indeed, asset managers could barely invest (no buy, no sell to avoid financial losses) and the asset management company was almost 'frozen'. The transformed investment process was submitted to consultants and clients for comment. New problems were raised which in turn guided the subsequent steps of the redesign process.

When you provide an asset manager with a ranking, he/she tells you that there is a problem. So it makes you study the ranking. In doing so, you identify other problems in the analysis, though it was not your first purpose. You shouldn't have found this mistake. But, by solving one problem, you created another one. (SRI Analyst)

Gradually, the goals of the three departments converged. In January 2008, the working group produced a new 6-step investment process (Figure 9.3). SRI analysts and asset managers agreed on the idea that SRI may be a means to select the most promising companies in the long term – financially speaking – whereas they first thought these objectives were contradictory. To achieve this compromise between SRI and financial performance, they decided to build a common analysis of companies based both on financial and SRI criteria. They worked on new SRI criteria they deemed essential for business reasons.

Whereas SRI analysis had previously preceded financial analysis, companies were now ranked using a decision matrix (Figure 9.4) that simultaneously took into account both the SRI and financial rankings. Since the SRI ranking had been redesigned according to the needs of asset managers, there were fewer contradictions between the two rankings.

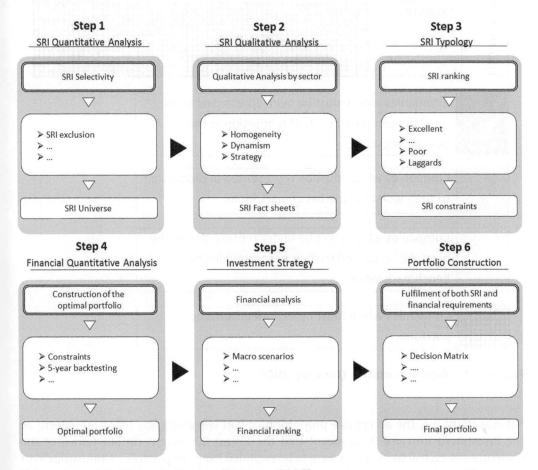

Figure 9.3   Investment process (January 2008)

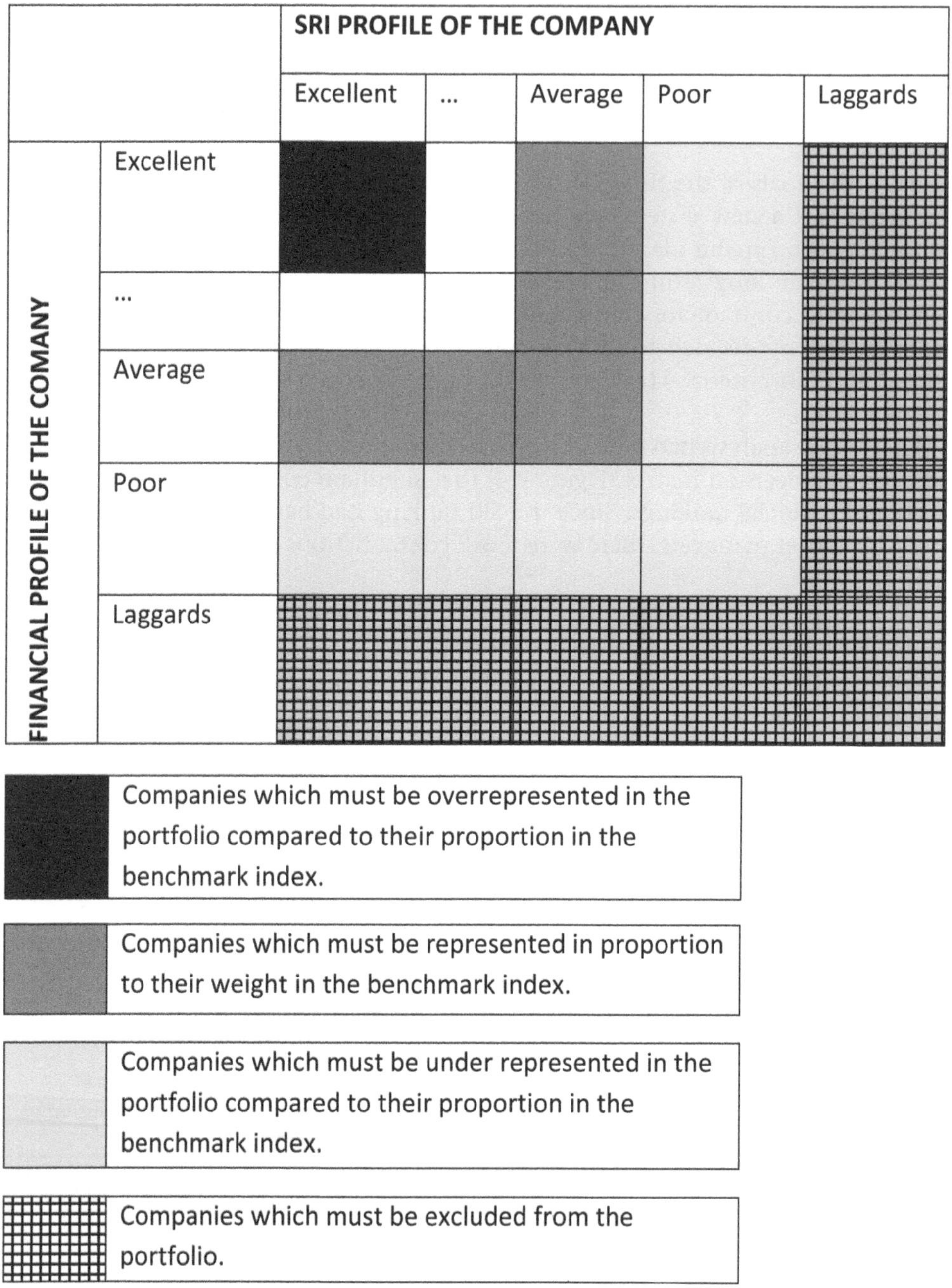

	SRI PROFILE OF THE COMPANY				
	Excellent	...	Average	Poor	Laggards
Excellent	███		▓▓▓	░░░	▦▦▦
...					▦▦▦
Average	▓▓▓	▓▓▓	▓▓▓	░░░	▦▦▦
Poor	░░░	░░░	░░░	░░░	▦▦▦
Laggards	▦▦▦	▦▦▦	▦▦▦	▦▦▦	▦▦▦

(row labels at left under heading **FINANCIAL PROFILE OF THE COMANY**)

███ Companies which must be overrepresented in the portfolio compared to their proportion in the benchmark index.

▓▓▓ Companies which must be represented in proportion to their weight in the benchmark index.

░░░ Companies which must be under represented in the portfolio compared to their proportion in the benchmark index.

▦▦▦ Companies which must be excluded from the portfolio.

Figure 9.4   Decision matrix (January 2008)

SRI selectivity (i.e. the acceptable proportion of 'SRI laggards') was set at 50 percent of the investment universe. This meant that the lowest 50 percent (in SRI terms) of the companies in each activity sector were to be excluded from the portfolio. Companies with the best SRI and financial profile would be overrepresented in the portfolio compared to their benchmark index. Companies with an excellent SRI profile but a very poor financial profile, or vice versa, would be excluded as 'laggards'. Other companies would be selected according to their SRI and financial profile.

Pragmatist Commentary – In this phase, we see the escalation of cycles of inquiry, where the problems arising from each solution immediately stimulated a new episode. But there is more yet to understand about inquiry, as it is a process that is mediated by language, routines, drawings, tools and other signs. Semiotic mediation has strong foundations in pragmatist thinking, especially Peirce's seminal work on the interpretation of signs (Peirce 1965: 2.227–273), where he argued that the meaning of a sign is determined by the situated context of its use. As such, this meaning is always evolving through usage. Semiotic mediations allow historic memory, action rehearsal and creative imagination, by making present in inquiry elements that are distant in time or space, such as past behaviors or imagined future situations.

Mead (1934) later proposed that mediations in the form of what he called 'significant symbols' provide the basis for mutual intelligibility and the social coordination of actions. He argued that significant symbols promote the development of reflexivity by allowing us to stand in someone else's shoes to gain a new perspective on events. Significant symbols are constructed transactionally, providing narrative objects that are accessible to a community of inquirers. Thus they not only mediate, but are also mediated by inquiry, which develops as a pluralist controversy between different interpretations of signs. It is the resulting ambiguities that admit the possibility of creative insight and learning. Conversely, in the absence of significant symbols, conversation is reduced to a series of reflex reactions that cannot produce new meanings. In the case of X Corporation, progressive cycles of inquiry produce new diagrams, new rules and new procedures, which then mediate further inquiry. The diagrams were constructed collectively, so their meanings are shared by everyone in the group. This is not to suggest, however, that every group member has an identical interpretation of the diagrams. Each member brings a different experience to situate their interpretation of the diagrams, and indeed, it is the exploration of differences between their interpretations that opens up possibilities for new thinking.

PHASE 5: TOWARDS CLOSURE

In January 2008, the investment process had been redesigned 'on paper', but had not yet been fully implemented. The working group first decided to conduct 'back-testing' (i.e. testing the new investment process on fictitious portfolios). As this was a first time methodological experience, they faced a number of unexpected problems (e.g. the choice of software or the selection of technical constraints), which prolonged the back-testing beyond what had been originally planned.

The new investment process was finally implemented in May 2008. However, two weeks later, the 50 percent SRI selectivity raised major problems: too many companies still had a contradictory SRI and financial profile. The working group then decided to lower SRI selectivity to 40 percent, then to 25 percent. Consequently, the investment process was less constrained in terms of SRI than had originally been anticipated: only 25 percent of companies in each activity sector were excluded for SRI reasons. In July 2008, the working group officially finished the task and the new investment process seemed to work in practice. The inquiry was concluded when the working group – and more particularly the CEO – judged that the investment process was sufficiently transformed to be convincing and commercially effective:

> *There comes a moment when you have to stop looking for something else, since it's no longer useful – you don't find anything further ... It's a bit like doing research. But I don't have to tell you that, do I? There comes a moment when you have something that you shouldn't try to improve. You must go with it and then ... carry on. (CEO)*

Pragmatist Commentary – Peirce (1965: 5.374–376) argued that inquiry comes to an end when the irritation caused by doubt is no longer sufficient to motivate further inquiring action. Here, we see that after a period of inductive confirmation of the chosen solution, X Corporation has reached a new point of equilibrium, albeit a temporary one, where the company's desire to continue to improve their investment decision-making process has to be tempered by other demands in the business.

Conclusion

In this chapter we have argued that pragmatism provides a very practical perspective on creativity by locating it in the everyday human practices by means of which people make sense of their situations. Using X Corporation as an illustrative example, we have shown that the pragmatist ideas of abduction, habit, inquiry, transactional meaning-making and semiotic mediation are all essential in coming to an understanding of creative action in organizations. Although the linear structure of chapter writing has forced us to elaborate each of these ideas in turn, we do not intend to suggest that they arise sequentially. Rather, we see them as intimately intertwined and mutually constituting. Overall, the case exemplifies an inquiry episode that begins with the disruption caused by the consultants' critique of the company's performance and ends with a return to habitual practice, albeit a different habit from that which was originally disrupted. Within this long-term episode which lasted for almost a whole year, there are many shorter cycles of abductive inquiry that attest to repeated occurrences of creative action embedded within the process of change at X Corporation. Thus we come to an understanding of organizational change as a continuous unfolding of creative actions that arise as people get on with plodding through their lives together. In this way, pragmatism demystifies creativity and suggests productive avenues for further research.

References

Bernstein, R.J. 1972. *Praxis and Action*. London: Duckworth.

Bohm, D. 1996. *On Creativity*. London and New York: Routledge.

Cook, S. and Brown, J.S. 1999. Bridging epistemologies: The generative dance between organizational knowledge and organizational knowing. *Organization Science*, 10(4), 381–400.

Corrington, R.S. 1992. *Nature and Spirit: An Essay in Ecstatic Naturalism*. New York: Fordham University Press.

Csikszentmihalyi, M. 1996. *Creativity*. New York: HarperCollins.

Czarniawska, B. 1999. Management she wrote. *Studies in Cultures, Organizations and Societies*, 5, 13–41.

Dewey, J. 1922 (1957). Human nature and conduct. *Middle Works*, (ed.) J.A. Boydston. Carbondale and Edwardsville, IL: Southern Illinois University Press, vol. 14.

Dewey, J. 1938 (1986). Logic: The theory of inquiry. *The Later Works, 1925–1953*, (ed.) J.A. Boydston. Carbondale and Edwardsville, IL: Southern Illinois University Press, vol. 12.

Dewey, J. and Bentley, A.F. 1949 (1991). Knowing and the known. *The Later Works, 1925–1953*, (ed.) J.A. Boydston. Carbondale and Edwardsville, IL: Southern Illinois University Press, Vol. 16, pp. 1–294.

Elkjaer, B. and Simpson, B. 2011. Pragmatism: A lived and living philosophy. What can it offer to contemporary organization theory? *Research in the Sociology of Organizations: Special Volume on Philosophy and Organization Theory*, (ed.) H. Tsoukas and R. Chia. Bingley: Elsevier, vol. 32, 55–84.

Hargadon, A.B. and Bechky, B.A. 2006. When collections of creatives become creative collectives: A field study of problem-solving at work. *Organization Science*, 17(4), 484–500.

Hennessey, B.A. and Amabile, T.M. 2010. Creativity. *Annual Review of Psychology*, 61(1), 569–98.

Joas, H. 1996. *Creativity of action*. Chicago, IL: University of Chicago Press.

Kilpinen, E. 1998. Creativity is coming. *Acta Sociologica*, 41, 173–9.

Lorino, P., Tricard, B. and Clot, Y. 2011. Research methods for non-representational approaches to organizational complexity: The dialogical mediated inquiry. *Organization Studies*, 32(6), 769–801.

Mead, G.H. 1934. *Mind, Self and Society*, (ed.) C.W. Morris. Chicago, IL: University of Chicago Press.

Peirce, C.S. 1965. *Collected Papers of Charles Sanders Peirce*, (ed.) C. Hartshorne and P. Weiss. Cambridge, MA: Belknap Press of Harvard University Press.

Simonton, D.K. 2003. Scientific creativity as constrained stochastic behavior: The integration of product, person and process perspectives. *Psychological Bulletin*, 129(4), 475–94.

Simpson, B. 2009. Pragmatism, Mead, and the practice turn. *Organization Studies*, 30(12), 1329–47.

Sternberg, R.J. and Lubart, T.I. 1999. The concept of creativity: Prospects and paradigms, in *Handbook of Creativity*, (ed.) R.J. Sternberg. Cambridge: Cambridge University Press, 3–15.

Tsoukas, H. and Chia, R. 2002. On organizational becoming: Rethinking organizational change. *Organization Science*, 13(5), 567–82.

Weick, K.E. and Roberts, K.H. 1993. Collective mind in organizations: Heedful interrelating on flight decks. *Administrative Science Quarterly*, 38(3), 357–81.

Woodman, R.W., Sawyer, J.E. and Griffin, R.W. 1993. Toward a theory of organizational creativity. *Academy of Management Review*, 18(2), 293–321.

10 *Organizational Learning: Knowing in Organizing*

ULRIK BRANDI AND BENTE ELKJAER

Introduction

In this chapter we introduce a theoretical framework for organizational learning with a point of departure in American pragmatism. We address two interrelated conceptual issues. First, we clarify the relationship between pragmatism and organizational learning, emphasising the learning aspect. We trace the impact of pragmatism on several of the founding figures of organizational learning like Herbert Simon, Chris Argyris and Donald Schön to the works of John Dewey. Their focus on organizational learning is to enhance respectively organizational decision and communication processes through inquiry into organizational systems and mental models. Second, we highlight the organizing element in organizational learning. Although acknowledging the above mentioned founding figures' point of departure in pragmatism, we find their concepts of organizational learning grounded too firmly in an understanding of organizations as rational systems and individuals as cognitive beings. This means that organizational learning becomes a question of individuals' adaptation, detecting and correcting dysfunctional behaviors leaving out the organizing of enterprises. Therefore, we have turned towards a pragmatist inspired understanding of the sociology of work in order to see process, conflict, situations and events as units of analysis. We illustrate this through an analysis of organizational learning in a contemporary enterprise. We propose a point of departure in the time-space relations in learning, knowing and organizing as a way to overcome the separation between individuals' learning and organizational systems.

We see our contribution to organizational learning as connecting insights from the sociology of work to understand learning in enterprises departing from the organizing of work, rather than in individuals' cognitive abilities with the pragmatist notion of knowing through inquiry into uncertain situations and events. In other words, our introduction of a theoretical framework for organizational learning embedded in pragmatism develops an elaboration of the two concepts that comprise organizational learning: knowing and organizing. To begin, we elaborate on the theoretical framework introduced above structured around the concepts of inquiry and organizing. This is followed by an illustration of how this pragmatist inspired organizational learning framework may be used in an analysis of a case study of organizational change in a Danish biotech/pharmaceutical company. We argue that this is one way to connect organizational learning and knowing to the content of and purpose of work, organizing and management.

Inquiry as the Pathway to Knowledge

Learning through inquiry is a core idea in pragmatism developed by John Dewey (Dewey 1916 (1980), 1938 (1986); Dewey and Bentley 1949 (1991)), which we find, for example, in the works of Herbert Simon (1947), influenced by Dewey's contributions to psychology and human conduct (Cohen 2007a, 2007b; Kerr 2007; Langley et al. 1995). Inquiry for both Dewey and Simon is seen as the core element for knowing, for generating new habits and routines in enterprises and lives. Simon used inquiry to unlock learning in decision-making, which he explains as a process consisting of three phases: from intelligence to the development of designs to deciding which design to be implemented (Langley et al. 1995). There are, however, fundamental differences between Dewey's and Simon's conceptualizing of inquiry. Dewey (1922 (1988)) viewed inquiry as an interplay between habits, emotion and intelligence (cognition) and action based upon an equal relationship between the three, whereas Simon emphasises the cognitive aspect of inquiry (Cohen 2007a, 2007b). It was only later that Simon and his colleagues from the Carnegie School (e.g. Cyert and March) began to see how habits, shaped by collective and organizational rules, procedures and routines, were relevant and significant for organizational learning and change (Cohen 2007a).

Chris Argyris and Donald Schön represent another strand of the organizational learning literature that makes explicit reference to pragmatism in their work on action theory, action science and organizational learning (Argyris and Schön 1978, 1996). They suggest: 'We use 'inquiry' here not in the colloquial sense of scientific or juridical investigation but in a more fundamental sense that originates in the work of John Dewey (1938): the intertwining of thought and action that proceeds from doubt to the resolution of doubt' (Argyris and Schön 1996: 11). For Argyris and Schön inquiry is characterized by a combination of mental reasoning and action, triggered by surprise or mismatch between expected and actual outcomes in organizational actions. Inquiry is a process in which organizational actors play an active part in their attempts to resolve the problem ('error') that caused the surprise or mismatch. For Argyris and Schön, however, the relation between thinking and action is sequential: first comes mental modelling (cognition); second, this is followed by action, whereas for Dewey thinking and action are intertwined and cannot be separated (Dewey 1896 (1972)).

Although acknowledging the intellectual debt to these founding figures within the field of organizational learning, it is possible to see that Simon, Argyris and Schön all take their point of departure in individuals and their mental models as guiding actions. In other words, learning is understood to be closely related to individuals' problem-solving capabilities and firmly grounded in a rationalist notion of learning and knowledge construction. Organizations are treated as learning systems in which individuals act on behalf of the enterprise, thereby creating an analytical separation between the individual and the enterprise. For Dewey, this analytical separation is not in line with real life enterprises in which you cannot tell where one (individual) ends and the other (enterprise) begins because they are mutually constituted in voices and actions (Dewey and Bentley 1949 (1991): 101–2). A fundamental premise for understanding inquiry from a pragmatist perspective is that learning and knowing is accomplished in and through practice, through 'transactivity' with the world, and not solely through passive thinking or observation of the world (Putnam 1994: 152). Dewey writes that our capacity to inquire is naturalistic, and hereby rooted in nature. Inquiry is, however, not something that is brought to nature and 'man' from the outside. Instead, 'it is nature realizing its own potentialities on behalf of a fuller and richer issue of events' (Dewey 1929 (1984): 171). Inquiry does not operate as an isolated function in a biological system, but is a mode of action that is socially and culturally conditioned and has cultural as well as social outcomes. Inquiry may focus on the creation and use of new plans, ideas and theories aimed at dealing with indeterminate situations. Hence, the primary aim of inquiry is to attain judgments based on the selection and organizing of different kinds of means to make the indeterminate situation determinate. Dewey defines inquiry as:

> ... the controlled or directed transformation of an indeterminate situation into one that is so determinate in its constituent distinctions and relations as to convert the elements of the original situation into a unified whole. (Dewey 1938 (1986): 108)

Following this definition, organizational learning is understood as a process that transforms an uncertain organizational situation into a more settled situation or event by creating and employing knowledge that may subsequently result in changing organizational habitual practices. But what is the processual character of organizational learning? A core issue is that the inquiring process in an organization is affected by many different individual, social, cultural and material aspects to be understood, related and studied in order to understand the situation and the enactment of inquiry as organizational learning and new knowledge. Thus, organizational learning is characterized as a continuing process of (re-)constructing organizational knowledge vis-à-vis confusing or uncertain situations when established routinized or habitual activities are interrupted (Brandi 2010). Pragmatism assumes no a priori propositions or categories and no universal cognitive structures or mental models that shape knowledge. This means, for example, that organizational knowledge is not defined beforehand as the sum of individual learning but that organizational learning derives from lived experience in which humans are at work with their environments on a continuous basis (Dewey 1925 (1981), 1925 (1984), 1938 (1986)). This accentuates an experimentalist type of reasoning in Deweyan pragmatism based on 'what-if' relations (Elkjaer 2009; Marres 2007).

Social Arenas/Worlds as Organizing for Learning

A source of inspiration in order to understand the mutual constituency between individuals and organizations is to be found in the sociology of work, more specifically the Chicago School of sociology or by those scholars known as the 'interactionists' (Fisher and Strauss 1978). This work draws explicitly on Dewey, especially what is sometimes called Dewey's social-psychological account (Dewey 1922 (1988)) and on George Herbert Mead (Clarke 1991; Strauss 1993). Thus, Adele Clarke and Anselm Strauss focus upon actions and interactions, and how these processes organise work. They use the term 'social arenas/worlds' to understand the organizing of work in which commitment to action is the central tenet. The notion of social arenas/worlds is applied to understand social organization and organizing as it unfolds amongst members of and in the context of organizations. It is the social worlds organized in social arenas that are the locus of analysis because one cannot understand an individual social world in isolation, because social worlds are always embedded in larger social arenas (Clarke 1991). It is important to note that social worlds are not social units or structures but are made up by a recognizable form of collective actions and transactions shaped by commitment to organizational actions and practices (see also Becker 1970). Important features of social worlds are that they are not bounded by geography or formal membership but by the limits of effective communication. Thus, a social world is an interactive unit, a 'universe of regularized mutual response, communication or discourse' (Shibutani 1955). As a result, social worlds influence the meaning that people impute on events and are defined as:

> (g)roups with shared commitments to certain activities, sharing resources of many kinds to achieve their goals, and building shared ideologies about how to go about their business. (Clarke 1991: 131)

From a social arenas/worlds perspective, the processes of power, tensions, competition and negotiation are stressed. These processes unfold within and between social worlds, creating arenas of social worlds and subworlds, in potential creative tension. In social arenas 'various issues are debated, negotiated, fought out, forced and manipulated by representatives' of the participating social worlds and subworlds (Strauss 1978: 124). Thus, the use of the notion of social arenas/worlds helps us to understand that participation not only involves striving for harmony, but also tensions and conflicts reflected in the different commitments to organizational actions and values (Elkjaer and Huysman 2008; Hendley et al. 2006).

Strauss characterises social worlds by means of three concepts. The concept of trajectory denotes that every social world unfolds processually. Strauss defines trajectory as:

> (1) the course of any experienced phenomenon as it evolves over time and (2) the actions and interactions contributing to its evolution. That is, phenomena do not automatically unfold nor are they straightforwardly determined by economic, political, cultural, or other circumstances; rather, they are in part shaped by the interactions or concerned actors. (Strauss 1993: 53–4)

Hence, the phenomenon at the center of trajectory does not unfold through an 'internal logic' but is shaped through actions and interactions with other kinds of aspects making up social worlds. This leads to the next fundamental concept: the conditions that create the possibility for social worlds to emerge. Strauss suggests that a social world includes: the sharing of resources, information and assumptions; common activities or work objects; technologies and signs; spaces and buildings; people; plans and rules; and a certain division of labor (Strauss 1978: 122, 1982: 357). Finally, Strauss stresses the significance of negotiation as the third concept. Negotiation is a fundamental process that illustrates both the dynamic and political characteristics of social worlds. Every social world is characterized by intersections and segmentation, caused by both internal as well as external (between social worlds) conflicts and contradictions, which convey negotiations and give rise to processes of segmentation/intersecting. The processes of segmentation/intersecting are, through its dependence on negotiations or processual ordering, as Strauss later argued, a highly political process.

The sociology of work developed by Clarke and Strauss (and others) embraces aspects of conflict theory. The generic social process is assumed to be negotiations within intergroup conflicts and tensions unless and until data prove otherwise. It is also a theory that transcends the division between structure and process, and Strauss uses the term 'processual ordering' to capture this conceptually. The field of organizing work is viewed as a 'field of battle' (Clarke 1991: 129) and it is the commitment to collective action that structures human social life. Concepts to analyze organizing include the 'conditional matrix', which is the structural or spatial conditions of the organizing processes and 'trajectories', which help us to analyze organizing in time flows that stretch back in history, grasp the present and open up to the future.

Making meaning and, in our terms, learning or knowledge construction, is experimental and played out as a 'what-if' game about how things are and could be otherwise. The questions asked include who/what are in the situation or event, and what are they doing that may be termed 'learning'. We suggest working with notions of 'tensional tales' and 'wrestling voices' inspired by pragmatism in discourses and practice to include the temporal, the trajectory of events, and simultaneity in space within situations and events. In the remainder of this chapter, this work will be illustrated by data taken from a case study in which we examined organizational learning opportunities within an enterprise in the midst of restructuring. Here we show that organizational learning opportunities are not only to be understood as evolutionary and bound up with organizational development over time, but also as simultaneous opportunities for infusing tensions and conflicts with meaning. This is one way to work with organizational learning through organizational changes in which learning is 'pulled out' of the individual and situated within organizational processes and conditions.

Organizational Change in a Biotech/Pharmaceutical Enterprise

Data presented below is drawn from a case study we conducted in Medindu (fictive name), an enterprise within the biotech/pharmaceutical industry (for details about the study, see Brandi and Elkjær 2011).[1] Medindu's headquarter is in Denmark and there are a number of subsidiaries and distributors all over the world. There are about 1,300 full-time employees in Medindu and about 400 of these are located in Medindu, Denmark. In our study we have limited ourselves to the Danish site, the production and R&D departments as well as the HR department. Our Key informant was the HR consultant of the Danish site, and we focused upon two habits as the turning point for gathering data and a 'keyhole' into the organizing of work in Medindu: 'induction' and 'management loyalty in a process of organizational change'.[2] The data used in this chapter was gathered threefold:

1. participating in meetings with our key informant and the site manager;
2. observations from field work primarily in the HR department and from following an introductory training program for newcomers;
3. analysing documentary material.

The bulk of the data is, however, drawn from interviews, which we undertook in two rounds. We have interpreted our data in two steps:

1   We would like to express our gratitude to a former colleague from the Copenhagen Business School, Professor Jesper Norus, who helped us in the early phases of the project and who passed away much too young.

2   The reason for this focus was due to the project being a part of an international comparative research project about the development of management practices in enterprises under the management of Professor Elena Antonacopoulou. Our part of the project was focussed upon the relation between change and learning. The grant number was: RES-331-25-0024.

1. a phenomenological approach to analysing qualitative data in order to reduce the quantity of the texts, asking the question: what does this sequence of text say about the organizing of work in Medindu? (Giorgi 1975; Kvale 1996);
2. we read the selected text looking for tensions in and between social worlds by way of descriptions of commitment, work content and the organizing and management of work.

We gathered data at a time when many of the employees and management had a foot in the past and present as well as having ideas about the future. Here we noted a great willingness to talk about the organizational changes in the enterprise. The orientation in time is our background for identifying the 'tensional tales' between social worlds, and the 'wrestling voices' are identified within the social worlds in which differences in commitment, work content and the organizing and management are played out simultaneously in space. We apply the notion of 'tension' as learning opportunities in time and the notion of 'wrestling' as learning opportunities in space.

Medindu – Before and Now

The story about Medindu begins with a Danish medical doctor (the founder: 1918–2006) who in the 1960s invented a way to diagnose cancer. This invention was the foundation of Medindu and is elaborated in a booklet written by a family member. In the booklet, we are told the story about the inventive researcher who began his business when he was still connected to a university in some small rented premises with just himself and a laboratory technician as the only employee. In the beginning, the company grew slowly but in 1971–72 the staff consisted of 19 people, mostly women. The 'Medindu spirit' is an important concept in the story of Medindu because it used to be a large 'family', an enterprise not solely focused on making money. Medindu used to be driven by a dual aim to create quality products and at the same time be a pleasant enterprise to work in. To produce quality products is to develop still more precise means for the diagnostics of cancer, thereby helping sick people. The attractive workplace is defined by its family belongings: 'Next to creating a good product is the goal to create a good healthy and fruitful atmosphere within the Medindu family' (from the booklet on Medinfo: 103).

When we visited Medindu in the winter and spring of 2006, we are entering an enterprise that had appointed a new CEO (August 2005) and been restructured (December 2005). In the descriptions of these changes the focus of the enterprise has changed to become market- and customer-oriented: 'Towards the end of the year, the management launched a series of initiatives to create a clearer focus for the business, shorter decision-making processes, clear division of responsibilities within the organization, and, not least, sharp customer and market focus' (Annual Report 2005: 10). The restructuring of the enterprise entailed a change from an 'inward' focus upon the quality of the product towards a more 'outward' oriented focus upon the value of the market. The Medindu spirit and the Medindu family concept were back-staged and family ownership replaced by professional management and ownership. The restructuring involved a division in sites and a formalization of responsibility and decision processes that no one in Medindu had ever experienced before. From these structural changes followed changes of management, and four out of seven top managers were replaced in less than a year. In the following, we elaborate on these changes by first interpreting them as tensions between social worlds, a former and a present Medindu followed by an interpretation of wrestling within these two social worlds.

Tensions between Two Social Worlds

It is important to stress that we are referring to a continuum between a 'before' and a 'now' which mirrors ideas about the future. But it is equally important to stress that although most members of Medindu can see some sense in changing the enterprise from an inward and research oriented focus to a more outward and market oriented enterprise, the ideas about the old Medindu are still very much alive. As such, it is possible to see organizational tensions between two identifiable social worlds.

One social world can be characterized as a commitment to development and production of products to serve people, while the other social world is committed to products aimed for sale in a still more competitive market in a professionally managed enterprise. This is what illustrates a tension between two social worlds, which is also a tension between an inward oriented focus upon coherence and community and an outward oriented focus upon market and competition. The changes are carried forward by new forms of organizing and management and have been initiated by the family's withdrawal from the enterprise. The background for terming it a 'tension' between the old and new Medindu is that employees and management can create meaning out of the new development but at the same time are deeply worried about whether this is the right way forward for Medindu. The tensions are further fuelled by the change in the former relations of power in the enterprise from R&D towards sales and marketing. In this overall tension between the two social worlds there are myriads of simultaneous wrestling between commitments, work content organizing and management. This wrestling tells a story of the changes, which brought the possibilities for problematizing the former positively connotation of the Medindu spirit, which for some also felt like a 'ghost' from the past, making it possible to become 'liberated' from the family membership in order to be committed to Medindu only as a workplace. This means that it is not possible to talk about a former 'good' enterprise that has changed to a 'bad' enterprise, but about different work content and ways of organizing work that hold possibilities for inquiry, for new interactions and, in turn, new habits.

Employees and managers who stress the research oriented foundation of Medindu trace it to the founder's impact, in spite of the fact that he and his family left the everyday life of the enterprise long ago. It is the liberation from the family and the need to establish a more competitive enterprise that informs the argument for moving the enterprise away from research and into a more competitive enterprise. As one study participant said: 'Before it was a family driven enterprise in which the focus was not so much upon surplus but about the production of good products. Now this has changed and we have to produce results' (site manager). The movement of Medindu away from research and into market orientation takes place with reference to the need to reduce the complexity of work in a research oriented enterprise, as revealed in this interview excerpt:

Somebody from a research unit who likes Medindu will call about a research project and don't we want to be part of that? Then there is a customer who wants some particular products and couldn't we produce them right away? And we could not continue like that. We somehow had to streamline the enterprise and everybody can see that. (Corporate HR Director)

Reduction of complexity is, naturally, always a management problem in any enterprise. In Medindu, the attempt to reduce complexity resulted in a focus upon sales of fewer products and, as a consequence, a reduction in research and researchers' former decision power within the enterprise. As such, the market orientation of the new CEO is ascribed much importance for the changes but there is also an understanding of how the still more competitive market relations have an impact on Medindu and that Medindu, in turn, cannot maintain its inward oriented gaze: 'We used to be number one but now we're number two. We've not managed to grow so much and the competition has become more severe, and new players have entered the market' (middle manager). In the old Medindu there was only one social world, the family and the research orientation. This was for most members easy to navigate in but as restructuring takes place a new social world appears. The new Medindu is, to a large degree, carried by a new generation of young managers, and they do not gain their power without resistance.

The tensions created through the new work content, and the organizing and management of work can be interpreted as tensions between a research and a market oriented enterprise, which is expressed as such by one interviewee: 'When people hear the word factory it's like a red rag to a bull. It's bugaboo for both the academic employees and the laboratory technicians. There's a great fear of standardization' (quality manager). This quote cannot be understood with reference to the relation between management and employees because these are 'voices' that do not sustain this classification. In our understanding, these tensions are important to work with because they can shape new possibilities for organizing Medindu. The organizational change disrupts understandings of what you do in Medindu, why you do what you do and how this new doing is being organized and managed. It is, in other words, a new story about work content and its purpose as well as of the organizing and management within Medindu. In Table 10.1, the two social worlds are summarized:

Table 10.1 Tensions between social worlds

Commitment to	The 'old' Medindu	The 'new' Medindu
What (content of work)	To develop products to help patients' cure	To sell products to customers
Why (purpose with work)	To make reliable cancer diagnoses	To create coherent customer solutions
How (organizing and management of work)	Organized as a family	Organized as a 'professionally' managed enterprise

We could finish our analysis here but that would be inadequate for examining the organizational opportunities for learning and knowing in the new organizing of Medindu.

As such, we use the above as a backcloth for analysing examples of 'wrestling' within the social worlds. Thus, we zoom in closer on the stories of commitments in the content and purpose of work, and the organizing and management of work.

Wrestling about the Content of Work

The content of the work in Medindu has not changed in any overall way because it is still possible to:

be dedicated to for what you do, cancer research, and it's great to contribute to doing good for sick people. (Team Manager).

The crucial point, and this is where it is possible to see wrestling, is whether the emphasis placed on content in Medindu first and foremost is to develop new products or whether it is to get the products marketed and sold. When the emphasis is placed upon product development, the employees in R&D speak loud and clear:

In R&D we've always been very critical towards the other functions in the enterprise because we knew the products so well. The other groups, on the contrary, never get mixed up with what we do. But is the enterprise does something that we don't like, we feel that it has to be voiced. (Middle Manager).

On the whole, the change in Medindu from being a research oriented enterprise to become more sales oriented meets resistance from the R&D people, creating what we term as 'wrestling':

Our founder was researcher and for many years Medindu has been very research oriented. Many ideas have naturally come from R&D and our marketing organization was relatively weak. Now we're about to turn it around but they (the marketing people) do not know our area very well yet. (Middle Manager)

This quote illustrates a change of a 'strong' and a 'weak' commitment, which has turned the power relation between the two social worlds around and with that, also the mandates to negotiate that members of the social worlds meet each other with. Before sales and marketing was in a weak or secondary position, whereas in the new organization they are at the core or the heart of the enterprise while the commitment directed towards research and product innovation has taken the secondary position. In the variations of commitments in Medindu's two social worlds we can see that the basic conditions for acting and interacting, for learning, knowing and creating new habits are up for negotiation. Both forms of commitment in the work of Medindu do not, however, hold the same status. Thus, central to the interpretation of the wrestling about work content is that, while it was previously legitimate to develop products that had a hard time finding their way into production, it is now a legitimate commitment in Medindu to work in order to become more efficient and business oriented:

*We are changing, we have to be more efficient and business oriented. We are in a rather
marked change process. We want that but right now we are not a homogeneous enterprise. (HR
Manager)*

New players enter the game, voices are 'wrestling' and the enterprise is moving in a new
or different direction.

Wrestling about the Purpose of Work

It is difficult to separate the content of the work in Medindu from its purpose because
they are two sides of the same coin. Both can be traced to its history and a great deal to
coincidence. The purpose of establishing Medindu can be traced back to the founder's
invention of a method to diagnose cancer, with the enterprise finding a niche space in
the market. Customers were both researchers who used the products of Medindu for
research, and hospitals that used the tool in laboratories to diagnose cancer. The primary
business area for Medindu is still cancer diagnostics but the work in hospitals become
still more automated, meaning the need has changed more towards so-called systems
solutions rather than the delivery of diagnostic tools:

*Today it's generally about automating as many of the manual processes in laboratories as
at all possible, and about going one step further and creating fully integrated systems. (From
company newsletter)*

This change in focus appears to be taking place at the expense of research and the support
of researchers:

*We no longer deliver so much to research as there is not so much money in that. (Corporate
HR Director)*

In line with the change in the enterprise's original aim, the content and purpose of work
in Medindu has had to adapt to new and profitable ways of working in hospitals. The
point of departure for 'wrestling' is the adaptation to new experiences and habits as well
as the ability to cope with a changing world. A crucial theme in the interpretation of
wrestling about work content is to be found in the two terms 'diagnose' and 'system
solutions' that characterise the purpose of work in the old and new Medindu social
worlds. 'Diagnose' is a term that refers to finding the cause of a problem or what an illness
is, that automatically creates pictures of doctors, nurses, illness and a patient. Contrary,
'system solution' refers to the optimizing of the arrangement or improved organization
of elements that automatically creates pictures of engineers, technician, consultant,
managers and a customer solution service. It is possible to see a marked change in the
purpose of work in Medindu. As such, there is a streamlining of the relation between
production and the sales of system solutions rather than the production of tools for
clinical diagnostic use, which the customers do not demand to the same degree as before.
In the old Medindu, the question behind all organizational learning and innovation
processes was: 'How will this tool work as a cancer diagnostic tool?'; in the social world of
the new Medindu, this questioned is reformulated: 'How will this tool be part of a system

solution package?' Thus, we are able to see two differences in the two social worlds' understanding of the enterprise's original purpose and how it is possible to witness the occurrence of organizational opportunities for learning.

Wrestling about the Organizing and Management of Work

A concrete expression of wrestling within organizing and the management of work is that a previous low turnover of personnel and a low ratio of absence in the enterprise have recently increased. This is a sign of certain dissatisfaction with the enterprise and our key informant tells us that both the Medindu spirit and the employee commitment 'belong to the past', whereas today 'more people regard what they do in Medindu as just an ordinary job' (HR Manager). The culture in Medindu was previously a research culture in which both researchers and laboratory technicians were committed to the development of new products rather than getting them sold:

> Before we could do as we liked, and if somebody had some fun ideas we could just materialise them. (Team Manager)

The emphasis was placed on customer care and the production of products of a high quality:

> We are known for our customer focus, and we deliver products of a high quality and provide good service ... We are not that fast but the quality is high. (Team Manager)

The changes in commitment in Medindu is related to the management of Medindu, the harsh market situation in which the products have to be sold, the wish to become quoted on the stock market and the need to streamline the enterprise strategy and decision processes that follows from that. In the old Medindu, 'the products almost sold themselves' (from meetings with our key informant). Some informants talk about the former 'discussion culture' in Medindu:

> When we began everybody had to agree about everything, and it was not sufficient with 80% in agreement, we had to be 100% in agreement. This could take two years to reach this kind of agreement, and then the project could be obsolete. (Site Manager)

Today this has changed and some comment that there is too little information and discussion in Medindu and that this has generated some insecurity. The organizing and management of Medindu creates wrestling voices about employees' and management' relation to their workplace, and new 'professional' decision processes are taking over a previous (for some) egalitarian discussion culture.

The interpretations in time focus on tensions before, now, after and between social worlds, whereas the focus on space and simultaneity expands the interpretations of the wrestling voices within the social worlds. The following examples can be used as illustrations: 'Be dedicated to cancer research' in order to 'do good for other people' in a 'research environment' versus 'work as any other work' in order to 'manage the competition' in a 'factory'. Another could be: 'Family members' participating in creating 'progress for mankind' in a 'home' versus 'proud employees' doing 'routine work' in an 'enterprise like all other enterprises'. Finally, a third illustration can be drawn as follows: 'Workers' participation in decisions' and 'treating all customers alike' in a 'democratic enterprise' versus 'only necessary information supplied', creating 'necessary differentiation of products and customers' rather than adhering to too many voices in a 'discussion club'.

The point is that learning opportunities can be conceptualized both by the change of an enterprise over time and as simultaneous voices about work content, purpose, organizing and the management of work. Organizational change does not only encompass tales of a before, present and after but also simultaneous voices in and around the space of an enterprise. This allows us to see learning opportunities not just in 'for or against' the old/new enterprise, but also in the simultaneous different voices about the doings and unfolding of an enterprise, as well as around the organizational why and how. These simultaneous wrestling voices are illustrated in a schematic way, in Table 10.2:

Table 10.2 Wrestling within social worlds

Commitment	Content of work	Purpose with work	Organizing and management of work
Example 1	'Be dedicated to cancer research' versus 'Work as any other work'	'Do good for other people' versus 'Manage the competition'	'Research environment' versus 'Factory'
Example 2	'Family member' versus 'Proud employees'	'Progress for mankind' versus 'Routine work'	'Home' versus 'Enterprise like all other enterprises'
Example 3	'Workers' participation in decisions' versus 'Only necessary information supplied'	'Treating all customers alike' versus 'Necessary differentiation of products and customers'	'Democratic enterprise' versus 'Too many voices in a discussion club'

Conclusion

In this chapter we have presented a theoretical framework for organizational learning founded in pragmatism that allows us to see organizational learning and knowing not just as the sum of individual learning that makes the individual the key agent of organizational learning, but also related to organizational attributes, the content and purpose of work, organizing and the management of work. We have hereby addressed a fundamental challenge within classical organizational learning theory that tends to individualise learning in organizational settings. In this chapter, we have demonstrated that inquiry and social arenas/worlds theory are two core concepts that are able to connect organizational members to their enterprises through work and the organizing of work. Moreover, this link is at the core of understanding organizational learning and knowing. It is argued that a pragmatist perspective of organizations and organizational learning directs attention to organizing processes in social arenas/worlds and learning possibilities from the arising tensions and wrestlings. Here we suggest that tense situations and challenging existing dominating habits provide occasions and opportunities for new organizational learning trajectories.

To demonstrate how a pragmatist approach contributes to understanding organizational learning through disorder and order, we have used an illustration from a qualitative case study conducted by the authors about organizational changes in an enterprise within the biotech/pharmaceutical industry. The illustration focuses on organizational change processes and how these changes can be understood as opportunities for organizational learning. From our analysis, we have shown that the organization has changed from being dominated by one social world into two social worlds: 'old' and 'new' Medindu, with different commitments, work methods, objectives, ideologies and status. Overall, we have showed in our analysis that Medindu has evolved from an enterprise focused on research and doing well for people and employees in Medindu to a company that primarily focuses on adapting to external market conditions and enhancing the competitive power of the organization. We have described this development as a movement in Medindu, from an internal focus to an external oriented enterprise.

We have shown how organizational learning transpires from tensions and wrestlings located within multiple times and spaces within processes of work and organizing. This approach to examining organizational learning takes learning out of its individually oriented learning approach into one in which learning includes processes of organizing by focusing on the work practices and the management hereof. In the changes within Medindu we can observe that change is a continuous process. For example, change in the organization's core product is constantly scrutinized. Further, this processual change is enacted between different aspects of the work practices within Medindu. We can observe the concrete negotiations between organizational members from 'old' and 'new' Medindu about how to understand the role of the core product, whether product innovation or sale is principal objective, how management should be conducted, whether Medindu is committed to serve patients or customers, and so on. Based on this illustration, we have argued that social worlds and its members constantly interact based on firm understandings of what it means to be a member of an enterprise that is understood in different organizational forms (for instance, 'old and new', 'spirit and ghost'), with different consequences in terms of how the organization has adopted new business models and responded to new demands in the health care sector. Organizational learning focused on work practices and processes of organizing holds potential for future research and interventionist practices that delves into organizational learning, rather than focusing on individual traits and abilities for learning as primarily a cognitive process. For us, it is the focus on work and organizing practices that makes learning in the workplace 'organizational' rather than 'individual'.

References

Argyris, C. and Schön, D.A. 1978. *Organizational Learning: A Theory of Action Perspective*. Reading: Addison-Wesley.

Argyris, C. and Schön, D.A. 1996. *Organizational Learning II: Theory, Method, and Practice*. Reading: Addison-Wesley.

Becker, H.S. 1970. Notes on the concept of commitment, in *Sociological Work. Method and Substance*, (ed.) H.S. Becker. Chicago, IL: Allen Lane, 261–73.

Brandi, U. 2010. Bringing back inquiry – Organizational learning the Deweyan way, in *Beyond Knowledge Management – Sociomaterial and Sociocultural Perspectives within Management Research*, (ed.) S. Jordan and H. Mitterhoffer. Innsbruck: Innsbruck University Press, 95–121.

Brandi, U. and Elkjær, B. 2011. Organisatorisk læring i organisatorisk forandring. *Tidsskrift for Arbejdsliv*, 13(2), 73–89.

Clarke, A.E. 1991. Social worlds/arenas theory as organizational theory, in *Social Organization and Social Process: Essays in the Honor of Anselm Strauss*, (ed.) D.R. Maines. New York: Aldine de Gruyter, 119–58.

Cohen, M.D. 2007a. Administrative Behavior: Laying the Foundations for Cyert and March. *Organization Science*, 18(3), 503–506.

Cohen, M.D. 2007b. Reading Dewey: Reflections on the Study of Routine. *Organization Studies*, 28(5), 773–86.

Dewey, J. 1896/1972. The reflex arc concept in psychology, in *Early Works*, 5, (ed.) J.A. Boydston. Carbondale and Edwardsville, IL: Southern Illinois University Press, 96–109.

Dewey, J. 1916/1980. Democracy and education: An introduction to the philosophy of education, in *Middle Works*, 9, (ed.) J.A. Boydston. Carbondale and Edwardsville, IL: Southern Illinois University Press, 1–370.

Dewey, J. 1922/1988. Human Nature and Conduct, in *Middle Works*, 14, (ed.) J.A. Boydston. Carbondale and Edwardsville, IL: Southern Illinois University Press, 1–227.

Dewey, J. 1925/1981. Experience and nature, in *Later Works*, 1, (ed.) J.A. Boydston. Carbondale and Edwardsville, IL: Southern Illinois University Press, 1–328.

Dewey, J. 1925/1984. The development of American pragmatism, in *Later Works*, 2, (ed.) J.A. Boydston. Carbondale and Edwardsville, IL: Southern Illinois University Press, 3–21.

Dewey, J. 1929/1984. The quest for certainty: A study of the relation of knowledge and action. Gifford Lectures, in *Later Works*, 4, (ed.) J.A. Boydston. Carbondale and Edwardsville, IL: Southern Illinois University Press.

Dewey, J. 1938/ 1986. Logic. The theory of inquiry, in *Later Works*, 12, (ed.) J.A. Boydston. Carbondale and Edwardsville, IL: Southern Illinois University Press, 1–539.

Dewey, J. and Bentley, A.F. 1949/1991. Knowing and the known, in *Later Works*, 16, (ed.) J.A. Boydston. Carbondale and Edwardsville, IL: Southern Illinois University Press, 1–294.

Elkjaer, B. 2009. *Pragmatism: A Learning Theory for the Future, in Contemporary Theories of Learning. Learning theorists … in their own words*, (ed.) K. Illeris. Abingdon, NY: Routledge, 74–89.

Elkjaer, B. and Huysman, M. 2008. Social worlds theory and the power of tension, in *The SAGE Handbook of New Approaches in Management and Organisation*, (ed.) D. Barry and H. Hansen. London: Sage, 170–77.

Fisher, B. and Strauss, A.L. 1978. The Chicago Tradition and Social Change: Thomas, Park and Their Successors. *Symbolic Interaction*, 1(2), 5–23.

Giorgi, A. 1975. An application of phenomenological method in psychology, in *Duquesne Studies in Phenomenological Psychology*, 2, (ed.) A. Giorgi, C.T. Fischer and E.L. Murray. Pittsburgh, PA: Duquesne University, 82–103.

Hendley, K., Sturdy, A., Fincham, R. and Clark, T. 2006. Within and beyond communities of practice: Making sense of learning through participation, identity and practice. *The Journal of Management Studies*, 43(3), 641–53.

Kerr, G. 2007. The Development History and Philosophical Sources of Herbert Simon's Administrative Behavior. *Journal of Management History*, 13(3), 255–68.

Kvale, S. 1996. *InterViews: An Introduction to Qualitative Research Interviewing*. Thousand Oaks, CA: Sage.

Langley, A., Mintzberg, H., Pitcher, P., Posada, E. and Saint-Macary, J. 1995. Opening up Decision-Making: The View from the Black Stool. *Organization Science*, 6(3), 260–79.

Marres, N. 2007. The Issues Deserve More Credit. Pragmatist Contributions to the Study of Public Involvement in Controversy. *Social Studies of Science*, 37(5), 759–80.

Putnam, H. 1994. *Pragmatism and Moral Objectivity*. Cambridge, MA, and London: Harvard University Press.

Shibutani, T. 1955. Reference Groups as Perspectives. *The American Journal of Sociology*, 60(6), 562–9.

Strauss, A.L. 1978. A Social World Perspective. *Studies in Symbolic Interaction*, 1, 119–28.

Strauss, A.L. 1982. Interorganizational Negotiations. *Journal of Contemporary Ethnography*, 11(3), 350–67.

Strauss, A.L. 1993. *Continual Permutations of Action*. New York: Aldine de Gruyter.

11 *Believing in a Pragmatist Business Ethic*

SCOTT TAYLOR AND EMMA BELL

Introduction

As the editorial introduction to this book makes clear, American pragmatism went through a period of scholarly decline in the middle of the twentieth century. When it was revived in the 1980s the work of one if its key contributors, William James, was presented as a minor component of the philosophical scheme. Even when James's work was read or interpreted, writers tended to neglect the roots of his writing on pragmatism and his desire to construct an epistemologically credible framework for analysis of the wider social significance of practising religious belief. James developed his version of pragmatism in response to two key questions he asked of the late nineteenth-century North American society he lived and worked in. First, he sought to understand religious belief as it was embedded in everyday social life as an action-guiding ethic. Second, James wanted to analyze how religious experience was understood in relation to the increasingly dominant perspective of positivist, post-Enlightenment rationality. Here we suggest that James's response to these questions and the philosophical system he developed to address them continue to have significant implications for analysing religious belief's influence on managing organizations. We interpret James's work to analyze a particular case, the approach to business ethics promoted by the City of London-based Christian Association of Business Executives (CABE).

Our aim is thus to present a reading of James's work that takes full account of the empirical puzzle that stimulated his philosophical writing on pragmatism. We do this in part because of an existing interest in James's ideas as a means of analysing the contemporary interplay of religious belief, organization, and ethics (Bell et al. 2012). However, here, we also want to focus on how pragmatism has been interpreted within the field of business ethics, primarily as a philosophical underpinning for stakeholder analysis (Wicks and Freeman 1998), and to argue that version of pragmatism neglects a key task, the assessment of the meaning of a proposition. According to our reading, a Jamesian pragmatist perspective on the ethical implications of managing and organizing involves at least as much focus on meaning as on the purpose or use-value of an action or principle. We illustrate this through analysis of recent CABE initiatives such as the *Principles for Those in Business*. We conclude the chapter by outlining the implications of a revised pragmatist perspective for the theory and practice of business ethics, concentrating on James's stated desire for scholars to focus on melioration in applied settings such as workplaces with the aim of 'improving and invigorating lived human experience' (Stroud 2009: 378).

William James and Varieties of Philosophical Belief

William James is renowned today for various aspects of his personal and working life: his family is central to nineteenth-century US intellectual life, he contributed to a remarkable variety of academic fields, his ability to communicate through his writing is striking to all of his readers, and his consistent inconsistency is often noted by contemporary scholars. For sociologists of religion, his argument that unmediated 'sensible experience' could be a legitimate epistemology of social inquiry to analyze religious and spiritual experiences (James 1902) continues to stimulate debate (Carrette 2005b). As James constructed this methodological position he was simultaneously trying to defend religious faith against the developing hegemony of positivist sciences in the late nineteenth century, particularly the desire expressed by the secular 'high priests' of that movement for tangible evidence of all knowledge claims (Hollinger 1997). Driven, in part, by his own religious beliefs and doubts, James wanted to retain the right to believe in the propositions framing religious belief without either empirical evidence or epistemic justification (Gale 1980) as a legitimate subject position in both society and scholarship.

The foundations of this pluralist perspective on belief and knowledge lie in James's early polemical writing, which encourages scholars to acknowledge the practical consequences of belief for individual psychology and social action (James 1897). In pursuing this argument, James sought to reconcile his lifelong religious sensibility with a commitment to social analysis as a scientific project (Hollinger 1997). He argued that a way through this intellectual and professional discomfort existed, by developing what Rorty (1997: 84) characterises as a 'utilitarian ethics of belief', but which others more sympathetically frame as a concern with asking: what difference does belief make? The argument is summarized with characteristic rhetorical skill by James when he suggests that religious beliefs should be judged by their 'fruits', not their 'roots'. In other words, religious experiences should not be accorded ontological privilege or dismissed as delusional fantasy, but attention must be paid to their utility or meaning.

These debates about the reality of religious experience and how to settle metaphysical disputes of meaning and truth initially took place privately within James's conscience as a social scientist with an uncomfortable sympathy for religious belief. However, publication of *The Will to Believe* (1897) and *Varieties of Religious Experience* (1902) brought James's then radical position to a wide audience. The perspective that was written into these books was founded on acknowledgement and exploration of the problematic epistemological status of religious belief, and by extension any other ethical or moral system. These arguments presaged his later (James 1907) formation of pragmatism as a philosophical ethic for the conduct of all social science. Thus James's version of pragmatism involves an understanding of ethics as *belief systems with a purpose*, with the purpose being the key means of deciding the truth of the ethical framework. It is, in other words, an anti-foundationalist perspective that does not examine the content of the belief system; rather, a pragmatist approach to (business) ethics involves analysis of the 'fruits' of the moral beliefs, their social, cultural, or individual effects, but not their philosophical or metaphysical foundation.

In this sense, social scientific analysis is taken to be a means of encouraging a practical focus on improving the conditions and conduct of social life (Wicks and Freeman 1998), through encouraging ethical agency and structural change. In business ethics, as in other ethical contexts, a pragmatist perspective may be a means of coming to terms with otherwise irresolvable debates of epistemology and metaphysics, orienting analysis towards the issue of how to lead better lives, 'imploring people to act as agents of social and political change' (Wicks and Freeman 1998: 129) to help cope with the world as we experience it every day. Our chapter continues by building on these arguments. First, we give a more detailed account of James's contributions to American pragmatism, paying particular attention to the ways his philosophical position rests on his desire to maintain religious belief as a legitimate subject position within modernity. Here we draw on a key reading of James's work by Ayer (1968). We follow this by outlining the argument that philosophical and political-economic pragmatism is essential to realizing the potential within corporate capitalism for development of an ethic that encourages individual liberty and virtue, drawing here on Livingston (1997). Within this, we present analysis of an example of this potential via a reading of the *Principles for Those in Business* published by CABE. We argue here that some form of belief, religious, spiritual or secular, is central to the possibility of a pragmatic business ethics. Finally we turn to the possible future interplay of American pragmatism, business ethics, and belief, suggesting how further analysis could contribute to understandings of the experience of capitalist wealth creation as an ethical act in post-secular societies.

Believing in American Pragmatism

As this book demonstrates, versions of pragmatism abound both in the first wave of nineteenth-century theoretical development and in late twentieth-century interpretations from within postmodern or post-structural frameworks. There is a continuous thread in all versions and interpretations – the way in which pragmatism demands links between epistemology and action. For us, Taylor (2004) summarises pragmatism's broadest implications most clearly. The idea of truth it contains does not rest on whether we get something 'right' in the sense of epistemological accuracy when we observe, think or talk about it. Rather, something is true if it 'works' for us as we make our way through the complexities of everyday life. This, in turn, implies that we cannot appeal to an absolute external reality to resolve disagreements, but must turn to an assessment of whether our truth helps us to live, and emphasises a key aspect of pragmatism's underlying realism. The idea that 'works' may be utilitarian in the sense of its material productivity, but its 'cash value', to use James's term, may also be ideational. In other words, we can live pragmatically in the pursuit of purpose or meaning as well as material wealth. It is this aspect of pragmatism that has been neglected in its adoption to analysis of business ethics.

As Taylor (2004) and many others also note (e.g. Ayer 1968; Carrette 2005b), religious belief sits at the center of James's entire written canon. He turned an inner debate, in which he sought to resolve personal doubts about how to believe as a practising scientist, outward. In doing this, James considered a division then dominating philosophy: the relationship between self and the world, including others/the other. From this starting point, James argues that in some domains it is impossible to establish certainty through truth. Put another way, James sought to suggest that sometimes faith is needed to enable creation of (social) fact in relation to the self. However, as Taylor emphasises, if we follow this process it does not imply we create a materialization of the fact. Faith does not, need not, perhaps should not, create something that we touch or see; it may, though, create an idea that helps us to live well and resolve otherwise irreconcilable differences through appeals to a pragmatist form of truth. This position, according to Taylor, brings together epistemology and ethics and allows us to analyze credibly without necessarily relying on empirical or scientifically robust evidence that satisfies a logical positivist.

Ayer (1968) provides a productive reading of James's pragmatism, as part of his pursuit of the notion of 'sophisticated realism'. He notes that James's version of pragmatism is best known for its basis in radical empiricism, which in turn underpins his pragmatist theory of truth. This is a term and an epistemology that James developed through his consideration of the varieties of religious experience (1897), his most detailed engagement with empirical fact and human experience in which he contrasted his emerging pragmatic position with abstracted logical formulations based on a priori arguments. As Ayer notes, James's objection to Hegelian a priori arguments was twofold: emotional and moral. James objected to the idea of both theological and philosophical synthesis, as they share a desire for transcendental intervention to resolve the evident contradictions of everyday life through divine or philosophical justification. In each of his key contributions to psychology, sociology of religion, and philosophy, James reiterated the damage that abstract thinking can do to our understandings of how life is lived and experienced. Logic will always be overwhelmed by the richness of human experience. In common with other readers of James's work, Ayer (1968) emphasises how all of his academic investigations were driven by his desire to understand religious experience, as either a philosophical position or as a phenomenal means of coming to truth. James suggested that belief lay beyond logic, rendering a substantial part of nineteenth-century theology redundant. Rather, James argued, we should find truth and proof of belief in the experience of 'inner reality' – and that experience should be accepted as valid in its reality and effects.

Thus James's solution to the intellectual problem of how to reconcile his and many others' simultaneous religious belief and commitment to rational-scientific forms of thought lay in pragmatism. In particular, as Ayer (1968: 196) writes, James's form of pragmatism enabled religious experiences to be understood as rationally defensible, if truth were taken to lie in what people believe to be significant, helpful or meaningful in everyday life:

> the implication here is not only that any adequate system of beliefs must satisf your moral requirements, as well as agreeing with the facts of sensory experience and maintaining logically correct relations between its constituent ideas, but that these three different needs are met by different kinds of propositions ... Thus, for James, it is an essential characteristic of religious and moral theories that their role is to satisfy our emotional and practical demands.

Many commentators note in James's and other pragmatists' ideas the danger of individualistic moral relativism. James's pragmatic theory of truth is, however, considerably more than the conventional summary of it as whatever is expedient and useful. As Ayer further notes, the empirical and philosophical objections to this position are so obvious that attributing it to James or any other pragmatist suggests they are at best naive, at worst dishonest or self-deluding. Rather, following the interpretation that Ayer develops, we prefer to think of a pragmatist notion of truth as resting on a desire to investigate and understand 'it' from the perspective of the individual engaged in everyday practice.

This then is the core of James's idea of the 'pragmatic rule'. A proposition may be accepted, or a belief accepted as true, if it 'works' as a way of making meaning out of the experience of reality. The reality may be empirical or metaphysical, material or spiritual; the rule remains the same. Ayer, broadly supportive of a pragmatist position and James's writing in particular, is nonetheless clear about flaws in its early twentieth-century expression. In particular, James's wish to retain a sense of truth or general principle, alongside the emphasis he wanted to place on experience, generates tensions. Notwithstanding, Ayer concludes that pragmatism contains enough to be taken seriously as a means of approaching ontological decisions or disputes. In particular, Ayer argued that the reification of whatever we decide to be real, or meaningful, may be a pragmatic decision, based on what we wish to believe, which is in turn founded on what is convenient or helpful to us as moral actors *in pragmatism as in other ethical frameworks*. The next section takes these ideas into the context of organizations, focusing on their intersection with the ethics in management and business.

Pragmatism and Corporate Capitalism

There is a strong argument to suggest that the nineteenth century is a pivotal point in the development of corporate capitalism (Jacques 1996; Shenhav 1999). Livingston (1997) argues specifically that the constitution of the corporation as a legal person in the late nineteenth century signalled the decline of market capitalism. Corporate legal personhood was an attempt to reconstitute ownership patterns and social relations in a pre-modern form. Livingston draws extensively on James's ideas, analysing events 'as if thoughts were things, and vice versa' (xxiii), expressing a fundamentally pragmatist method and sensibility. Further, he argues that pragmatism's origins are as 'a narrative of the transition from proprietary to corporate capitalism' (xxiv), an attempt to understand then-new nineteenth-century socio-cultural forms of economic life as embodied in the idea of the corporation. Importantly the emergence of the corporation involves constructing a different moral form, 'a transition to a social order and cognitive regime in which neither self not knowledge can be located or stabilized by reference to external necessity' (Livingston 1997: 201). As always, a pragmatist position may be dismissed as conformist, with James sometimes appearing to be a 'jolly preacher of "pragmatic adjustment" and positive thinking' (201). However, Livingston argues that this misreads James's work as it neglects the method he developed as a way to understand the 'possibilities residing in actually existing circumstances' (201).

Livingston goes on to argue that the form of capitalism we now have involves a resulting reconstruction of subjectivity (i.e., its fruits), whose method and standpoint (i.e., roots) lie in American pragmatic practice and philosophy. Those of us living with this form of capitalism should recognise that logic and reason are not sufficient to explain or even interrogate these new forms of self and knowledge. James's observation and associated argument as to the nature of the relationship between industrial society and self is pivotal. This essentially pragmatist position suggests that pre-pragmatist analysis of the emerging political economy of the nineteenth century assumed meaning or worth lay only in external material circumstances and conditions. This position, James repeatedly argued, ignores the rich and complex inner lives that people in industrial societies live beyond the material self. In particular, James suggests that the personality (his term for what we think of as subjectivity):

> *sanctioned by pragmatism is a more promising bearer of an intelligible morality than the progeny*
> *of Enlightenment, simply because it can treat inherited standards, customs and practices – and*
> *the communities that made them possible – as something more than an external constraint on*
> *its own content, development, or fulfilment. (Livingston 1997: 215)*

Above all, Livingston interprets James as challenging the Romantic critique of modern industrial life, in its idea(l) that an agent must withdraw from the grubby world of commerce in order to approach subjective truth or a self with integrity. This also emphasises a further aspect of pragmatism, that knower and known cannot be separated. Livingston and Ayer both note that logical philosophers, most prominently Bertrand Russell, dismissed pragmatism because it takes faith and belief seriously, instead of excluding them in favor of reason and 'real truth'. As we have seen, belief is an especially strong presence in James's version of pragmatism, leading to his contribution being dismissed or footnoted as an early attempt that can be neglected in favor of the writing of 'proper' philosophers such as Dewey. James is, as Livingston colorfully puts it, categorized as the 'demented uncle whose place in the [pragmatism] family tree is still in question' (1997: 227). Reclaiming James's version of pragmatism, as Livingston aims to do in relation to management and organization, implies a re-evaluation of the significance of experience and belief as a means of locating ethical reflection and subjectivity. James's pragmatist position, as an account and critique of modern subjectivity, enables the construction of a quite different ethical character.

Livingston's book apart, tracing the interplay of pragmatism and business ethics is relatively straightforward. European business ethicists pay little heed to it, focusing on the grander traditions of Aristotelian, Marxist, utilitarian, or deontological ethics (see, for example, Jones et al. 2005; Parker 1998). These authors tend to propose a way of getting away from the utilitarian bind that normative business ethics is prone to by engaging with historical and contemporary versions of virtue ethics. Thus in terms of European business ethics, pragmatism is largely absent.

In the US, however, the revival of philosophical pragmatism led by Rorty opened up an alternative means of considering the 'moral dimension' (Wicks and Freeman 1998: 124) of organizing, enthusiastically taken up by scholars with a taste for native theory. Initially, pragmatism was framed as an alternative to dominant positivist analyses of organization and management, as a means of avoiding what scholars labelled 'anti-positivist' options that deny the objectivity of science, such that an objective or accurate description of reality is rendered impossible, leaving us with the rather unsatisfactory tools of narrative, symbol and metaphor (see Wicks and Freeman 1998: 127 passim). For these authors, one problem (the impossibility of constructing an objective value-neutral social science of management) is replaced with another (relativism, in which researchers become 'lay theologians' promoting baseless belief systems).

The way out of this that these authors, and many others subsequently, propose (e.g. Nahser and Ruhe 2001; Jacobs 2004; McVea 2007) is a particular version of pragmatism. Ostensibly drawing on the work of Dewey, James and Rorty, contemporary American pragmatist business ethicists always return to what they define as its epistemological foundation: is this (data, data analysis, theory) useful in helping to create something better? Wicks and Freeman, in their keystone paper, are initially at pains to distinguish their new formulation from utilitarianism (1998: 129). However, they acknowledge that pragmatist ethics are defined by their contribution to the purpose of the community. This has subsequently been interpreted by those promoting pragmatist stakeholder analysis and its associated business ethic to locate shareholder value as the primary purpose of wealth-creating organizations – leading us back to utilitarianism as the key means of assessing the best, most justifiable way of defining how best to reach the ends of business. Moral legitimacy returns to the balance sheet, with means appearing only as entries that generate either profit or cost.

This is one concern about the co-option of pragmatism into analysis of business ethics. More significant for us here, though, is the way in which pragmatism is framed. As noted above, these scholars acknowledge James. However, the conception of pragmatism that underpins their approach to business ethics loses something significant along the way. We can see this most clearly in Wicks and Freeman's (1998) definition of pragmatic usefulness, as epistemological credibility based on reliability of information. This writes a very significant aspect of pragmatism out of the story, belief. To illustrate our argument here, we turn to the CABE and their *Principles for Those in Business* initiative.

Practising Ethics, Believing in Ethics

The global recession of the 1930s saw many Christian theologians and church members express hostility towards those profiting from the exploitation of labor and natural resources. The Christian Association of Business Executives (CABE) was founded in 1938 by a group of senior executives in London, with two purposes: first, as a spiritual community to support Catholics working in shareholder corporations; and second, as a means of reconciling the practice of capitalist industry and wealth creation with critique from officers of the church. In the time since its establishment CABE, ecumenical from around the time of the Second Vatican Council in the 1960s, has consistently sought to

> interpret business activity as a human response to God's imperative to renew the face of the earth and to undertake the creation and recreation of wealth as part of the process of building God's kingdom on earth. (Kiaer and Wright 2008: 2)

Members include senior figures from churches as well as business, and a series of books, pamphlets and guides to action set out the moral philosophy and ethics that the association promotes.

The practice of business ethics has always been central to the CABE community. The association was set up with a remit to explore the ethics of capitalism, this activity reaching a peak when members of CABE established the Institute of Business Ethics (IBE) in 1986 as an inter-faith initiative. The IBE started with a remit to publish religiously informed analyses of ethical issues in business and develop codes for organizational implementation. Helped by the increasing visibility of business ethics within the scholarly community, the IBE gained considerable corporate support within and beyond the Christian community, and was detached from CABE in 2000 to become an independent, secular charity and think tank.

CABE is unique in the UK as a nexus of religious belief, corporate practice, moral theology, economic theory, and influential businesspeople. It sits at the center of a loose institutional field populated by Christians concerned about the ethics of wealth creation in capitalist economies, publishes popular books and a quarterly journal, hosts workshops or seminars, and leads a network of religious and secular organizations (such as the IBE, the Transforming Business and Faith in Business initiatives at the University of Cambridge, and the Institute for Global Ethics). Here we focus on one aspect of recent CABE activity, a set of *Principles for Those in Business*.[1]

A PRAGMATIC PERSPECTIVE ON ETHICAL PRINCIPLES

The then chair of CABE, John McLean Fox, started to develop a set of principles during the late 1990s as a central part of his stewardship of the association. The final text, 31 principles designed to provide one for each day of the months, was published in 2006 and revised in 2010. They were:

> [d]esigned as a statement of corporate responsibility and personal values drawn from a Christian perspective ... a structured discipline to assist individuals and to complement at the personal level the commitment to ethical standards promoted by IBE for companies. (Wright and Kiaer 2008: 7)

Presented in a small leaflet that may be carried by adherents, the principles are the third key intervention that the association has made, following two commissioned books on the relationship between biblical teaching and wealth creation (Griffiths 1982, 1984) and the IBE's foundation in 1986. The principles are intended to 'embrace corporate responsibility and personal values, drawn from a Christian perspective' (1).[2] They are presented as a 'reminder of ... Christian vocation' (1), implying that it can sometimes be difficult to reconcile Christian teachings or ideals with everyday organizational life and actions. The ideas that Fox developed draw on his familiarity with Franciscan monastic practice. As with other monastic orders such as the Benedictines, community and lay members strive to live daily lives according to the ideals of the order as set out in a formal rule book. The CABE principles suggest that a Christian 'rule' for association members, and other Christians working in business, can be constructed and lived to the benefit of individual, business, wealth creation, and society. The relationship between the ethical frame that Christianity can provide and the ethics of free market wealth creation is highly significant. The front page of the Principles states business should be conducted 'honourably and responsibly' within a Christian ethical framework – in other words, a Christian ethic surrounds and defines the secular ethic of capitalism and wealth creation.

The month is divided into four aspects of rule and practice: Priority Aims, Corporate Values, Responsibilities to Stakeholders, and Personal Qualities. The principles begin and end with a biblical quote and there are eight other references to God or Christ. Each day is summarized in a key term, such as 'Serve wholeheartedly' (day 1), 'Diversity' (day 10), 'Community and environmental interests' (day 17), or 'Serving others' (day 23), followed by 50–100 words of text. Our reading of these texts suggests two key concerns in being Christian and being in business: self-other relations and self-wealth relations.

---

1   See http://www.principlesforbusiness.com/ and a subsection of the CABE website at http://www.cabe-online.org/index.php [both accessed 15 August 2011].

2   All page references to the Principles refer to the leaflet as it would be read if printed and folded.

Self-other relations appear in multiple entries. On day 21 (6), readers are encouraged to 'show a sympathetic response' to others met during the conduct of business, with the aim of building 'ongoing caring relationship[s]'. On day 10 (3), members of the association are reminded to be respectful of people regardless of race, color, gender, age and other social markers. Here we might be reading a tract on business ethics written by a follower of Kant, concerned only with transcendental ideals of behavior and thought and the application of duty-based rules. In contrast, self-wealth relations are more complex, and suggest a more two-directional pragmatic perspective. The idea of a pure capitalism is significantly attenuated here in, for example, day 3 ('Create wealth': 2) during which members should ask themselves whether the financial and operating returns being achieved will benefit all stakeholders appropriately. Similarly, on day 15 (4) readers should reflect on whether they are behaving responsibly towards 'Providers of capital' such that the long-term value of the business is being increased. We can read these and other examples as articulations of a relationship, within which religious ideals and neoliberal wealth creation principles are set alongside each other, in the hope of a synthesis. Both are *pragmatised* to acknowledge the need for both to work and be meaningful.

Belief and the Pragmatics of Business Ethics

We approached this chapter as a way of exploring the philosophical position that underpins William James's ideas about religious belief. With Cathy Driscoll, a colleague from St Mary's University in Canada, we have analyzed the practice of business ethics in three US multinationals through the lens that James's unique writings on belief provide (Bell et al. 2012). During that process, we were conscious of an epistemological hinterland, the philosophical foundations of James's work, that we were assuming. This chapter has allowed us to engage with pragmatism, and in particular the ways in which James's version of that philosophy is intertwined with his desire to understand religious belief in modern societies.

As James built his conception of pragmatism on belief, we have presented a brief illustrative analysis of an institution that approaches business ethics with belief in mind in a way that we suggest expressed both aspects of Jamesian pragmatism: the philosophical and religious. The CABE is not a high-profile organization in business schools or news media, but it has played a prominent role in the development of business ethics in the UK through the establishment (and subsequent disestablishment) of the Institute of Business Ethics. We read their *Principles for Those in Business'* as a manifestation of pragmatic business ethics. In this, they are an alternative to the more familiar pragmatism of stakeholder approaches to business ethics. This approach is also founded on a version of pragmatism; however, we find that perspective unsatisfactory because stakeholder analysis has written out James's contribution, and therefore the belief-based roots of American pragmatism. Further, the revival of pragmatist thought in the late twentieth century, when read alongside James's earlier writing on religion, suggests to us a need to rethink the position of belief in relation to the everyday business of ethical life in managed organizations. Organization, management and leadership can be analyzed in interestingly productive ways if we acknowledge that beliefs rather than positivist science provide the foundations for an ethical meta-commentary on practice (Chia 2003).

Conclusion

Finally, we want to consider what our account of American pragmatism, as read into James's books and secondary interpretations of them, means for researching management practice. We can gain a sense of this from recently published work by Scott Stroud, who is (significantly) a communication studies scholar rather than a business school-located business ethicist. Stroud (2009) writes conceptually of exactly what we have explored empirically in this chapter. He argues that James's version of pragmatism holds considerable potential for considering the ethics of management and organization; that there is little acknowledgement of James's work in existing accounts of pragmatism's potential alignment with business ethics; and that reading James has implications for both the substance and methodology of business ethics scholarship.

Stroud chooses to focus on James's notion of the 'ideal', in part as it has been neglected in the wider scholarly field of pragmatism. We have concentrated more here on belief and utility-as-meaning in lived human experience, following recent reconsiderations of James's writing (Carrette 2005a; Livingston 1997), but the relationship to the ideal is also crucial. James spoke of both as essential to his psychology and philosophy. In the end we are arguing for a reorientation of the representation of pragmatism in business ethics, that engages more closely with the intellectual and cultural context of James's early formulation and emphasises the 'applied' nature of such a reframing within lived everyday realities, with reference to an ideal (cf. Stroud 2009).

We have worked with a belief-based statement of what ideal ethical behavior in wealth-creating organizations might look like, commissioned by a low profile, high status British Christian executive association. In this analysis, we have suggested that pragmatism operates in two directions simultaneously; members of CABE are not simply exhorted to be pragmatic about their Christian beliefs, they are also inspired to *pragmatise* their business ethics and managerial actions. We believe this exemplifies James's philosophical precept of challenging categorical forms of ethic, and the notion of there being a single ideal ethical subject or act that we can all aspire to. We also think it is interesting because it exemplifies an interpretation of James's writing that sees ethical action happening in:

> the nexus between a consciously held ideal and the details of a concrete situation demanding action by the agent. (Stroud 2009: 387–8)

A 'Jamesian pragmatism for business ethics' therefore suggests we find an ethical position we are comfortable with as a belief, yet attempt to retain a sense of novelty in the coming together of the ideal and the habitual acts we are surrounded by every day. This is a form of reconstructive or poetic pragmatism applied to business ethics (Stroud 2009, drawing on Shusterman 2002). In other words, we retain the right to believe in an ideal as a non-rational act in a logical philosophical sense in the context of action, because there will not necessarily be a rational or empirical resolution to ethical questions and debates in the complex material social or cultural contexts of organization.

References

Ayer, A. 1968. *The Origins of Pragmatism: Studies in the Philosophy of Charles Sanders Peirce and William James*. London: Macmillan.
Bell, E., Taylor, S. and Driscoll, C. 2012. Varieties of organizational soul: The ethics of belief in organizations. *Organization*, 19(4), 425–39.
Carrette, J. (ed.) 2005a. *William James and the Varieties of Religious Experience*. London: Routledge.
Carrette, J. 2005b. Passionate belief: William James, emotion, and religious experience, in *William James and the Varieties of Religious Experience*, (ed.) J. Carrette. London: Routledge, 79–96.
Chia, R. 2003. From Knowledge-Creation to the Perfection of Action: Tao, Basho and Pure Experience as the Ultimate Ground of Knowing. *Human Relations*, 56(8), 953–81.
Gale, R. 1980. William James and the Ethics of Belief. *American Philosophical Quarterly*, 17(1), 1–14.
Griffiths, B. 1982. *Morality and the Market Place*. London: Hodder and Stoughton.
Griffiths, B. 1984. *The Creation of Wealth: A Christian's Case for Capitalism*. London: Hodder and Stoughton.
Hollinger, J. 1997. James, Clifford, and the scientific conscience, in *The Cambridge Companion to William James*, (ed.) R. Putnam. Cambridge: Cambridge University Press, 69–83.
Jacobs, D. 2004. A Pragmatist Approach to Integrity in Business Ethics. *Journal of Management Inquiry*, 13(3), 215–23.
Jacques, R. 1996. *Manufacturing the Employee: Management Knowledge from the 19th to the 21st Century*. London: Sage.
James, W. 1897. *The Will to Believe*. London: Longmans Green.
James, W. 1902. *The Varieties of Religious Experience: A Study in Human Nature*. London: Longmans Green.
James, W. 1907. *Pragmatism: A New Name for Some Old Ways of Thinking*. London: Longmans Green.
Jones, C., Parker, M. and ten Bos, R. 2005. *For Business Ethics*. London: Routledge.
Kiaer, C. and Wright, S. 2008. *The History of the Christian Association of Business Executives*. London: CABE.
Livingston, J. 1997. *Pragmatism and the Political Economy of Cultural Revolution, 1850–1940*. Chapel Hill, NC: University of North Carolina Press.
McVea, J. 2007. Constructing Good Decisions in Ethically Charged Situations: The Role of Dramatic Rehearsal. *Journal of Business Ethics*, 70(4), 377–90.
Nahser, F. and Ruhe, J. 2001. Putting American Pragmatism to Work in the Classroom. *Journal of Business Ethics*, 34(3/4), 317–30.
Parker, M. (ed.). 1998. *Ethics and Organizations*. London: Sage.
Rorty, R. 1997. Religious faith, intellectual responsibility, and romance, in *The Cambridge Companion to William James*, (ed.) R. Putnam. Cambridge: Cambridge University Press, 84–102.
Shenhav, Y. 1999. *Manufacturing Rationality: The Engineering Foundations of the Managerial Revolution*. Oxford: Oxford University Press.
Shusterman, R. 2002. *Surface and Depth: Dialectics of Criticism and Culture*. Ithaca, NY: Cornell University Press.
Stroud, S. 2009. William James on Meliorism, Moral Ideals, and Business Ethics. *Transactions of the Charles S. Peirce Society*, 45(3), 378–401.
Taylor, C. 2004. What is pragmatism?, in *Pragmatism, Critique, Judgment: Essays for Richard J. Bernstein*, (ed.) S. Benhabib and N. Fraser. Cambridge, MA: MIT Press, 73–92.
Wicks, A. and Freeman, R. 1998. 'Organization Studies and the New Pragmatism: Positivism, Anti-positivism, and the Search for Ethics. *Organization Science*, 9(2), 123–40.

12 *The Practice of Government Finance*

JOHN R. BARTLE AND PATRICIA M. SHIELDS

Making the fiscal system work is, after all, a large part of making democracy function. (Musgrave and Musgrave 1973: xiv)

Introduction

Pragmatism is a philosophy that emphasizes learning through action and building a knowledge base from experience and reflection. It is a potentially compelling approach to public administration generally, and to government finance specifically (Shields 2008). The approach is consistent with Musgrave and Musgrave's (1973) insight about the nature and purpose of a fiscal system. Numerous theories have been applied to government finance. As a philosophy, pragmatism is an overarching construct under which different theories can fit. A practitioner can 'test' a theory to see if it is useful in resolving their problem but if it is not, they can move on to use another theory. Whether a theory is true or false as a matter of epistemology is generally not the concern of a manager; rather the question is: is it useful or not in guiding action? Managers of one government may operate productively under the guidance of one theory, while those in another may follow a different theory. Thus pragmatism is a broader explanation that accommodates the local relevance of different theories.[1] The goal of positive social science theory should be to explain social actions and advance a framework so an observer can develop a model that allows for description and understanding to a broader audience. To advance practice, the theory must first take into account practice. We believe that the overarching framework of pragmatism allows for this. In fact no single theory is likely to be able to explain the breadth of practice of government finance, because practice varies greatly over time and cross-sectionally. Neither is any single discipline likely to successfully advance a theory that generally explains government finance. This potential needs to be explored and its implications articulated. This chapter attempts to do so. It begins with a critique of existing theories of government finance. It then develops the philosophy of classical pragmatism, and then assesses the viability of this approach to understanding government finance.

---

1   Specifically, we are referring to the classical pragmatism of John Dewey, William James, Charles Sanders Peirce and Jane Addams. We are not referring to neo-pragmatism of Richard Rorty. For an extended discussion of the difference between these versions of pragmatism and their application to public administration see Shields (2003, 2004, 2005), Whetsell and Shields (2011) and Miller (2004, 2005).

A Critique of Existing Theories

There is a vast literature on government finance. We look at three large areas of theory: public finance; public financial management; and public budgeting. As a whole, we refer to these three areas as 'government finance'. Public finance (PF) is an applied field of economics, and was the first of these areas to fully articulate a coherent theory. Public financial management (PFM) draws more from public administration and is a largely normative theory of 'good' ways to manage the finances of government, as well as specific tasks such as cash management, debt management and procurement. Public budgeting is a collection of theoretical perspectives applied to the formulation, adoption, implementation and evaluation/audit phases of budgeting.

The dominant theories of PF and PFM are largely normative. They focus on prescription, drawing from certain sets of values and serve as models of practice. Existing theories are also largely ahistorical and generally do not take into account change over time. However, the historical development of government budgets and financial practices runs contrary to many of the prescriptions of these normative theories. The dominant theory of PF is also divorced from considerations of tax administration. Of course, in practice, a fiscal policy must be administratively feasible to be implemented, so this is a serious omission. In contrast, theories of public budgeting are more diverse, but many also focus on values from different disciplines. In addition, budgeting has been influenced by reform movements in government, which have then spurred budget reforms. By their nature, these reforms are normative and idealistic, rather than descriptive. Historically, budget reform has spawned a set of budgetary methods that are employed in varying degrees in governments.

We do not seek to abandon these valuable contributions to practice. However, government finance theory fails to describe and explain adequately the practices of the field. In some cases, the norms prescribed may not be shared by government officials and citizens, and thus policy prescriptions from theory become unhelpful. We believe theory should guide practice, but theory must also be informed by practice, and too often in this field theory has given practice scant attention. We seek to establish a better basis to understand the structure and evolution of government finance, and to help practitioners face difficult situations that call for workable solutions.

PUBLIC FINANCE THEORY

Arguably the most influential book of the twentieth century in the area of government finance was Richard Musgrave's *The Theory of Public Finance*. Musgrave's (1959) approach was largely normative, and explicitly so. Economic efficiency and equity were his core principles. His view of equity was somewhat paternalistic; for instance, he argued that merit goods were a meaningful concept and that the state should promote the consumption of these worthy goods. His classic three branches of a fiscal department (allocation, distribution, and stabilization) are not a description of any government organization, but rather a framework of what, in his mind, a good government should do. The task of each branch attempts to serve the normative goals of efficiency, equity and stable economic growth. Therefore his approach is largely normative. Undoubtedly many practitioners were helped by his approach, as it provided a balance for two compelling social values. It is, however, a rather single-minded view of government. As Buchanan has pointed out, it idealizes a unified government with strong leadership. Where power is more diffuse, the logic of fiscal policy and institutions is likely to be less coherent.

While current texts have different emphases and many stress equity less than Musgrave, the concept of economic efficiency is still dominant in most all PF texts.[2] For example, Anderson (2003: 4) cites some key questions of PF:

> What role should the government play in the economy relative to markets? What services should the government provide and how should those services be financed?

Notice the use of the word 'should', implying a normative approach and central control. He also declares that:

> in public finance our objective is to advance the goals of economic efficiency and equity through the appropriate design of public sector programs and financing. (2003: 6)

Such a model is a useful guide for developing a set of 'best practices' that government should consider. But as anyone who has seen the making of tax and budgetary policy knows, broad social values often give way to the power of interest groups, citizens' concerns, and administrative reality. What are fiscal officials to do when 'best practices' are not politically acceptable, or are in conflict with other powerful interests? These texts often use the assumptions of neoclassical economics to ask questions about how to enhance efficiency. It needs to be emphasized that efficiency is a normative value. While some PF texts rigorously 'prove' certain 'optimal' policies, this does not necessarily make the approach acceptable or even feasible. Of course that is not necessarily the goal of such theories: scientific advancement is the main purpose. Public choice theory is an interesting mixture of positive and normative theory. Many public choice inquiries (see, for example, Mueller 2003) posit certain assumptions, and then seek to predict relationships and outcomes. Public choice theory is sometimes normative when it uses logical derivations to make a case for a certain preferred policy prescriptions, such as limits on taxes or restrictions on bureaucratic behavior. This theory is sometimes positive when it examines institutional arrangements to examine their effects, either by the use of logic or with evidence.

James Buchanan described the genesis of public choice theory as a specification of constitutional and other rules for making fiscal choices, as well as an investigation of their consequences, in the tradition of the original designers of the US Constitution. He also argued that his constitutionalist approach was more consistent with American values:

> I think there is a fundamental difference between American and European attitudes ... on constitutional structure ... Americans have a sense that constitutions are needed to constrain politicians. You [Europeans] don't really have that tradition, and in the sense that it is the fundamental break between Richard Musgrave's position and mine. He trusts politicians; we distrust politicians. (Buchanan and Musgrave 2001: 88)

Public choice denies the viewpoint that government is a 'benevolent despot' that will act to correct market failures and make distributional judgments in an even-handed way. From this perspective, one:

---

2   See, for example, Rosen (1995), Ulbrich (2003), Gruber (2005) and Fisher (2007).

ceases to see government as standing apart from the economy adjusting, correcting, and fine-tuning the economy. Rather, one sees it as being thoroughly enmeshed in the economy. (Levy 1995: 95)

It is argued that this is a better way to understand why certain government policies exist. Some elements of public choice theory have real practical merit to the practitioner, such as voting models, agenda control, rent seeking, principal–agent relationships, and models explaining government growth. Right or wrong, it also presents an alternative worldview that may be consistent with the perspective of some actors, and therefore can be relevant. Casual evidence, such as the popularity of tax and expenditure limitations, suggests that the beliefs of many voters and elected officials are roughly consistent with public choice theory. Nevertheless, public choice is heavily burdened by its strong assumptions about human behavior and the assumptions of synoptic rationality and self-interest. The normative frameworks of PF focus on efficiency, equity and economic growth but often do not support an experimental or explanatory approach to addressing public finance problems. There is a disconnection between the theories and how we approach practice. Further, the utility of theory to practitioners is likely to be limited because the solutions arrived at in this approach do not give sufficient consideration to the context of the problems practitioners face.

PUBLIC FINANCIAL MANAGEMENT THEORY

The public financial management (PFM) theories of tax and expenditure policy and administration also tend to be normative, although the norms are different to those in the PF literature. The dominant 'best practices' framework is based on values such as managerial control, legal compliance, and implementation of accounting standards (Bartle and Ma 2004). This explains, in part, the divergence between PF and PFM textbooks as the normative basis of the two approaches draws from different values. The different approaches of the disciplines therefore create a theoretical divergence between policy and management that does not exist in practice. Making policy and carrying it out are not as separate in practice as they are in theory. For example, Coe's (1989: 5) textbook 'is written to give students the financial management skills and analytical techniques they will need on the job'. In the chapter on accounting he asserts, 'A well-designed and well-managed accounting system also helps to ensure proper stewardship over public funds' (6). Similarly, Mikesell's (2011) text is oriented to giving students the skills needed to work as fiscal analysts. It does survey current practices and identifies its differences from best practice. Reed and Swain's book has a more pragmatic focus, as it defines PFM as a technical field, that is, one concerned with 'how things are done with money' (Reed and Swain 1997: 2). It focuses more on legal constraints, politics, financial concepts, and public organizations more broadly. While some scholarship in this area is more based on the study of practice (debt management, purchasing, and pensions), much of PFM is focused on best practice which may or may not be feasible or common for practitioners. There is room to improve our understanding of PFM by studying how practice has developed over time and why there is variation among governments.

PUBLIC BUDGETING

Public budgeting theory is more heterogeneous, as different theories have been applied and have been shown to have some merit. Bartle (2001) and Khan and Hildreth (2002) review some of these theories, including incrementalism, real time budgeting, the organizational process model, the greedy bureaucrat model, the median voter model, principal agent model, transaction cost theory, interpretive theory, postmodernism, punctuated equilibrium, and portfolio theory. This broad range of theories suggests the pluralism in this area. This is healthy and perhaps helpful for the practitioner as different theories are accessible for consideration and experimentation. Another source of budget theories is Alan Schick's very influential 1966 article which established a periodization of American (mostly federal) budgeting and the associated orientations of budgeting:

- control, ranging from 1920 to 1935, and focused on financial control;
- management, from the New Deal until the 1960s, focused on using financial resources to meet the goals of the organization;
- planning, beginning in the Kennedy-Johnson administration, and focused on optimizing resource use in pursuit of policy goals.

Others have identified different orientations since then. But earlier (1930), Mabel Walker, identified four other periods of American municipal budgeting:[3]

- honesty: employing the budget as a means to combat corruption (1840–1900);
- economy: 'the attitude was to keep the tax rate down regardless' (Walker 1930: 13);
- efficiency: 'the taxpayer gets full value received for every dollar expended by the city' (ibid);
- proportion: 'balance in the administration of the city's affairs' so that different pressures and interests are satisfied as well as possible (Walker 1930: 14).

Taken together, she identified these four standards of ideal fiscal administration: 'honesty, economy, efficiency, and proportion' (Walker 1930: 15).

Whether Schick or Walker correctly identified these periods is not the issue here. The seven values they identified are all salient ones that may be used in government finance, and not just in the US. Some of the theories reviewed by Bartle and Khan and Hildreth may serve the same purpose. These values and theories are then starting points for practitioners to consider in defining their own approach. They also present a tentative framework that a manager can share with colleagues and citizens to help them understand the value trade-offs in any decision. This can lead to a meaningful dialog that can achieve a balance among compelling frameworks. Theorists can help practitioners by identifying potentially relevant values in any decision, and demonstrating the trade-offs among these values. In the words of Charles Beard, 'budget reform bears the imprint of the age in which it originated' (cited in Schick 1966). The popularity of different reforms during different time periods indicates that they were temporal solutions to the problems of the day. Certainly not all governments embraced these reforms, but

---

3   She did not specify the time periods corresponding to the second through fourth periods.

practitioners learn from their neighbors as well as from their experience. An answer that worked for a neighboring government might be worth a try. Thus solutions spread if they solve the problem facing the practitioner. Over time, as the problems facing practitioners change and new solutions are suggested, a different reform develops for a new age.

Many practical problems of government finance are considered within a deliberative framework that includes staff meetings, public hearings; and voting by city councils, legislatures, and school boards. Existing theories do not explicitly take this into account. If, as Musgrave and Musgrave (1973) suggest, fiscal systems are a 'large part of making democracy function', government finance theories need a philosophical perspective that incorporates democracy in its many forms (participatory or representative). An overarching theoretical perspective that is problem oriented, pluralistic, democratic, provisional, and tied to a legal and constitutional framework would be a valuable addition to government finance. The classical pragmatism of Pierce, Holmes, James, Dewey and Addams offers such a perspective.

Pragmatism

Dwight Waldo linked public administration to pragmatism, noting that pragmatism 'as a body of literature cannot be compressed and reconciled in short space' (Waldo 1948: 83).[4] To make sense of pragmatism, it is useful to begin with inquiry and its role in resolving problematic situations. Pragmatism uses a problematic situation as a starting point for inquiry. Pragmatic inquiry incorporates a scientific approach and broad participation. Ultimately, problematic situations are resolved through action. Hence, pragmatism is well suited for the dynamic, decision-filled world of government finance. In addition, pragmatism emphasizes learning through doing and making. Although government finance is a process, it is filled with deadlines and products which are sources of problematic situations such as budget documents, financial statements and revenue estimates. Financial managers do and make these documents. Theory is important because it can guide the doing and making. It can also be used to make sense of the results or consequences of these actions. Theory does not represent truth rather it enables reflection on past decisions, is a guide to action, and a prism to interpret consequences.

Classical pragmatism is also a philosophy that focuses on the tools that facilitate doing and making, which resolve problematic situations. Pragmatism approaches the problematic situation using an experimental approach to inquiry. Action is placed within a broad experimental context. Did the action result in the expected outcome? Action guided by an experimental logic resolve the problematic situation. Then, the action is evaluated in light of consequences. Various theories of government finance

---

4   He went on to attempt at least a sketchy description 'But we are on safe ground to say that pragmatism is a protest against rationalism, against *a priori* methods of thought, and habits of mind. Its test of truth is usually considered to be chiefly "workability" or "cash value"; an idea is true if it "works", if it has desirable effects when tried, it places emphasis on experience, and is hence characterized by empiricism. Intelligent use of experience in testing for truth is an experiment; so "experiment" is a term frequently found in pragmatic writings, Since the truth of an idea is determined by (or is) what it does, it is in some sense an instrument. Impatience with the "abstract" or "theoretical",and use of such terms as scientific, experience, empirical, practicability, experiment – these characterize the pragmatic temper' (Waldo 1948: 83).

may be used by a practitioner. As long as theories are useful, they serve to order the information an actor receives and guide their resolution of problematic situations. Other actors may use other theories, which present a challenge in communicating and resolving a problem. There is no reason to believe that any particular theory will be relevant in any case.

CHARLES SANDERS PEIRCE

Charles Sanders Peirce originally conceived of pragmatism as a philosophy of science with a logic of inquiry at its center.[5] He began by criticizing ways of thinking which 'fixate' belief systems, thus making them impervious to fresh evidence. Peirce draws a distinction between doubt and belief and the impact each has on action.

> Doubt is an uneasy and dissatisfied state from which we struggle to free ourselves and pass into the state of belief; while the latter is calm and satisfactory state ... The irritation of doubt causes a struggle to attain a state of belief. I shall term this struggle Inquiry. (1955a: 10)

Inquiry using the methods of science is the best way to 'satisfy our doubts' (Pierce 1955a: 18). When belief states exist, habits of mind provide stimulus for action. When belief/habits are disturbed, a problematic situation emerges. The problematic situation is resolved through inquiry. The process of resolution can result in new belief systems and new habits. One might speculate that accepted budgeting and financial management practices used by government such as accounting systems, budgeting practices, and performance budgeting, are the manifestations of organizational belief systems or habits that make the system work. Inquiry and the problematic situation arise when the standard operating procedures of a practice break down and a search for new tools to resolve the problem begins. The focus on inquiry/action also encourages reflective thought, imagination, and creativity (Joas 1996).

For Peirce, the scientific method represents the opposite of individualism. 'What distinguishes it from all other methods of inquiry is its cooperative or public character' (Buchler 1955: x). The classic example of the three blind men trying to describe an elephant is illustrative. Each describes the elephant from his own limited perspective (small tail, big ears, etc.). The story's moral is that we are all trapped inside our limited selves, and cannot know the truth. If, however, we allow the three blind men to talk to each other, to compare perspectives, to argue, to test new hypotheses, to behave like a community of scientific investigators it is possible to imagine that the blind men will eventually overcome their limited perspectives and come to a truer sense of the elephant. In the same way, a budget director, agency head, and accounting director may all see a problem from different perspectives drawing from their theoretical frameworks. Until they approach a problem using a cooperative method of inquiry, they are likely to 'talk past' each other and not be able to reach a consensus to resolve the problem. Instead the problem remains unresolved, or one imposes their view on the others.

---

5   From a public administration perspective, what is also interesting about Pierce is his 30-year employment with the US government as a physicist, astronomer, inventor and occasionally, an administrator. He worked at the United States Coast and Geodetic Survey, currently the National Geodetic Survey (Dracup 1995).

Peirce (1955b) also argued ideas have clear meaning when applied – that is in their effect or consequences. For example, a temperature of 90 degrees is hot if one is playing football. It is cool if one is drinking tea. Apart from the context and practical consequences terms like hot, cool and 90 degrees have little meaning. Using this logic both guiding norms and theories of government finance should be considered in context and by their effects or consequences.

JOHN DEWEY

Dewey extended Pierce's scientific logic of inquiry to practical reasoning and social problems. The struggle to see the elephant becomes the struggle to *use* the elephant in everyday life. Hence, unlike earlier philosophers such as Plato, Aristotle, Decartes, and Kant, Dewey's real interest is *not* truth rather the social grounds of belief. He (1938: 14) used 'warranted assertability' as the test for the social grounds of belief.[6] The methods of science retain their centrality but the focus of science is no longer the 'discovery of nature's eternal laws'. Rather, emphasis shifts:

> to the formulation of theories motivated by the desire of human beings to predict and control their natural and social environment. (Posner 1995: 390)

Dewey's philosophy presupposes a:

> specific theory of self and community … for Dewey social institutions are better understood as experiments in cooperation … rather than as embodying some timeless order. Human development requires cooperation. (Seigfried 1996: 92, emphasis added)

Hence, Dewey emphasized the role of community in inquiry:

> An inquirer in a given special field appeals to the experiences of the community of his fellow workers for confirmation and correction of his results" (Dewey 1938: 490, emphasis added).

John Dewey and Jane Addams use this focus on the community (in inquiry) to develop a rich theory of participatory democracy (Shields 2006). The notion of democracy usually alludes to ideas of representation and voting. Participatory democracy falls outside this schema and is conceptualized as a way to communicate and cooperate. It is an ongoing daily process – a way of life. It is:

> the day by day working together with others. Democracy is the belief that even when needs and ends or consequences are different for each individual, the habit of amicable cooperation – which may include, as in sport, rivalry and competition – is a priceless addition to life. (Dewey 1998)[7]

Dewey and Addams' inclusive organic conception of democracy can be applied as financial officers work with each other, across organizational boundaries, and with the public. It

---

6   Dewey (1938: iii) acknowledged Peirce's influence in the Preface of *Logic*.

7   For an extensive discussion of Dewey's notion of democracy and how it can be used as a source of objectivity in public administration see Hildebrand (2008) and Ansell (2011).

is helpful because it places the 'public' front and center – something missing from many theories of government finance. Returning to Musgrave and Musgrave's (1973) insight, Dewey and Addams show us a way to link the 'working fiscal system' with a 'functioning democracy'.[8]

OLIVER WENDELL HOLMES JR.

As mentioned earlier, PFM emphasizes legal compliance and implementation of accounting standards. Further, Buchanan links PF theory to a constitutional framework. The contribution of another founder of classical pragmatism, Supreme Court Justice Oliver Wendell Holmes Jr. also demonstrates the applicability of classical pragmatism to the legal nature of government finance theory and practice (Shields 2008).

In his most famous passage of the *Common Law*, Holmes asserts, 'the life of the law is not logic: it has been experience' (Holmes 1881: 1). He believed the method of solving legal problems (finding an established rule and applying it logically to the facts) 'was not as certain as the formal statement of rules and facts in judicial opinion, nor as the statement of rules in treatise or the statute book made it appear' (Patterson 1953: 467). Holmes emphasized the distinction between the law that 'is' and that 'ought to be'. He believed that when laws (what ought to be) are implemented they are changed. When social conditions change or new values emerge, courts are asked to interpret and change the boundaries of the law. This is the boundary a practicing financial officer must navigate as they implement tax, expenditure, auditing, and accounting principles. This logic applies to the multitude of rules, regulations and standards confronting government finance.

FOCUS ON THE PRACTITIONER

Many academic theories of government finance attempt to generalize about the processes and outcomes in the field, but do not focus on understanding the day-to-day tasks and motivations of practitioners. While academics spend lots of time arguing about theories and methodology, practicing financial managers are often stuck with the messy jobs of producing budgets or implementing tax changes. Academic theories struggle to provide a framework that incorporates practitioner experience or helps practitioners keep an eye on the big picture while navigating the narrow, day-to-day world. Classical pragmatism provides a strategy that can help financial managers recognize and resolve problematic situations as they go about the practical day-to-day business of implementing programs, preparing financial reports, balancing budgets, and considering revenue options. It does this in a context that encourages democracy and dialog, and recognizes the web of networks that enrich and complicate their world, thus the emphasis on the community of inquiry is more appropriate than a single theory.

As a practicing financial manager looks at the action-oriented, adaptable and ever-fluctuating environment described by classical pragmatism he knows this is his world.

It is a complex world not amenable to understanding much less conquest, by any one formula or singular approach; but rather where old arsenals quickly rust ... In this world the most

---

8   For an extensive discussion of Jane Addams notion of democracy see Addams (1902) and Shields (2006).

consistent success arise from the application of robust beliefs and techniques inaugurated at the three-way intersection of ... experience, common sense and hard-nosed science. (Brom and Shields 2006: 312)[9]

It is based on the history and cultural setting of each manager because it sets the context of what is possible, and therefore relevant to be considered. Therefore different experiences in different places are likely to lead to different understandings of what theory is workable.

John Winfrey (1998) outlines a similar approach to public policy that he calls a pluralistic approach to social ethics. While he acknowledges the relevance of several philosophical approaches to ethics, he argues that:

those theories that attempt to derive all rules from a single, fundamental principle are unsuccessful ... We have argued that the relative weights given to each moral principle may change according to the situation. Thus our approach must be pluralistic *in the sense that no one ordering of principles is available. Similarly, it must be* intuitionist *in the sense that, when no strict ordering is available, one must use her or his own considered judgment ... Although no set weights can be assigned to moral principles, our judgments as to how they should be balanced in various situations become better informed with experience. (Winfrey 1998: 3 and 16, emphasis in original)*

His argument is similar to ours as he attempts to provide an approach to the resolution of contentious policy issues in a society where values diverge. Similarly, we believe that different perspectives that have served to organize action, research and learning in this field need to embrace the intuitionist and experience-based approach. Winfrey's approach also uses the metaphor of balance in making public decisions. Just as judges balance competing principles of justice as applied to a specific case, so too must government managers. Thus, rather than applying one theory to a problem without dialog with other stakeholders, a practitioner needs to listen to differing values and then balance them to resolve a problematic situation.

THEORY, PRACTICE AND PRODUCT

Dewey turns the Greek way of knowing on its head to demonstrate the practical nature of science as well as the intimate connection between practice and scientific inquiry. The Greeks classified ways of knowing using the terms *theoras*, *praxis* and *poiesis*. *Theoras* (or theory) is derived from the Greek word for god (Hickman 1990: 108). Theory dealt with the divine and the 'fixed essence' of nature. Foundational notions of knowledge are derived from this tradition (Hickman 1990: 83). *Praxis* (or practice) indicated the concrete deliberative exercise of an art or science. *Poiesis* (or product) is associated with productive activities (Shields 1998). The hierarchy of Greek social organizations reflected the privileging of *theoras* vis-à-vis praxis or *poiesis* (Hickman 1990: 109). The esteemed philosopher engaged in *contemplation* (finding truth in theory), the artisan (architect, ship designer, sculptor – budget process designer) engaged in *making*, and the craftsman (carpenter, stone cutter, accountant, budget officer) engaged in *doing*. This philosophic

---

9   The basis of this assertion is largely intuition rising from experience. 'This is not enough to form belief, but enough to meet the pragmatic threshold for initiating an exploratory inquiry' (Brom and Shields 2006: 312).

formulation, reinforced by Greek social structure, created a 'division between practice and theory, experience and reason' (Dewey 1938: 73). According to Dewey (1938), science and experimentation which necessarily involved making and doing was not valued in Greek society. Because the social structure devalued doing and making, Greek society placed little value on scientific discovery.

Perhaps more importantly, the worlds of practice and production were devalued leading to common dualisms such as theory/practice, academic/practitioner, and policy/administration. From this ancient perspective, practice and practitioner (financial managers) are worth-less. Dewey argued that the privileging of theory placed roadblocks in scientific discovery and inquiry generally. His important insight about science is that it inverted the ancient hierarchy. Theory no longer had to deal with final certainty but instead became a tool of scientific investigation propelled by the interactions between practice and production. As a tool, theory was valued for its practical consequences and its usefulness (Hickman 1990: 99). This orientation makes sense for government financial managers because, like all managers, they are focused on solutions to problems and cannot be wedded to academic theories to guide their action when the elected officials and citizens they serve need a solution to a problematic situation. Theory is a tool, not an ideology.[10]

HOTEL CORRIDOR

William James (1907: 54) uses a hotel corridor metaphor to illustrate how pragmatism's pluralistic (inter/multidisciplinary) orientation connects to the problematic situation. Consider a patient with back pain (problematic situation). The patient walks the corridor owning the pain. The hotel rooms represent different paradigms such as chiropractic, orthopedic, physical therapy, acupuncture as well as different ways to diagnose and treat the pain. The person with the back problem knows when relief occurs. The ultimate test of the value of an approach to the treatment of a back problem is practical – the relief of pain.

In the case of financial management, the practicing financial manager owns the problem as he travels a hotel corridor looking for ways to reach resolution. Theories from economics, operations research, organization theory, accounting and other disciplines are found within rooms connected to the corridor. All the rooms open out to it and all the rooms can be entered. The problematic situation brings the manager to the corridor and gives them the right to move freely from room to room. The theories inside the rooms are judged by their usefulness in addressing the problem. The tools of theory and methods found in the rooms are combined and tested using practical outcomes as criterion of truth. Thus pragmatism views theories as practical tools that can be drawn from a pluralistic tool box. Further, the problematic situation as a starting point is easily applicable to the complex nature of government finance. For example, public financial management problems transcend scale (small city, state agency, Department of Defense). Problems can also be either concrete or abstract.[11] These theoretical tools may need to be drawn from existing theories or fashioned on the spot. The value of pragmatism is that it helps practitioners recognize that new and better conceptualization is necessary. It also

---

10   For an extensive discussion of pragmatism as a philosophy of science for public administration see Shields (1998).

11   The recognition of the need to find a new theory is an example of an abstract problematic situation.

encourages them to find or develop the needed tools. Importantly, Dewey distinguishes between abstract and concrete thinking. He notes that each is useful in resolving the problematic situation. The issue here is that the practicing financial manager's thoughts must be tethered to the post of 'use' (problematic situation). But, if the tether is too short, it is quite difficult to really see creative ways to resolve the problem. Theory enables the practitioner to lengthen the tether and bring more critical thinking skills to the problematic situation.

Using pragmatic logic, one would not expect a unifying theory of government finance. Rather, the field is organized around the principle that theories are useful and should be judged by their usefulness in resolving problems. Unity is achieved because the pragmatic financial manager owns the corridor and understands how to use and combine the tools in the rooms as they address small, large or 'wicked' problems. Across the community of practitioners, there is sharing of information to see what others are doing and what works. However, each manager needs to adapt other solutions to their own administrative and political situation, and to indigenous beliefs, customs, and practices. Luckily, pragmatism provides a forum for reflective thought and encourages creativity and imagination, all of which should help practitioners adapt existing theory and apply it to their situations, taking into account past experiences and insights from colleagues.

Assessment

Pragmatism is not new to this field; it is over 80 years old. In his 1926 book, *Municipal Finance*, A.E. Buck wrote:

> The approach is from the pragmatic point of view, emphasis being placed on practical and efficient financial administration. The method of treatment is empirical; theory is reduced to a minimum. The criteria used are based on experience and practice. (Buck: v)

In 1930, Mabel Walker wrote:

> If a budget clerk were to carefully search through the archives of public finance, economic theory and municipal government, he would find pitifully little to assist him in the all-important question of dividing up the city's revenues. His adoption of rule-of-thumb devices to tide him past the crucial points is the most that could be reasonably expected ... To understand municipal budget making it is necessary to visualize this tremendous pressure that is being exerted from all sides – the pressure of organized interests, of ambitious department heads, of civic groups, of official prejudices, of the political potency of a low tax rate, even of public opinion where not represented by any of the above. The final budget will be the resultant of these forces and not the outcome of a dispassionate evaluation of the various functions. (Walker 1930: 29 and 47–8)

She dismisses utility theory from economics as 'a pleasing theory but not a practical one for budget makers'. Pragmatism is 'cruder and simpler' (Walker 1930: 86). Coherent, logical theories that are used in government finance are pleasing, as Walker says. A more pluralistic approach that embraces multiple theories is messy. Certainly a good theory should not become a monolithic belief system. However, a primary goal of theorizing in an applied field such as government finance should be to describe and explain what we observe. Existing theories have some descriptive and explanatory power, but that power is limited. An approach such as Walker's that balances the pressures of different stakeholders is more likely to describe the outcome and be useful to practitioners.

Some theories of government finance suffer from being too abstract and are imported from other disciplines causing too much separation from the environment. These theories tend to cling to the assumptions and values of their discipline. As a result, they have a weaker ability to describe and explain the practices and outcomes of government. Instead, explanatory theories can draw from the worldviews of practitioners. Multiple frameworks represent the different professions and viewpoints and will shift over time. While some questions are conducive to disciplinary theories, attempts to understand and explain why something happened often require an understanding of locally held beliefs and relationships.

> The pragmatist's real interest is not in truth at all, but in the social grounds of belief ('warranted assertibility'). This change in direction does not necessarily make the pragmatist unfriendly to science, but it shifts the emphasis in thinking about science from discovery of nature's eternal laws to the formulation of theories motivated by the desire of human beings to predict and control their natural and social environment. (Posner 1995: 390)

One shortcoming of this approach for a theorist is its greater degree of complexity. Rather than employing one theory, the pragmatic approach sees many potentially relevant theories, reducing its generalizability. But existing theory tends to produce anomalies which confound theorists. A generalizable theory with weak explanatory power may be more deceptive than it is worth. A second limitation of this approach is that normative recommendations are less obvious for those advising governments, as the recommendations have to be made consistent with local context, politics and history. However, many generic recommendations provided by outside advisers without an understanding for the local context are simply ignored after the expert leaves town. Recommendations that are crafted for the local situation have greater potential to endure.

Conclusion

A pragmatic philosophy of government finance is designed to serve practitioners, not theorists. But if it does so, then it should have empirical validity and so be helpful to theorists as well. Further work needs to articulate the organizing principles of this approach and the means by which we can test for empirical validity. And some coherence is still needed to organize thinking in the field that could easily be overwhelmed by numerous theories. However, empirical accuracy is more important than theoretical tidiness in developing a positive model. We believe this approach is more accurate and useful.

A good theory of government finance needs to explain the historical development of fiscal policy and administration. It is not obvious how this will be done, but the influence of any government's constitution on government finance is both a historical beginning point as well as an institutional framework of powers and constraints. Also, the seven values identified in the discussion of public budgeting theory are associated with different time periods and seem to be enduring values in government finance, at least in the US. Whether they truly are values that government managers have employed is an important question to answer.

This approach also suggests the importance of the democratic process. Practitioners actively test their theories in discussions with other stakeholders and in professional networks. This process of authentic dialog allows an effective manager to discard unworkable ideas and hone workable ones. Essentially it is an open and extended process of compromise that seeks to balance the relevant considerations. Further, good managers seek to find creative approaches that might blend two or more sets of values into an innovative solution (Joas 1996). In contrast, an adherent to a normative theory would presumably expect others to accept their values without argument. This is undemocratic, unrealistic, and generally inaccurate. A good manager has to adapt to value systems they may not necessarily agree with as elected officials come and go, mandates are handed down from superior governments, and public opinions shift. If they want to keep their job, they must understand these other viewpoints and be flexible. They may choose to disagree in certain instances, but a veteran manager knows that there is risk in doing so. Moreover, a 'pleasing theory' that does not work is utopian in the truest sense of the word; it is a luxury a manager cannot afford. Applying the philosophy of pragmatism to government finance has potential to address some of the weaknesses of existing theories, and provide an overarching framework that reconciles policy and administration, and theory and practice. It should be more empirically accurate and historically relevant. Most important, it should inform the practice of government finance.

References

Addams, J. 1902. *Democracy and Social Ethics*. New York: Macmillan Co.

Anderson, J.E. 2003. *Public Finance: Principles and Policy*. Boston, MA: Houghton Mifflin Co.

Ansell, C.K. 2011. *Pragmatist Democracy: Evolutionary Learning as Public Philosophy*. Oxford: Oxford University Press.

Bartle, J.R. 2001. *Evolving Theories of Public Budgeting*. Oxford: Elsevier.

Bartle, J.R. and Ma, J. 2004. Managing Financial Transactions Efficiently: A Transaction Cost Model of Public Financial Management, in *Financial Management Theory in the Public Sector*, (ed.) A. Khan and W.B. Hildreth. Westport, CT: Praeger Publishers, 1–23.

Brom, R. and Shields P. 2006. Classical Pragmatism, the American Experiment and Public Administration, in *Handbook of Organization Theory and Management: The Philosophical Approach*, 2nd edn, (ed.) T. Lynch and P. Cruise. New York: Taylor and Francis, 301–22.

Buchanan, J.M. and Musgrave, R.A. 2001. *Public Finance and Public Choice: Two Contrasting Visions of the State*. Cambridge, MA: MIT Press.

Buchler, J. 1955. *Philosophical Writings of Peirce*. New York: Dover Publications.

Coe, C.K. 1989. *Public Financial Management*. Englewood Cliffs, NJ: Prentice Hall.

Dewey, J. 1938. *Logic: The Theory of Inquiry*. New York: Holt, Rinehart and Winston.

Dewey, J. 1998. Creative Democracy: The Task before Us, in *The Essential Dewey: Volume I, Pragmatism, Education, Democracy*, (ed.) L. Hickman and T. Alexander. Bloomington, IN: Indiana University Press, 340–44.

Dewey, J. 1998. Philosophy and Democracy, in *The Essential Dewey: Volume I, Pragmatism, Education, Democracy*, (ed.) L. Hickman and T. Alexander. Bloomington, IN: Indiana University Press, 71–8.

Dewey, J. 1998. Pragmatic America, in *The Essential Dewey: Volume I, Pragmatism, Education, Democracy*, (ed.) L. Hickman and T. Alexander. Bloomington, IN: Indiana University Press, 29–31

Dracup J. 1995. History of Geodetic Surveying: Part II Following in Hassler's Footsteps. *American Congress of Surveying and Mapping Bulletin*, July/August: 15–19.

Fisher, R.C. 2007. *State and Local Public Finance*, 3rd edn. Mason, OH: Thomson.

Gruber, J. 2005. *Public Finance and Public Policy*. New York: Worth Publishers.

Hickman, L.L. 1990. *Dewey's Pragmatic Technology*. Bloomington, IN: Indiana University Press.

Hildebrand, D.L. 2008. Public Administration, as Pragmatic, Democratic and Objective. *Public Administration Review*, 69(2), 222–9.

Holmes, O.W., Jr. 1881. *The Common Law*. Boston, MA: Little Brown.

James, W. 1907. *Pragmatism: A New Name for Some Old Ways of Thinking*. Cambridge, MA: The Riverside Press.

Joas, H. 1996. *The Creativity of Action*. Chicago, IL: University of Chicago Press.

Khan, A. and Hildreth, W.B. 2002. *Budget Theory in the Public Sector*. Westport, CT: Westwood.

Levy, J.M. 1995. *Essential Microeconomics for Public Policy Analysis*. Westport, CT: Praeger Publishers.

Miller, H. 2004. Why Old Pragmatism Needs an Upgrade. *Administration and Society*, 36(2), 243–9.

Miller, H. 2005. Residues of Foundationalism in Classical Pragmatism. *Administration and Society*, 37(3), 360–74.

Mikesell, J.L. 2011. *Fiscal Administration: Analysis and Applications for the Public Sector*, 8th edn. Boston, MA: Wadsworth.

Mueller, D.C. 2003. *Public Choice III*. New York: Cambridge University Press.

Musgrave, R. 1959. *The Theory of Public Finance*. New York: McGraw-Hill.

Musgrave, R. and Musgrave, P. 1973. *Public Finance in Theory and Practice*. New York: McGraw-Hill.

Patterson, E.W. 1953. *Jurisprudence: Men and Ideas of the Law*. Brooklyn, NJ: The Foundation Press.

Peirce, C.S. 1955a. The Fixation of Belief, in *Philosophical Writings of Peirce*, (ed.) J. Buchler. New York: Dover Publications, 5–22.

Peirce, C.S. 1955b. How to make our ideas clear, in *Philosophical Writings of Peirce*, (ed.) J. Bulcher. New York: Dover Publications, 23–41.

Posner, R. 1995. *Overcoming Law*. Cambridge, MA: Harvard University Press.

Rosen, H.S. 1995. *Public Finance*. Chicago, IL: Irwin.

Reed, B.J. and Swain J.W. 1997. *Public Finance Administration*, 2nd edn. Thousand Oaks, CA: Sage

Schick, A. 1966. The Road to PBB: The Stages of Budget Reform. *Public Administration Review*, 26(6), 243–58.

Seigfried, C.H. 1996. *Pragmatism and Feminism: Reweaving the Social Fabric*. Chicago, IL: University of Chicago Press.

Shields, P.M. 1996. Pragmatism: Exploring Public Administration's Policy Imprint. *Administration & Society*, 28(4), 390–411.

Shields, P.M. 1998. Pragmatism as Philosophy of Science: A Tool for Public Administration. *Research in Public Administration*, 4, 195–226.

Shields, P.M. 2003. The Community of Inquiry: Classical Pragmatism and Public Administration. *Administration & Society*, 35(5), 510–38.

Shields, P.M. 2004. Classical Pragmatism: Engaging Practitioner Experience. *Administration & Society*, 36(3), 351–61.

Shields, P.M. 2005. Classical Pragmatism Does Not Need an Upgrade: Lessons for Public Administration. *Administration & Society*, 37(4), 504–18.

Shields, P.M. 2006. Democracy and the Social Feminist Ethics of Jane Addams: A Vision for Public Administration. *Administrative Theory & Praxis*, 28(3), 418–43.

Shields, P.M. (2008). Rediscovering the Taproot: Is Classical Pragmatism the Route to Renew Public Administration? *Public Administration Review*, 68(2), 205–21.

Ulbrich, H. 2003. *Public Finance in Theory & Practice*. Mason, OH: Thomson.

Waldo, D. 1948. *The Administrative State: A Study of the Political Theory of American Public Administration*, 2nd edn. New York: Holmes Meier Publishers.

Walker, M.L. 1930. *Municipal Expenditures*. Baltimore, MD: The Johns Hopkins Press.

Whetsell, T. and Shields, P.M. 2011. Reconciling the Varieties of Pragmatism in Public Administration. *Administration & Society*, 43(4), 472–83.

Winfrey, J.C. 1998. *Social Issues: The Ethics and Economics of Taxes and Public Programs*. New York: Oxford University Press.

13 *A Pragmatist Approach to Emotional Intelligence and Managerial Regret*

ROSA SLEGERS

Introduction

"Intelligence loves simplicity," writes Henri Bergson (1946 [1934]: 249), summarizing William James's pragmatist outlook, "it seeks to reduce effort, and insists that nature was arranged in such a way as to demand of us, in order to be thought, the least possible labor." When the intellect encounters what James calls "vagueness," (i.e. experiences that muddle the neat simplicity of what it deems "rational") it tends to dismiss these complications as irrelevant. This chapter focuses on the concept of "emotional intelligence" as it is commonly understood in organizational contexts and explores the temptation to use this concept to simplify, categorize or even reject vague and unruly sensations as they occur in the work place. A particular kind of regret will feature as an example of such unwelcome sensations. James's pragmatism shows that the acknowledgement of "emotional vagueness" in general and this kind of regret in particular, both make a difference in our experience (a pragmatist requirement) and enriches the decision-making process in a way that benefits the organization. It will be suggested that a pragmatist approach to the emotions, which allows room for the vague and on occasion resists the intellect's simplifying, labor-saving inclinations, can only be put into practice by managers with "tough-minded, empiricist temperaments."

Emotional Intelligence

"Emotional intelligence" has become a mainstream concept and the idea that (corporate) leaders need to be "in touch" with (some of) their emotions, in order to be 'good' at what they do, has achieved common sense status. Researchers have proposed different models of emotional intelligence and the ways it can be measured, but authors on the topic generally agree about two common core components: "awareness and management of one's own emotions and awareness and management of others' emotions" (Extein et al. 2006: 240). Daniel Goleman is commonly credited with popularizing the notion of "emotional intelligence" in the mid-1990s (Goleman 1995), though the term had appeared in earlier scholarly research (DiPaolo et al. 1990). It is this popularized account of emotional intelligence that is often encountered in organizations, but it would be wrong to suggest that this conceptualization is the only (let alone the best) "version" of emotional intelligence available today. Since this chapter deals with emotional intelligence as it is most commonly employed in organizations, these other voices in the emotional intelligence debate (often more rigorous and critical than Goleman's) fall outside the scope of the argument presented here. Goleman's theory of emotional intelligence encompasses the components mentioned above. As he explains in a "primer" on emotional intelligence, "the ability to manage ourselves and our relationships effectively consists of four fundamental capabilities: self-awareness, self-management, social awareness, and social skill" (Goleman 2000a: 83). Since Goleman introduced the term to a wider audience, "emotional intelligence" has taken on a life of its own, and the way in which the concept is commonly understood in business may differ from Goleman's theory as he originally formulated it. It is informative to look at both Goleman's own claims and the way in which the theory is commonly interpreted.

Where businesses are concerned, the advantage of emotional intelligence is understood primarily in terms of the strategic benefits: experienced CEOs know when to trust their emotions, hunches, or intuitions, and this enables them to make the right, profitable decisions. Goleman (2000b) argues that leaders who use emotional intelligence to create and maintain a pleasant working environment will see a pay-off in financial terms. Furthermore, giving employees the feeling that they are appreciated has been shown to improve employee retention, workplace morale, and motivation (Goleman 2000b: 86). Considering our own everyday experiences, these observations will hardly come as a surprise: we often "trust our gut" when making big decisions and are more likely to try harder at our jobs when we feel that our efforts are being noticed and that our contribution is recognized and valued. Everyone benefits from an "emotionally pleasant" work environment, and so-called "emotionally intelligent" bosses and managers play an important role in bringing this about. This rather common sense observation is merely a starting point, however; what remains to be clarified is what, exactly, we mean when we call someone 'emotionally intelligent' in a business context and how the concept of emotional intelligence is captured in guidelines for managers. For now, it is sufficient to merely point to the vaguely defined concept of emotional intelligence as it features in everyday (business) language and organizational behavior.

Emotion is traditionally regarded as separate from (or even opposed to) reason or rationality, but according to William James we should be suspicious of any strict division between supposedly separate abilities. Rationality, he claims, is a sentiment: we call something rational when it fits in with our assumptions and prior beliefs. The sentiment of rationality is "a strong feeling of ease, peace, rest" while we reserve the word "irrational" for things that baffle us and are to novel or irregular to accept. James adds that "the transition from a state of puzzle and perplexity to rational comprehension is full of lively relief and pleasure" (James 1956: 63). Our intellect is the ability that allows us to find this relief and is therefore greatly valued. But this account shows that "intelligence," according to James, cannot be divided up into an emotional and a rational ability: we call rational what puts our minds at ease and our emotions are an indispensable part of what we call reasoning. As James explains in "The Stream of Thought" (1977: 72): "All Reasoning depends on the ability of the mind to break up the totality of the phenomenon reasoned about, into parts, and to pick out from among these the particular one which, in our given emergency, may lead to the proper conclusion. Reasoning is but another form of the selective activity of the mind."

Neuroscientist Antonio Damasio has shown that even the simplest decisions we make are not only informed by, but predicated upon, our capacity to attach emotional value to different options. Like James, Damasio blurs the line between reason and emotion, stating that "certain aspects of the process of emotion and feeling are indispensable for rationality" (Damasio 2006: xxiii). In line with the theory James puts forth in "What is an Emotion?," Damasio describes feelings as cognitive: they are "the sensors for the match or lack thereof between nature and circumstance" (2006: xxv). Damasio discusses the famous case of Phineas Gage who suffered serious brain damage in a railway blasting accident in 1848, yet remained in full possession of his motor, speech, and reasoning skills. It soon became evident, however, that Gage was no longer able to make sound decisions in either his professional or his social life and his friends did not recognize him as the same person. Drawing parallels between Gage's case and modern cases of similar brain damage, Damasio shows that in these patients emotions are reduced or absent, and that this absence results in an inability to assign different values to different options. This makes the patients' "decision-making landscape hopelessly flat" (Damasio 2006: 51) and leaves them unable to ever make up their mind about even the simplest things. Findings such as Damasio's show that we do not have a choice to involve our emotions in our decision-making process: they are always already part of it. In fact, with the capacity to attach emotional value to different phenomena in our experience blocked or lessened, we become very poor decision-makers. William James, foreshadowing many recent findings in neuroscience, presents a philosophical approach to the role of the emotions in decision-making and so provides us with a pragmatist framework for emotional intelligence.

In "What is an Emotion?," James remarks that "the nervous system of every living thing is but a bundle of predispositions to react in particular ways upon the contact of particular features of the environment" (James 1884). Recent empirical research supports James's notion that certain parts of "the world's furniture" trigger in us a response while other parts do not: we appear to be predisposed to respond to certain parts of the world in particular ways. For example, it is easy for us to cultivate a fear of snakes, but not a fear of flowers (Haidt 2001). We may even go so far as to claim that it is "reasonable" to feel fear at the sight of a snake in the wild, while it is unreasonable to feel fear at the sight of a daisy. However, the fear we feel at the sight of a coiled snake on our path is not induced by reason: we know now that the emotion experienced in this situation is immediate and the result of a much more primitive and much faster process in the brain than the conscious thought: "This is a snake; I should be careful" (Haidt 2001; Prinz 2009). James's observations a century earlier led him to much the same conclusion: emotions, he claims, are immediate, strong, bodily sensations and have little or nothing to do with reason. An emotion may lead us to come up with a conscious, reasoned explanation, but the emotion itself is not something rational.

> If we fancy some strong emotion, and then try to abstract from our consciousness of it all the feelings of its characteristic bodily symptoms, we find we have nothing left behind, no 'mind-stuff' out of which the emotion can be constituted, and that a cold and neutral state of intellectual perception is all that remains. (James 1884: 195)

Prinz largely agrees with James but phrases the issue in more contemporary terms. In his defense of an emotionist account of ethics, Prinz summarizes the issue as follows:

Evidence from neuroscience shows that we don't need the neocortex to trigger a bodily response that, when experienced, would be identified as an emotion ... I submit that no bona fide emotion is disembodied. Every apparent candidate proves visceral to the core. (Prinz 2009: 58–60)

If the emotions themselves have little to do with reason, and if emotional intelligence as it is commonly understood consists of both the awareness and the management of these emotions, what might this kind of "intelligence" look like from a pragmatist perspective? A study of James's account of the intellect and its role in sifting through the multitude of sensations we experience every minute will be useful in formulating a response to this question.

The Intellect and the Sensible Flux of Experience

About our sensations, James writes:

That they are is undoubtedly beyond our control; but which we attend to, note, and make emphatic in our conclusions depends on our own interests; and, according as we lay the emphasis here or there, quite different formulations of truth result. (James 1978: 118)

Accordingly, the existence of emotions is beyond our control, but which emotions we take seriously within an organizational context will depend on our interests. As a consequence, we will hold certain emotions to be useful and correct, appropriate, and conducive of truth, while others will be considered irrational, inappropriate and an obstacle to truth. That the emotions are key to many if not all life decisions can hardly be disputed, but some still want to see the workplace as separate from the rest of our experience. Preferring to see ourselves as rational creatures, we might like to think of our professional decisions as independent of our emotions, believing that we reach "objectively true" conclusions as a result of a reasonable thought process. The idea that the workplace is, or should be, an emotion-free, rational environment is still prevalent despite the rise in interest in emotional intelligence (cf. Fineman 2004). James would point out that there is no contradiction here: over time, and with new research finding its way into public common sense, certain emotions lose their status of "irrational" and start forming a part of what it means to be a well-functioning member of an organization. These "productive," "positive" emotions are no longer regarded as an obstacle to being a good manager, employee, or executive, but are instead considered an asset. This, James would remark, results in a new truth, one formulation of which could be: "emotional intelligence is important to the success of an organization." But *which* emotions are considered part of "emotional intelligence," and *how* is it decided whether an emotion should be taken seriously or rejected as irrelevant? This, in James's words, depends on our interests, and it is these interests that should be subjected to closer scrutiny.

From the multitude of sensations experienced every minute, we pick out those that serve our interests while we ignore, repress, or simply fail to notice those that we cannot use. As James puts it, "we receive ... the block of marble, but we carve out the statue ourselves" (James 1978: 119). The intellect is utilitarian through and through, and its need for clarity can easily blind us to the fact that the clear picture we discern does not necessarily correspond to a "clear reality," but simply to those (aspects of) sensations that we think are important. Now that claims like "emotional intelligence is important to the success of an organization" have received the status of "truth," emotions in the workplace are evaluated differently than they were before. Plunging "forward into the field of fresh experience with the beliefs our ancestors and we have made already," we are apt to notice some things and not others. What we notice, in turn, "determines what we do; what we do again determines what we experience." If the traditional view states that organizations should be run by "level-headed" people who make decisions using "calm, rational judgment," and if this kind of judgment is understood to involve something like "pure," emotionless reason, then we are apt to act in ways that we feel are in accordance with this belief. And so James remarks that:

> from one thing to another, although the stubborn fact remains that there is a sensible flux, what is true of it seems from first to last to be largely a matter of our own creation. (James 1978: 122)

New truths spread like grease spots, according to James, "staining" the stock of old beliefs already in place. A new truth can only take hold if it can be absorbed by our already established truths with a minimum of adjustments. Consequently, a new truth can only be recognized as a truth because it is not actively repelled by the beliefs we already hold, and this applies to the (relatively) new beliefs about emotional intelligence as well. Emotional intelligence has become mainstream and, to return to James' description, is being absorbed by, and added to, the body of pre-existing beliefs like a slowly spreading stain. One should therefore expect that the new truths pertaining to emotional intelligence do not constitute a radical break with the long-accepted truths that were held (implicitly) even before the first organization and management theories came about. Seen in this light, it is no wonder that we speak of emotional *intelligence* – the very phrase itself suggestive of what James calls the utilitarian nature of the "rational" mind. If indeed rationality is a sentiment, as James suggests, then it is the intellect's task to ease our mind and to make us feel like the world "makes sense." The intellect's means of achieving this lie in the construction of useful shortcuts or concepts that lead us from one part of experience to another, insuring that we are not perpetually overwhelmed by the sensible flux. One of the questions to be addressed, then, is what shortcuts are constitutive of the concept of emotional intelligence as it is commonly understood. Awareness of the conservative, utilitarian, and selective character of our intellect and its role in shaping expectations about organizational behavior may help us notice and appreciate other parts of the "sensible flux" we encounter on the work floor. Before discussing the feeling of regret as an example to illustrate this point in the next section, a few concrete examples will be used to set the stage.

In the *Harvard Business Review* article "Why Repressing Emotions is Bad for Business," Daniel Shapiro (2009) argues that:

> emotional investment can improve your relationships, increase trust, and promote satisfying, enduring agreements … Fostering positive emotions – making people feel upbeat and engaged – can be one of the greatest sources of value for your organization.

Shapiro points out that on the one hand, emotions play a role in business, whether we like it or not. This is in line with James and Prinz. On the other hand, however, we can use emotions to our advantage and not only create value for the organization but also save ourselves from lawsuits brought by disgruntled (former) employees. Like James, Shapiro recognizes that emotions simply "happen" and are an unavoidable part of our work life. Like Goleman, Shapiro points to the use of the emotions for the bottom line. Certain emotions are considered to be more in line with the interests commonly shared by organizations and are therefore considered positive, while other emotions are deemed negative or even destructive and should therefore be avoided. As a consequence, there might be the sense that the accepted emotions have their appropriate time, place, and function: the right emotion at the right time signifies emotional intelligence, while unruly emotions, cropping up when they are undesirable, annoying, or distracting, are considered unreasonable or irrational.

In "When to Trust Your Gut," another article representative of the mainstream status of emotional intelligence, Alden M. Hayashi (2001) asks what can be gained from the study of the successful CEO's decision-making processes. Talking to a CEO who made a bold but wildly profitable decision after the fact does not necessarily make one much the wiser: what, exactly, does it mean to "trust one's gut," and how does one know it is time to trust it? From the overwhelming amount of data available to a manager, constituting the "sensible flux" of the workplace, what sensations does the successful manager notice, disregard, act on? There is no hard and fast rule, which is exactly the important point from a pragmatist perspective.

No checklist can sum up what is means to be a "good" leader or manager because the specifics change not only from one situation to another, but also from one moment in time to another. To say that a manager "needs emotional intelligence" to be successful only appears like a clear requirement at first glance, but as soon as one tries to pin down what exactly this capacity called "emotional intelligence" might mean, it appears that no definition can quite capture it (Fineman 2004: 721). Emotional intelligence is (or rather, should be) what James calls a *vague* concept, rich and complex but blurry in its outline. Our utilitarian intellect will attempt to "clean up" the notion of emotional intelligence and neatly define it, making it appear "rational." James's ideas about what he calls "the vague" or "vagueness" will now be applied to the emotion of regret specifically.

Regret and Vagueness

What does one mean when one says that one is experiencing regret? Taking into account James's remarks regarding the sensible flux, it is clear that no two experiences of regret can be exactly alike. The feeling of regret depends on a host of sensations particular to an individual, and these sensations themselves vary with time and experience. Because our intellect is utilitarian and tends to use concepts and abstractions to cut through the confusing multitude of the sensible flux the emotions, too, are indicated by words that appear to pick out a clearly defined part of reality but in fact merely point to a wide range of related but hard-to-define sensations. Any attempt to define an emotion ends up somewhere in between a generalization very far removed from our actual experience, and a description of a specific sensation so closely linked to particular circumstances that it can no longer be called a definition. It is not within the scope of this paper to study the different definitions of regret commonly occurring in the psychological and philosophical literature, but merely to pick out one possible form that regret might take in an organizational context. This particular kind of regret will then be considered through the lens of James's theory to enrich a pragmatist perspective on emotional intelligence sketched above.

Consider a manager and an employee meeting for a performance review. The employee's work has been mediocre at best, and the manager is aware of this. Knowing they will hurt the employee with their honest feedback, and knowing that they will feel uncomfortable having caused this hurt, this manager foregoes giving the feedback altogether. Rationalizing this course of action (or rather: lack of action), the manager may tell themselves that the employee in question would not have been able to handle the feedback, would have acted out, or soured the workplace atmosphere with passive aggressive behavior. Furthermore, they could reason, the feedback might not have been necessary anyway since the existing problems might take care of themselves over time. Or the manager might justify their decision not to be honest by telling themselves that the employee would not be able to improve their work even if they did take the feedback seriously and tried to act on it. A host of other arguments might be involved to "rationalize" the decision, all meant to justify the fact that no honest feedback was given. The manager in this situation exemplifies the pattern that has been called the "my-side bias:" the tendency to "search for anecdotes and other "evidence" exclusively on [the] preferred side of an issue" (Haidt 2001: 821). Haidt explains that people often engage in post-hoc reasoning to justify their beliefs and that "the goal of thinking is not to reach the most accurate conclusion but to find the first conclusion that hangs together well and that fits with one's important prior beliefs" (2001: 821). In this case, the manager's prior beliefs may include the idea that they are a kind and patient boss and this idea may be at the center of a multitude of dependent beliefs about the ways in which they should behave. Being the cause of an employee's hurt or serious discomfort does not fit with these beliefs and so reasons have to be found to justify the decision not to give feedback.

The manager in this situation anticipates feeling (great) discomfort at the hurt which the employee is expected to feel as a result of the honest feedback, and the desire not to feel this discomfort is so strong that the intellect selects those elements from the sensible flux that can be used to justify not giving the feedback. The "that" of the sensations experienced by the manager cannot be helped; it is, as James points out, beyond their control (James 1956). The feeling of nervousness, discomfort, frustration, etc. that accompanies the idea of having to give feedback is there, as are all the other sensations that more or less directly constitute this particular experience: the (nervous, overly confident, distracted ...) employee, the memory of a fight at breakfast that morning, the information about first quarter earnings just received, etc. The "which" of the sensations, however, is at least to some extent up to the manager: which sensations are deemed relevant, important, and pertain to the situation at hand? To feel like they have a grasp on the situation, the manager must get rid of all the "noise," block out "irrelevant" sensations and engage only those facets of the situation which are to-the-point, rational, and clearly defined in their decision-making process. But how do they know which elements in the stream of data are relevant? As James points out, "no one ever had a simple sensation by itself. Consciousness, from our natal day, is of a teeming multiplicity of objects and relations, and what we call simple sensations are results of discriminative attention, pushed often to a very high degree" (1977 [1904]: 21). The manager's set of prior beliefs predisposes them to single out those "simple" sensations that encourage the sentiment of rationality and give a sense of ease, peace, and rest. Haidt would remark that this shows that "the reasoning process is more like a lawyer defending a client that a judge or scientist seeking truth": arguments come into play to justify a foregone conclusion (Haidt 2001: 820). James's concept of vagueness is helpful here.

As William Gavin explains in *William James and The Reinstatement of the Vague*: "The vague ... refers to a situation that has not degenerated into an overly false clarity, and to one that does not intend to come up with final certainty" (Gavin 1992: 3). When we talk about the emotions and emotional intelligence in an organizational context, these concepts are likely to take on an appearance of "overly false clarity." Articles or management books which sum up, often in a number of steps or a list of concerns, what emotional intelligence *is*, or how one can *become* emotionally intelligent, easily give the reader the impression that what is at stake is something neatly defined and easily achieved, if only one follows the recipe to the letter (e.g. Caruso and Salovey 2004; Goleman 2000b; Lynn 2007; Mersino 2007). James reminds us that the richest and most personal sensations escape the analytic and seemingly conclusive approach proposed in coaching materials. The issue, then, is as Gavin phrases it: "How can one be articulate about the inarticulate, or clear about the vague, without undermining or 'explaining away' what it is that one wants to preserve?" (Gavin 1992: 4).

In a study about the "Consequences of Regret Aversion: Effects of Expected Feedback on Risky Decision-making," Marcel Zeelenberg et al. (1996) argue that people will "always tend to make regret-minimizing choices (rather than risk-minimizing choices)" (1996: 153). It is observed that regret "can affect people's choices before their decision is made, when they anticipate the regret they may feel later (if the decision turns out badly)" (1996: 155). These "anticipatory aspects of regret" are part of a process in which we compare the actual consequences of our actions to what might have been had we chosen to act differently. Regret occurs when this comparison shows that the alternative course of action would have been better. It is also assumed (in both the article and in regret theory in general) that "the emotional consequences or decisions are anticipated and taken into account when making decisions." People, in short, are "regret-averse," and avoid acting in ways that they know they might regret later. This relates to the example of the manager described at the top of this section: they anticipate feeling regret as a result of giving honest feedback and tell themselves that withholding the honest but painful feedback will result in a better outcome, thereby forestalling the feeling of regret. But is the manager preventing themselves from feeling regret, or some other kind of discomfort, and what might be the difference between the two? One could argue that the manager anticipates feeling regret primarily at causing their own discomfort; the prospect of having to hurt the feelings, pride, or ego of the employee is merely the occasion of this discomfort. The regret at stake is very different in nature if it is experienced by a manager who decides to give honest but painful feedback, knowing that it is the right thing to do. They regret hurting the employee, but the anticipation of this hurt does not keep them from acting honestly. It is this latter kind of regret which will be considered from a pragmatist perspective in what follows.

To better understand the pragmatic import of this kind of regret in an organizational context, it serves to pick out a few issues raised by the study cited in the previous paragraph. It is important to note that the study uses a rather narrow definition of the word "regret." The definition is never clearly stated but can be deduced from the study itself: from the way the experiment is set up, it appears that regret is taken to apply to situations in which one knows that one could have been better off (financially, in the case of the study) if one had acted differently. The term "regret," like all concepts, acts like a shortcut: it allows us to pick out a certain set of sensations to which the term applies without having to go through all the particulars. But, as is commonly the case where our utilitarian intellect is concerned, much is lost in the process: the shortcut is convenient, and clearly "works" for the purposes of the study, but what is measured is not regret in all its personal complexity but rather a small facet of one very particular kind of regret, tested in a laboratory setting. Compare the regret one might feel about investing in money markets (when it has turned out that investing in bonds would have been more profitable) to the regret experienced by the manager who has to give difficult and painful feedback to an employee. The word "regret" can be applied to both situations, but rather than a clearly defined, analytical concept, it turns out to be a shortcut that points us to a very large, diverse, and rich field of sensations. When a manager knows that honest feedback is in order, and that to withhold the feedback would be selfish (i.e. out of a desire to avoid discomfort) and even unkind or unfair (because the feedback might actually help the employee improve their performance and in the long run even keep their job), they may still regret the hurt caused by their actions, even though they do not doubt their actions were the best possible under the circumstances. Regret is here experienced not as remorse or because a different course of action would have led to a better outcome, but because hurt was inflicted in the course of doing what was right.

In attempting to get a grip on regret, James would say, we are entering the domain of the vague, and the more acutely regret is felt, the vaguer the sensation becomes. Not because the feeling is only fleeting or peripheral but because it is so intense, rich, and multifaceted that it escapes exact definition and analysis. But the vaguer the sensation, the less useful from a purely utilitarian perspective. After all, what purpose is served by this kind of regret, which supervenes on an action that, from an organizational standpoint, should not be regretted? If indeed the action was the best one possible under the circumstances, regret may seem not merely unnecessary but even irrational or counterproductive. Because we tend to be regret-averse (as is apparent not only from the study cited above but also from our everyday experiences), anticipatory regret may be an obstacle to us acting as good managers who need to give honest feedback and fire employees when necessary. As a result, regret is marked as a "negative emotion" and is not commonly featured in articles praising emotionally intelligent leaders. "Emotional intelligence" is itself a shortcut to those emotions which fit in with the already accepted truths about organization theory – the more "rational," "productive," and all-round "useful" emotions that help get results. But what difference would it make, pragmatically speaking, if room was made in organizations for the "vaguer" emotions such as regret? What changes would occur in our experience if emotional intelligence was taken to be a vague rather than a clear-cut requirement for organizational success? James's distinction between the tough – and the tender-minded temperament provides a helpful perspective on these questions.

Managerial Temperament

James remarks that:

the human race as a whole largely agrees as to what it shall notice and name, and what not.
And among the noticed parts we select in much the same way for accentuation and preference
or subordination and dislike. (James 1977: 71)

Since it is "far too little recognized how entirely the intellect is built up of practical interests," we are largely unaware of this selective tendency and mistake the shortcuts embedded in everyday language for reality itself (James 1956: 84). The practical bent of our intellect is useful and indispensable, but it should not lead us to disregard the vague. Rather, James proposes a *Weltanshauung* called "radical empiricism" which incorporates the utilitarian perspective but does not exclude those parts of the sensible flux which escape conceptualization:

To be radical, an empiricism must neither admit into its constructions any element that is not directly experienced, nor exclude from them any element that is directly experienced. For such a philosophy, the relations that connect the experiences must themselves be experienced relations, and any kind of relation experienced must be accounted as 'real' as anything else in the system. (James 1977: 194–5)

We must come to recognize, according to James, that though conceptual processes can categorize, define and interpret facts, "they do not produce them, nor can they reproduce their individuality. There is always a *plus*, a *thisness*, which feeling alone can answer for" (James 1977: 455). It was suggested above that it is precisely this "plus" or "thisness" which easily gets lost in the emotional intelligence literature: the clearer one tries to be about the emotions, the harder it is to do justice to their inherent vagueness. Goleman's (2000b) famous article "Leadership that gets results" can serve as an example. Listing the traits that belong to an emotionally intelligent leader, Goleman mentions "self-awareness," which includes "emotional self-awareness: the ability to read and understand your emotions as well as recognize their impact on work performance, relationships, and the like." James shows us that the manner in which we read and understand our emotions and their impact depends very much on our prior beliefs: we are predisposed to notice some elements in the flux of sensible experience but not others, and we choose to accept as evidence or justification those things that conform to our prior convictions. The manager who decides not to give the painful feedback perhaps understands their emotions as indications that the feedback should not be given, though this is by no means the only possible reading – it in fact betrays a "my-side bias." When asked to defend their decision, the manager might point to another trait listed by Goleman, self-control: "the ability to keep disruptive emotions and impulses under control." Labeling the discomfort they feels at the prospect of giving negative feedback as a disruptive emotion, they can feel justified in "keeping it under control," which here entails not acting on it. Furthermore, they might argue that they are displaying what Goleman calls organizational awareness: "the ability to read the currents of organizational life, build decision networks, and navigate politics" (Goleman 2000b: 85). Delivering the unwelcome feedback, the manager might argue, would be to go against the currents and disrupt politics. Emotionally intelligent leaders are capable of "developing others" and have a propensity to "bolster the abilities of others through feedback and guidance." But the manager may respond by suggesting they reserve their honest feedback for those who can handle it, and that this particular employee lacks abilities to be developed, and so one could go on. There is no doubt that the traits listed by Goleman are all valuable, but since they are abstract concepts they can be used to justify decisions one would be hard-pressed to call truly emotionally intelligent (whatever our exact understanding of the term).

The kind of regret described above is a feeling that springs from empathy with those who have come to harm because of one's actions, even though one has every reason to believe that those actions were right under the circumstances. Rather than dismiss all vague sensations because they appear to serve no straightforward purpose from a conservative organizational perspective, the pragmatic method asks us to consider *why* the vagueness in this particular case will likely be dismissed as "irrelevant" or "irrational." What interests are served in ignoring vagueness?

In *The Present Dilemma in Philosophy* (1977 [1907]), James describes how our response to vagueness depends on what he calls our temperament: some people are "tough-minded empiricists" and take seriously their sensations in all their diversity, richness, and vagueness, while other are "tender-minded rationalists" who are always drawn to clear explanations, systems, and abstractions (1977 [1907]: 19). A discussion of these temperaments in an organizational context will make clear what difference it makes, pragmatically speaking, to allow for vagueness where it comes to the emotions.

James states that we are all inclined to espouse those theories most closely related to the way in which we are accustomed to perceive the world. Rationalists tend to look for clear principles and final answers, hoping to find something absolute which they can then call God, Matter, Reason, etc. Having found this principle, they can be at rest because they have come to the end of a metaphysical quest. Empiricists, on the other hand, are never "done" because there are always new facts presenting themselves, calling for different theories, concepts, and shortcuts to help us deal with the sensible flux around us. For most of us, our temperament is a mixture of the two, but we do tend to be inclined one way or the other. This "potentest of all premises" – the fact that our like or dislike of a theory depends not primarily on "logical" reasoning but on our inclinations, expressed in our "temperament" – is rarely mentioned in philosophical discussions (James 1977 [1904]: 11). James clearly sides with the empiricists and agrees with them that "the actual universe is a thing wide open, but rationalism makes systems, and systems must be closed" (James 1977 [1904]: 20). Even a quick overview of James' descriptions of the two temperaments gives us reason to believe that organizations are, per definition, geared to the tender-minded, rationalist temperament. For an organization of any kind to run smoothly, clear rules and procedures need to be followed and respected so that quantifiable results can be attained. Though there has been an increase in attention for those leaders (political and corporate) who get results by following their gut even if doing so defies convention, the common sense opinion is that an organization should be orderly, transparent, and effective. James has shown that this common sense perspective is often not as straightforward as it seems, and we can now see that this is because the common sense understanding of an organization tends to be tender-minded. Organizations and the people working there are defined in terms of their functions and goals, and the words used to describe these functions and goals are themselves shortcuts. A manager, for example, is quite obviously in charge of (a group of) employees and has to ensure and aid both their productivity and well-being. But what does this mean in practice? To look at what it might mean to be a 'good' manager means to dip into the sensible flux of experience, picking out those elements that we connect to an employee's "well-being" and "productivity." But what data from the flux present themselves as ready candidates depends on our temperament: the tender-minded rationalist will select a smaller set of data because of their more narrow perspective than the tough-minded empiricist. Whereas the former will refer to a list of principles (the company's mission statement, Goleman's list of emotionally intelligent leadership traits, a chart provided by the organization to measure well-being and productivity), the latter will be open to data that lie outside these parameters and would not be far from obvious to the tender-minded rationalist.

A pragmatist like James would most likely agree that it is important for an organization's principles and goals to be clear and for an organization's employees to work efficiently, but the tough-minded pragmatist temperament would not stop there. A tough-minded organizational theorist would want to ask, for example: what does it mean to look out for an employee's well-being and productivity? No checklist can provide an answer here, even if the list includes items meant to help the manager assess the employee in an emotionally intelligent way. Any interaction with the employee takes place amidst a multitude of sensations, some clearly defined and "rational," some vague and "irrational." Which ones are deemed relevant depends on the manager's temperament, experience, beliefs, and a host of other factors, some of which might not even be known to the manager's conscious mind. The idea that the success of any such interaction can be guaranteed through the use of a checklist may be appealing to a tender-minded manager. But the tough-minded empiricist would remark that though this way of thinking might provide a tender-minded manager with peace of mind, it will also have the effect of limiting the manager's perspective to what they expect to see based on the checklist. Any assessment circumscribed by (seemingly) clear parameters will result in (seemingly) clear results – results that leave no room for the vague.

Conclusion

The most usual way of handling phenomena so novel that they would make for a serious rearrangement of our preconceptions is to ignore them altogether, or to abuse those who bear witness for them. (James 1978 [1904]: 54)

In considering the particular kind of regret that one feels when one "did the right thing" but caused others harm nonetheless, this tendency to ignore "useless" or "irrational" feelings is evident. What, after all, is the point, from an organizational perspective, to feel regret when one did nothing wrong? The tender-minded response to this feeling would be to push it away or, if one's temperament were particularly rationalist, to not even consciously register the emotion. Going by a set of organizational principles alone makes one's professional life more comfortable, at least on the surface. Pragmatism as James describes it, however, is more demanding.

Pragmatism's "only test of probable truth is what works best in the way of leading us, what fits every part of life best and combines with the collectivity of experience's demands, nothing being omitted" (James 1978: 44) The sensible flux within an organization includes emotions and our experience demands that we acknowledge all emotions, including the ones which are not "useful," strictly speaking, in terms of profit. A tough-minded empiricist in a managerial role will not exclude parts of experience from consideration but "try to interpret each notion by tracing its respective practical consequences" (James 1978: 28). The tough-minded empiricist will always remain wary of the utilitarian tendencies of the intellect. The emotions are vague, and vagueness is usually at odds with the sentiment of rationality. We are inclined, therefore, to come up with shortcuts, lists, and guidelines to "regulate" emotional intelligence and make it appear like a straightforward, analytical concept. But the tough-minded empiricist recognizes that we are never done, and that absolute truth does not exist. This insight both complicates and enriches the popular emotional intelligence literature commonly encountered within organizations since it encourages a vague, Jamesian perspective on the emotions. Organizational theory is prone to rationalist tendencies, seeing reality as "ready-made and complete from all eternity." For the organizational pragmatist, however, "it is still in the making, and awaits part of its completion from the future" (James 1977: 123).

References

Bergson, H. 1946. *The Creative Mind.* Translated by M.L. Andison. New York: The Philosophical Library.

Caruso, D. and Salovey, P. 2004. *The Emotionally Intelligent Manager: How to Develop and Use the Four Key Emotional Skills of Leadership.* San Francisco, CA: Jossey-Bass.

Damasio, A. 2006. *Descartes' Error.* London: Vintage.

DiPaolo, M., Mayer, J. and Salovey, P. 1990. Perceiving Affective Content in Ambiguous Visual Stimuli: A Component of Emotional Intelligence. *Journal of Personality Assessment,* 54(3), 772–81.

Extein, M., Weissberg, R.P., Cherniss, C. and Goleman, D. 2006. Emotional Intelligence: What Does the Research Really Indicate? *Educational Psychologist,* 41(4), 239–45.

Fineman, S. 2004. Getting the Measure of Emotion – And the Cautionary Tale of Emotional Intelligence. *Human Relations,* 57(6), 719–40.

Gavin, W.J. 1992. *William James and the Reinstatement of the Vague.* Philadelphia, PA: Temple UP.

Goleman, D. 1995. *Emotional intelligence.* New York: Bantam Books.

Goleman, D. 2000a. *Working with Emotional Intelligence.* New York: Bantam.

Goleman, D. 2000b. Leadership That Gets Results. *Harvard Business Review,* (78)2, 78–88.

Goleman, D. 2006. The Socially Intelligent Leader. *Educational Leadership,* 64(1), 76–81.

Haidt, J. 2001. The Emotional Dog and Its Rational Tail: A Social Intuitionist Approach to Moral Judgment. *Psychological Review,* 108(4), 814–34.

Haidt, J. and Joseph, C. 2004. Intuitive Ethics: How Innately Prepared Intuitions Generate Culturally Variable Virtues. *Daedalus,* 133(4), 55–66.

Hayashi, A. 2001. When to Trust Your Gut. *Harvard Business Review,* 79(2), 59–9.

James, W. 1884. What is an Emotion? *Mind,* 9(34), 188–205.

James, W. 1956. The Sentiment of Rationality, in *The Will to Believe and Other Essays in Popular Philosophy.* New York: Dover Publications.

James, W. 1977. *The Writings of William James: A Comprehensive Edition,* (ed.) J.J. McDermott. Chicago, IL: University of Chicago Press.

James, W. 1978. *Pragmatism and the Meaning of Truth.* Cambridge: Harvard University Press.

Jackman, J. and Strober, M. 2003. Fear of Feedback. *Harvard Business Review,* 81(4), 101–11.

Lynn, A. 2007 *Quick Emotional Intelligence Activities for Busy Managers: 50 Team Exercises That Get Results in Just 15 Minutes.* New York: Amacom.

Mersino, A. 2007 *Emotional Intelligence for Project Managers: The People Skills You Need to Achieve Outstanding Results.* New York: Amacom.

Prinz, J. 2009. *The Emotional Construction of Morals*. Oxford: Oxford University Press.
Shapiro, D. 2009. Why Repressing Emotions is Bad for Business. *Harvard Business Review*, 87(11), 30.
Zeelenberg, M., Beattie, J., Van de Pligt, J. and De Vries, N. 1996. Consequences of Regret Aversion: Effects of Expected Feedback on Risky Decision Making. *Organizational Behavior and Human Decision Processes*, 65(2), 148–58.

14 *Developing Collaborative Power in Working Life: Linking American Pragmatism and Action Research*

TORE HAFTING AND ERIK LINDHULT

Introduction

Power is a central concern and topic in the social sciences. Although American pragmatism has experienced a renaissance in recent decades, evident within the social sciences generally and in organization studies in particular, it is interesting to note that American pragmatist philosophy is largely absent in academic discourses on power. Power is considered an under-developed theme in American pragmatist thought (Mills 1964). Furthermore, there has been continued critiquing of 'pragmatic acquiescence', the tacit assent and compliance with established powers (Hildreth 2009). Early critical theorists, such as Horkheimer and Marcuse, dismissed pragmatism as a continuation of utilitarian thought and thus as being part of ideologies of the status quo (Joas 1993). Some critically oriented researchers today still argue that insufficient attention is paid to the structures of power in society (White 2004). Power thus seems to be a weak spot in American pragmatism. This begs several questions: Is there a pragmatist understanding of power to be recovered, or is this absence rather a failing of pragmatist thought?

American Pragmatism and Collaborative Power

Power is clearly not a primary theme in American pragmatic thought (Mills 1964), particularly in its Weberian understanding (going back to Machiavelli 1532), which sees power as part of coercive social relations: power as the capacity of agents to impose their will despite resistance from others (Weber 1947: 152). This is the dominant understanding of power in academic discourse relating to organization studies, although conceptions of power vary greatly (Clegg 1989; Clegg et al. 2006; Clegg and Haugaard 2009; Foucault 2000; Lukes 1974). What seems to be pragmatic acquiescence in the eyes of critics, however, can be interpreted as an impetus to find alternative perspectives to and on power in order to establish more fruitful social relations. For instance, there are researchers making efforts to restore the status of Dewey in the discourse on power. Recent interpretations of Dewey argue that there are sufficient conceptual resources in Dewey's works to provide the basis for a forceful, pragmatically oriented conception of power (Allen 2008; Hildreth 2009; Kadlec 2007; Rogers 2009). In addition to illuminating Dewey's theory of power – as power by some groups *over* others rooted in social structures – there is also a Deweyan account of transformative power with others (Kadlec 2007). This concept of power is vital to Dewey's creative project for participatory and inquiry based democracy (Bohman 1999; Caspary 2000; Westbrook 1991).

In this chapter we argue that American pragmatism can inspire and support an important shift in prevailing social science discourses on power towards non-coercive, collaborative understandings of power consistent with a participatory democratic politics and way of life (Dewey 1939a, 1939b). In order to trace a pragmatist understanding of power, we focus on two thinkers. First, John Dewey, in his extensive writings, has emerged as one of the leading thinkers to explicitly touch upon the issue of power. Second, Mary Parker Follett who, as we maintain, can and should be counted as one of the leading figures in American pragmatism. She can in several respects be considered a female counterpart to Dewey in terms of making pragmatist points of departures relevant for a progressive and participation-based democratic society. Dewey and Follett both focus on power as capacity instead of coercion; they can be seen as complementary in the clarification of non-coercive understandings of power (Dewey 1916a, 1916b; Follett 1924). Dewey can be said to implicate a collaborative conception of power linked to participatory democratic politics. Follett is more specific in focusing on and working out a non-coercive conception of power, and can be said to address specific dimensions not worked out by Dewey from a pragmatist point of view, e.g. a relational and activity based point of departure. Follett is particularly interesting because of her invention of a concept of power as 'power-with', which makes significant contributions to a pragmatist understanding of the concept and its practices. Where Dewey relies on social and cooperative intelligence as an alternative to coercive power and force (Dewey 1927), Follett offers processes of circular response through which interests are integrated and power-with is developed instead of power-over (Follett 1924).

We relate these debates to action research. The link between action research and pragmatism has been made in order to clarify how theory and practice, research and development are interconnected (see also Eikeland 2001; Greenwood 2002), but the connection to American pragmatism in relation to the theme of power is under-developed. The purpose of this chapter is to draw out an understanding of non-coercive, collaborative power from the works of Dewey and Follett, and illustrate its relevance for the analysis of power in the domain of action research. We focus briefly on the Scandinavian collaborative action research tradition (Hafting 2004a, 2004b, 2006, Lindhult 2005), demonstrating how a pragmatist conception of power can illuminate the action research practices and processes, and can clarify and develop the insights developed by and from Dewey and Follett. The issue of power in industry and working life is a link which we examine, as this is an area in which unequal power relations are particularly prevalent. This observation has been made both by Dewey and by scholars in the Scandinavian tradition, and thus identifies this as an area in need of social transformation (Dewey 1935; Emery and Thorsrud 1976).

Dewey on Social Power and Intelligence

Dewey shows less concern with the issue of power as compared to Follett. In his primary work on democratic theory, *The Public and its Problems* (1927), power is surprisingly not indexed and the concept is only touched upon in some peripheral sentences, used mostly to refer to conscious attempts by agents to influence and control conditions to achieve desirable ends. Dewey conceptualises power in a manner similar to Follett, as 'power to', described as the 'effective means of operation; ability or capacity to execute ... It means nothing but the sum of conditions available for bringing the desirable end into existence' (Dewey 1916a, 1916b). Power and freedom for Dewey are closely connected, as liberty 'is power, effective power to do specific things' (Dewey 1946: 111). As we are interested in power in an organized context, the social character of power as a capacity in relation to others is brought to the fore. Sympathetic commentators agree that this topic is not clearly described in Dewey's thoughts on power, where he seems to be content to focus on expediency and efficiency in achieving the desired ends (Allen 2008; Hildreth 2009). One person's expedience, however, could be based on the submission of others. Dewey wants to define the concept of coercion as force used to constrain others, something which comes close to the common Weberian definition of power as the capacity of agents to impose their will despite resistance from others (Weber 1947: 152). This form of power leads to restrictions on the growth of individual capacity, something recent commentators see as Dewey's implicit critical standard (Kadlec 2007; Midtgarden 2012).

Dewey took up the issue of social power in relation to appreciation and a critique of liberalism in particular. The concept of power was useful in this context because of how the 'power to', in progressive liberal politics in American democratic society, lent legitimacy to efforts to restrict the liberty of others. As Dewey understands liberty not in an abstract sense, but as the power to do specific things, there was a glaring inequality in the distribution of such powers in contemporary society (Dewey 1946: 112). It is quite clear for Dewey that the liberal tradition has made considerable contributions to the liberty of individuals. From the beginning, however, there has been an internal split within liberalism between an economic, laissez-faire strand, desirous of freedom from government interference, and a humanitarian strand working toward equal liberty for all. In its atomistic focus on the individual, liberalism tended to propagate the 'dogma of the freedom of the industrial entrepreneur from any organized social control', and 'ignore the immense regimentation to which workers are subjected, intellectual as well as manual workers' (Dewey 1946: 124). This was opposite to his strong participatory ideal of democracy, which argued 'the necessity for the participation of every mature human being in the formation of the values that regulate the living of men together', implying 'that all those who are affected by social institutions must have a share in producing and managing them' (Dewey 1946: 58). Coercion is not only physical, as 'the very fact of exclusion from participation is a subtle form of suppression', a form of coercion which is more effective than overt intimidation and restraint. As Dewey remarks:

> When it is habitual and embodied in social institutions, it seems the normal and natural state of affairs. The mass usually become unaware that they have a claim to a development of their powers. Their experience is so restricted that they are not conscious of restriction. (1946: 58)

And it is not only the individuals who are deprived:

> ... *it is part of the democratic conception ... that the whole social body is deprived of the potential resources that should be at its service. (Dewey 1946: 58)*

This shows Dewey's rich understanding of power in operation in the context of industrial relations. It has a critical focus on the participation and growth of all in a transformed society based on a democratic claim on the development of individual power, which will also enrich society. Hildreth (2009) points to the possibility of explicating a conception of power from Dewey's theory of experience, both enhanced and restrained by habits, institutions and culture, which shares similarities to Foucault (2000). Hildreth's analysis points to the potential for the development of a pragmatist conception of power in line with recent proposals by theorists of power in organizations (Clegg et al. 2006; Gordon 2009). Dewey's basic concern, however, is not the investigation of the circuits of power of the prevailing coercive systems in organizations and society (e.g. Clegg 2009a; Foucault 2000). Instead, in line with his participatory democratic and pragmatist orientation, Dewey's concern is the transformative need and potential to change the system, to open it up for freedom, creativity and growth (Dewey 1935). Dewey argues for a reformed liberalism which both reformulates its doctrine and reconstructs its existing practices in a direction of increased social control and increased collectivism of effort. Dewey specifically argues that 'social power' is needed to change institutions in order to achieve a more balanced and equitable system of liberties (1935: 113). Liberalism has to become radical so that 'instead of using social power to ameliorate the evil consequences of the existing system, it shall use social power to change the system' (1935: 132).

The type and form of power needed to accrue social power and achieve social control appropriate for a reformed liberal democracy is not sketched out by Dewey, but we can recognise different dimensions of it in his writings. First, social control is based on a vision of improved social knowledge to control consequences. It is a kind of knowledge and insight which did not yet exist (Dewey 1927: 166), but was the promise of the emerging social sciences, as well as an improvement in the intelligent use of the fruits of the natural and industrial sciences. Second, there is an emphasis in liberalism on maximum reliance on intelligence: 'The unremitting use of every method of intelligence that conditions permit, and to search for all that are possible' (Dewey 1946: 139). This can be understood to entail the development of experimental inquiry and its use in changing conditions, as well as the generation of effective social intelligence. The improvement of the methods and conditions of debate, discussion and persuasion are fundamental in this context. By maximising the development of experimental and cooperative inquiry and intelligence, a creative democracy where all share and participate in the improvement of society can be furthered. Third, it is the basis for the formation of democratically organized publics as agents in democratic social control. By being able to recognise consequences and their causes in uncontrolled social forces, publics can be formed which, through free communication, education and inquiry can form intelligent opinions as a basis for policies which can improve the social control of conditions (Dewey 1927). Fourth, as a remedy to laissez-faire liberalism, there is a need for power to change the distributions of power. There is a need, also, for an alternative system of social control which can bring equal liberties to all. Social control is thus not only a matter of increasing liberty as the power to do, but also the need to restrict the power of some – Dewey is pointing to industrial entrepreneurs in particular – in order to improve liberty of the many.

Social power is expressed in the procedures and methods employed to achieve change and transformation toward an improved system of social control. Dewey argues that liberalism stands for democratic methods of effecting social change and achieving social control. It is a slow process but can still achieve radical change: 'It is all a question of what kind of procedures the intelligent study of changing conditions discloses' (Dewey 1927: 138). It is closely connected to experimental inquiry and problem-solving. The movement toward social control, appropriate to a transformed liberal society, needs a cooperative social effort, 'a new kind of politics', where change is brought about by diverse combinations and coalitions of social groups, organizations, institutions and government (Caspary 2000; Hildreth 2009). Dewey indicates the advisability of a broad coalition of groups and classes which have an interest in change, although that would require seemingly extraordinary efforts to achieve. In this transformative cooperation, a more collaborative relationship between scientific experts and the public is also necessary. The relationship of the expert to the citizen was a fundamental issue for both Dewey and Follett, in the face of the technocratic movements gaining in popularity at the time (Dewey 1927; Follett 1924: Chapter 1). The core medium here is free inquiry, communication and education so that the public will be able to be informed of consequences and develop and exercise their combined intelligence. There is a division of responsibilities where experts can provide consequential knowledge and the public the information of need – 'where the shoe pinches' – and 'judge the bearing of the knowledge supplied by others upon common concerns' (Dewey 1927: 209).

The method of change is based on Dewey's view of scientific inquiry, which is realised in exploratory experimentation in natural settings. His definition of inquiry is the transformation of indeterminate situations into resolved or determined situations. Inquiry is operationally directed by ideas which, in the transformation, are translated into intended effects (Dewey 1939a). In Dewey's view of inquiry, the point of departure is invention and experimenting with new organizational forms, practices, processes and policies. Inquiry can thus involve bold innovations which are successively evaluated and experimentally improved based upon experience gained. Such social invention produces novel effects which can be appreciated based on intentions, values and potentials of solving problems. Because of the indeterminateness of social situations, the experimentation can involve exploration both in means and goals (Caspary 2000). The experimentation can be repeated, varied, further improved and refined until the sought-after effects can be reliably reproduced and stabilized in reflectively settled practices which are able to solve significant problems. Such practices simultaneously produce improved social control of conditions. We can recognise here the pragmatic inspiration for action research which was emerging contemporaneously, on the eve of the Second World War.

Follett on Power – From Power over to Power With

Mary Parker Follett's work has seen a revival in recent years, as her work on power has become a focal point for many writers. It has also been proposed that her writings provide the pragmatic conception of power which had theretofore been lacking (Pratt 2011). This section focuses on this conception of power and what it adds to Dewey's understanding of social power. Contemporaneous to Weber's influential post-World War I work (Weber 1922, 1968), Follett introduced a new conception of power: 'power-with'. Follett is largely in agreement with Weber concerning the centrality of power in social relations (Follett 1924: xii). The two diverge, however, in that what Weber authoritatively defined as power for the social science community – i.e., the capacity of agents to impose their will despite resistance from others (Weber 1947: 152) – Follett conceptualized this as just one form of power – power over. To Follett, power means 'the ability to make things happen, to be a causal agent, to initiate change' (Graham 1995: 101); this need not include placing impositions on others. She, like Dewey, criticises traditional coercive forms of power and their limits while also conceptualizing a distinct alternative to them. The principal goal is not to reveal the workings of coercive power in order to achieve further liberation from it, or even to balance or transfer power in its traditional forms. The core issue is *how to develop power*, and particularly a power that is 'co-active' rather than coercive. In her words: 'Genuine power can only be grown; it will slip from every arbitrary hand that grasps it; for genuine power is not coercive control, but coactive control' (Follett 1924: xiii).

Follett shifts from a dominant discourse on power, in which what she calls coactive control is an expression of a conception of power which is an alternative to a coercive one – 'power with'. She starts from a kind of Nietzsche-like understanding of power as a constitutive part of life processes, power as something necessary for growth and the development of capacity for creating life values. Power develops from the increasing control of circumstances gained by performing activities which lead to valued results. For instance, through specialized training, experience gained from competitions, appropriate nutrition and so on, an athlete can improve the standards and consistency of their performance. This is in line with Dewey's focus on individual growth as the normative point of departure.

In social and organizational life, there is often a dependency on coordinated activity involving a number of actors and groups. In the network of social life, the control able to be sustainably developed is accessed through the interweaving of activities and the progressive integration of potentially diverse desires and interests. The power that can be developed is thus described as integrated control, leading to concerted and controlled activity. What Follett sees in science as well as in social life, however, is 'power over' – different ways of manipulating or exerting power to satisfy the desire of the agent. In describing power in this manner, Follett raises an argument previously expressed by Machiavelli: 'Any attempt at arbitrary control sets up antagonisms in the other person or group that will defeat you in the end' (Follett 1924: 190). Rather than using strategies of domination to overcome resistance – like Machiavelli and later Weber – Follett focuses on the conditions needed to generate the form of power which leads to valid and legitimate control – concerted, coactive control. As such, 'power with' is best understood by the idea of integration. Follett provides an example of its workings based on her own experience in a library:

> In the library today, in one of the smaller rooms, someone wanted the window open, I wanted it shut. We opened the window in the next room where no one was sitting. This was not a compromise because there was no lopping off of desire; we both got what we really wanted. For I did not want a closed room, I simply did not want the north wind to blow directly on me; likewise the other occupant did not want the particular window open, he simply wanted more air in the room. (Follett 1924: 184f)

It is this type of process – interweaving different wants, desires and interests – that Follett sees as a core feature in cultivating power as 'power with' instead of 'power over'. The library illustration points to the creative aspect of integration, focused on the positive value of the conflict in relation to the development of power. As Follett saw it at the time, the then-emerging field of psychology in particular served to clarify the role of integration as a process. Psychology thus offered hints of a new conception of power. This is most clearly expressed in the concept of circular response, in which a response is based on the fact that each party's successive responses are related to and build upon not only the other party's most recent response but all earlier responses, and the relation between them evolving along with the situation. Circular response thus implies a progression of relating and integrating. It is this progressive experience which continuously creates plus values. It is thus a matter of creative experience, where participants collaboratively engage in the creative and unifying processes which coordinate both activities and desires. By creating an alternative form of action – or of co-action – participants' fostered concerted and coactive power, in the sense that their different activities come to be coordinated. The greater the extent to which each individual is empowered, the more coactive control it is possible to attain. The process of developing power as power-with through progressive integration can be seen as a sequence of cooperative empowerment processes, processes Follett sees as constitutive for democracy in both society in general and in organizational life in particular. It is both freeing and coordinating in processes where the total power of all is increased without the hampering force of power over.

Follett is well aware of the option of calling in a scientific expert, assuming 'the rule of the modern beneficent despot, the expert' (Follett 1924: 1) who, by revealing the truth, can help to overcome differences, produce unanimity of opinion and tell us what to do. To Follett, however, this signifies a desire to waive responsibility, to subjugate people to an Orwellian world. Follett points out that facts and power are intimately connected – e.g. in choice, interpretation and relation to desires – implying that fact-finding alone cannot solve the issue of how best to integrate diverse interests. The point of accurate information is not to overcome differences but to give legitimate and fruitful voice to difference, and find ways to gain the plus value of difference and conflict. This is the central focus of progressive integrative processes aimed at developing power with. There is no vicarious experience, however, implying that the experiences of all are needed – in Follett's words: 'that is all that democracy means' (Follett 1924: 19).

In her later writings, Follett was able to clarify and apply her understanding of power in the context of industry and working life. Concerning the industrial context, Follett had a more optimistic view than Dewey based on her acquaintance with contemporary business realities. She saw the common understanding of industrial democracy – that 'the power now held by owners and managers should be *shared* by the workmen' – as only a partial truth. According to Follett, this partial truth obscures the important truth that 'power is self-developing capacity' (1995: 113). Rather than focusing on sharing and transferring power – which would be illusory, as power is based on capacity – democratization should come from within, by jointly developing power, particularly through self-governance. From her understanding and observation of power, Follett was able to underscore the idea that 'over' and 'under' in business ought to be replaced by integrating capacity, organized in such a way so that both individuals and the organization are empowered. Her focus on the collaborative generation of power in industry made her a forerunner of paradigms related to the organization of work which were to be developed after her death in 1933, which served as an important impetus to the human rights movement, and to the industrial reform movements of the 1960s. The Scandinavian tradition of collaborative action research focused on democratizing working life was just one such branch of this reform movement (Emery and Thorsrud 1976), a tradition which, as we will see, has expanded Dewey's and Follett's idea of developing collaborative, non-coercive power.

The Scandinavian Tradition of Action Research

Collaborative power in American pragmatism is best illustrated by providing examples of contemporary applications of the Scandinavian tradition of action research in working life. We also intend to clarify and develop insights from Dewey and Follett in relation to action research while acknowledging that the tradition draws inspiration from a variety of intellectual sources (Reason and Bradbury 2008). We have previously addressed the concept of collaborative power as developed by Follett, as well as her view on democratization in working life (O'Connor 2000). Follett argued that, in order to attain tangible results, the work group has to be the point of departure for the cultivation of the types of collaborative power which facilitate the integration of interests. There are some similarities of reasoning on collaborative power between Follett and the context and practice of action research. Advocates of identifying collaborative power in action research presume that the parties of working life, by and large, have unified interests in general issues such as efficiency, earnings and secure employment (Gustavsen 2011; Gustavsen and Hunnius 1981). In line with Follett, the argument goes that workers and management have more power to exercise together than they possess separately (Boje and Rosile 2001). The goal of collaborative power is not to affect the private ownership of business, but to change the functioning of the firm within existing rights (Broström 1982; Engelstad 2004; Engelstad et al. 2009). Marxist critics of action research contest the presumption of unified interests between workers and capital owners (Gaventa and Cornwall 2001; Gran 1978). The ideology of common interests is reinforced in enterprise development programs. Moreover, the profit of capital owners will increase and alienation of wage labor remain unchanged.

The Scandinavian tradition of action research is based on cooperation between parties at the level of the department, organization, network of organizations and regional development coalition (Asheim 2011; Gustavsen 2001a; Gustavsen et al. 2008). In the early 1980s, parties arrived at an agreement on enterprise development which was essentially an amendment to The Basic Agreement in working life (Gustavsen 2001a). The intention was to lay the groundwork for a larger number of enterprises to join development programs focused on innovation. Enterprise 2000 in the 1990s and Value Creation 2010 in the 2000s are examples of national, multi-site, long-term innovation programs in Norway (Gustavsen et al. 2001; Ekman et al. 2011). The programs both comprised research groups scattered across the country. A considerable number of action research projects were implemented during their respective periods of operation, with researchers primarily concerned with ensuring that the effects of projects were as comprehensive as possible (Gustavsen 1996; Gustavsen 1998a; Gustavsen et al. 2008).

The regional development coalition is an example of how issues of scope are reflected in contemporary practicing of action research (Ennals and Gustavsen 1999; Gustavsen 1998a). For the purposes of this analysis, we intend to relate Dewey's concept of social and cooperative intelligence to the regional development coalition. A development coalition is defined as:

> bottom-up, horizontal co-operations involving the participation of a wide range of actors in a local or regional setting, ranging from work organizations inside firms via inter-firm networks to different stakeholders at the regional level to initiate and promote learning-based process of innovation, change and improvement. (Ennals and Gustavsen 1999, quoted in Asheim 2011: 44)

This aspect of collaborative power reflects the capacity to achieve goals by uniting the capabilities of traditionally divided groups with diverse interests. The achievements of a coalition are understood as discoveries based on experimental inquiry in which a multitude of actors have contributed so that the coalition might gain control over the social consequences of institutions (Hildreth 2009). Intelligence in this context is the pooled knowledge of organizations, and it forms the foundation from which coalitions can reach toward new insights and constructive solutions to pressing problems. A regional development coalition consists of learning organizations drawn from enterprise networks and public and private agencies in the region (Asheim 2011; Gustavsen 1998b; Shotter and Gustavsen 1999). The coalition contains and can draw upon a range of theoretical approaches and research methods pertaining to the economic development of regions, in addition to insights gained through action research into working life. A learning organization is dynamic and flexible, and is one 'that facilitates the learning of all its members and has the capacity to continuously transform itself by rapidly adapting to a changing environment through innovation' (Asheim 2011: 37). Innovation here is understood as interactive learning processes, and embraces organizations regardless of the level of investment made in research and development. The regional development coalition represents a high degree of complexity in terms of situations, actors and projects. Action researchers point to the limitations of the non-coercive practices of collaboration, contemplation and democratic dialog when power plays and strategic actions dominate the coalition (Johnsen and Normann 2004).

Dewey's concept of publics (1927) has been elaborated previously, and is raised here in connection with the theory and practice of democratic dialog in action research (Leirvik 2005; Pålshaugen 2002). The similarities of thought between the theoretical traditions are striking, despite their different origins. According to Dewey, publics are arenas of free expression of opinions, and learning can occur in and on a multitude of areas within a given society. These public spheres are of vital importance to and for a sustainable democracy and are a prerequisite for both experimental inquiry and social and cooperative intelligence. Democratic dialog is a method useful in the development of participatory democracy at the workplace, as it encourages the unified efforts of participants (Gustavsen 1985; Shields 2003). The method is considered to be unique to the Scandinavian tradition of action research, as it attempts the egalitarian mobilization of the capacities of all parties through open and broad discussions held on equal terms (Naschold 1992; Gustavsen 2001b; Habermas 1984, 1987). The aim is to generate the coordinated understanding and practical agreements necessary for joint reform action.

According to Dewey and Follett, democracy and participation are intrinsic values which facilitate human growth, learning and prosperity in organizations. All concerned parties are entitled to join by virtue of their experience, knowledge and skills, in order to fulfil their potentials both individually and collectively. The excluding of participants represents the exercising of power and serves to inhibit the growth, development and learning of the individual. We relate these basic principles of pragmatism to the role of employee participation in action research (Gustavsen 2001c). Enterprise Development 2000 and Value Creation 2010, both mentioned above, are central to these efforts (Gustavsen 1988, 1991, 1992). In principle, all concerned parties should take part in the organization's development processes. This represents a change of emphasis from the formal employee representation to direct participation (Wilkinson and Dundon 2010). The individual worker, meanwhile, is largely responsible for creating a sustainable business and workplace. A shift away from viewing employee participation as an intrinsic value to a means for creating value of the firm is connected to this (Qvale 2000a). The focus on value creation has a stronger appeal among business managers, and is vital to recruiting sufficient numbers of enterprises to participate in development programs. The shift of view on employee participation represents a pragmatic adaptation to the basic principles of participation. The crucial role of participation in action research is more conditioned by the interests of modern business in a globalized knowledge-based economy (Fudge et al. 2006; Giddens 2000). Bipartite collaboration, democratic dialog and employee participation in action research have in common elements of a pragmatic interpretation, adoption and practice.

Case Study

A case is drawn, albeit briefly, from the regional development coalition of the Grenland region in Norway in order to empirically illustrate concepts of integration, intelligence, participation and power as formal proprietary rights. Collaborative power is suggested by the cooperation between departments, enterprises, public agencies and action researchers. The strategy was to start with the strong concentration of processing plants because they were regarded as the 'spearhead' of industrial development and expected to create spin-off for establishing new companies (Qvale 2000b, 2007; Gustavsen et al. 2008; Qvale 2011). The plants are producing paper and pulp, gas, steel and chemical plastic solutions. The processing industry was chosen by virtue of its political position and strength in the region. Companies joined the VC2010 program and, later on, the coalition. The purpose of collaboration among the companies was, in part, to enhance the cost efficiency of plants and secure employment in the future. The cost-efficiency plan suggested reductions of costs by pooling services, workshops, maintenance and supplies. The trade unions accepted the plan because they were assured that the number of jobs in the short term would not be reduced by downsizing and in the long-term more jobs were to be created. The agreement on the plan between the parties has to be understood in the light of collaboration of more than 50 years in the region.

A democratic dialog conference was held in 2005 with 120 participants representing the processing plants along with external stakeholders of the region (Qvale 2007). The conference presented a break-through of the regional development coalition, and a high degree of agreement was achieved on topics of common concern. The participants at the conference discussed projects of the infra-structure of the region in a broad sense. The projects ranged from roads, harbors, railways and gas pipes to attractive place of living. As a result of this participation, many parties of the regional development coalition found they improved their competitive advantage. Furthermore, existing places of work were secured and new job opportunities were created within the region. However, two major corporations decided to shut down their plants, and about 1,000 workers lost their jobs. These actions caused strong protests and political demonstrations and the activists demanded that government intervene. At the same time, new forms of organizations emerged as joint services were introduced among the plants in order to secure employment rather than reduce it by outsourcing. The development processes of coalition came to a halt by 2008, because three major petrochemical plants were bought by a British group and changes in management in other plants and institutions occurred (Qvale 2011). For our purposes here, the case study draws attention to the possibilities and constraints of collaborative power, discussed in the next section.

Discussion: Possibilities and Constraints of Collaborative Power

The possibilities of collaborative power are firstly suggested by the regional development coalition. It is an empirical example of Dewey's social and cooperative intelligence and public sphere in which actors debate industrial development and innovation of a region. The coalition represents pooled knowledge of a variety of organizations enabling them to control the social consequences of efficiency of corporations and employment. Intelligence is exhibited as numerous conditions coalescing to a mobilization of forces making a difference in the industrial development. The bipartite cooperation in the regional development coalition facilitated that the processing plants regained their competitive advantage and employment was secured. Joint services were created among the plants which enabled them to avoid downsizing. In line with Follett, this is an example of successful integration of interests by the fact that owners of plants reduced labor costs and workers retained their jobs (Dewey 1939c). The finding in the case is contrary to the general assumption that it is impossible to arrive at integration in cases of downsizing (Nohria 1995).

Key features of collaborative power elucidated by Follett include processes of circular response and integration of interests. A recurrent theme in this case study is the collaboration between management and workers at the level of work organization, enterprise, organizations and the regional development coalition (Asheim 2011). The coalition suggests how power is developed collaboratively in which all parties will equally benefit. It is presumed that the pursuit of profit can be reconciled with securing employment (Follett 1918). The coalition facilitates learning among the member organizations which enable them to accommodate internal and external change and innovation. From one perspective, management and workers appear to have gained more power together, rather than divided.

Crucially, however, it must be acknowledged how the case study reveals the limitations of collaborative power. The first concerns the focus of employee participation in action research, here directed towards the value creation of enterprise. This meaning of participation is different from that of Dewey and Follett who stress that participation has an intrinsic value as human growth, development and learning. Perhaps this observation is the most obvious example of the tacit assent and compliance with established powers which the critics of Dewey termed 'pragmatic acquiescence' (Hildreth 2009). Nonetheless, there is an interesting dual element of employee participation in the case study which we will relate to Dewey's theorising on the role of habits and power (Dewey 1937 in Hildreth 2009). Dewey elaborates that individuals are simultaneously vehicles and subjects of power which is suggested by the long traditions of collaboration between the trade union and management. The trade union accepted the cost-efficiency plan, but demanded in return that management ensured and created new jobs which turned out to be partially fulfilled. On the one hand, traditions exert power over individuals by having them appear to comply willingly. On the other hand, traditions serve as a basis for empowering individuals by providing them with new possibilities.

Power exercised as proprietary rights based on law are suggested in the case by the fact that the owners either decided to close or sell major processing plants, leading to job losses. These actions influence and change the discussions on industrial development and innovation in the regional coalition (Hardy and Phillips 2004). Collaborative power is to a large extent not based on law, but on informal networks of social relationships in the community, in which actors are working together, exchanging experience and knowledge (Clegg et al. 2006, 2009b; Haugaard 2003). Limiting then is the presumption that it is feasible to have knowledge evenly distributed among actors in the network (Flyvbjerg 1998; Foucault 2000). Insufficient attention is paid to power conceived as knowledge residing in the formal proprietary rights of business owners. These rights are conceived as 'normal' or 'natural' and are therefore taken for granted in the discussion among the participants in the regional development coalition. This view is consistent with the Marxist critique of action research which we mentioned previously (Gaventa and Cornwall 2001; Gran 1978). The objective interests of workers and capital owners are contradictory and hence the basis of collaboration is absent. Competition and the pursuit of profit in business have to be replaced by production based on social needs and planning.

Another limitation of collaborative power, related to the one above, refers to Follett's focus on authority rather than power (Clegg et al. 2006; Lukes 2005). Power is defined as A having power over B when actions of A result in actions of B opposite to his or her interests. The concept of authority is not distinct from power because authority is one of many forms of power as coercion, force and manipulation. Follett argues that authority is based on functions and those employees who are most competent on a matter are entitled to make decisions (Follett 1995; Urwick 1949). The procedures are based on competence and cooperation and the individuals concerned comply with the decisions because they are regarded as legitimate. Authority, conceived in this way, implies that managers positioned lower down in the organization are relieved from the functions of their associates. Follett anticipated decentralized decision-making and the growing responsibility of contemporary knowledge-based organizations (Nohria 1995). This is suggested in the case study in terms of decision-making procedures which were delegated from plant management to lower levels of the organization (Qvale 2011). However, authority as decentralized decision-making and as the responsibility of supervisors and workers appears to exert weak influence on the formal right of owners to make decisions on restructuring, downsizing, selling and closing plants. The critique points to the implications of collaborative power, of which one concerns the practice of attaining voluntary consent by associates (Clegg et al. 2006; Lukes 2005). The brutal aspects of the economic system as coercion and force are avoided by the means of those with power, who can move others to willingly comply with visions and goals of the powerful. However, it is reasonable to interpret Follett's view on authority as being based on agreement among those concerned, so that authority is not exercised as power (Lukes 2005). Follett stresses that authority is the development of collaborative power internally in organizations on par with the informal social networks of the community.

Finally, we relate the limitations of collaborative power suggested by proprietary rights to Dewey's critique of liberalism (Dewey 1935). Dewey criticised the laissez-faire liberalism of his day in the US. One of his concerns was that government did not interfere with the business of employers. The liberty and hence power of other groups in society such as workers was restricted, as noted in our case study (Dewey 1939c). The Norwegian government did not interfere with downsizing, closing and selling of plants by the business owners in the region. This occurred despite the fact that strong interest groups attempted to persuade the government to step in and intervene. Notable then is that Dewey advocated a radical form of liberalism implying a redistribution of power enabling freedom to all people on an equal footing. With these limitations in mind, it is clear that the development of collaborative power is challenging, requiring ongoing effort to address its shortcomings.

Conclusion

We have provided an understanding of collaborative power based on concepts put forth by John Dewey and Mary Parker Follett. Further, we have related collaborative power to the theories and practices of the Scandinavian action research tradition in working life. Collaborative power is here understood as 'power in the making'. Its chief merit is ensuring, first and foremost, cooperation between parties. The significance of collaborative power is more broadly applicable than the local communities in which the concept was originally developed. The concepts of circular response and integration of interest are useful in analysing collaborative power at the micro, meso and macro levels of society. What is more, the concept of intelligence fits well with the theory and practice of the regional development coalition in action research. The focus here is on how the knowledge of various groups of people is or can be pooled, in order to control the consequences of social institutions. This leads us to critiques of collaborative power which assert that knowledge is unevenly distributed across social networks. Powerful people are, by virtue of their proprietary rights, able to change and reduce the effects of collaborative power. Indeed and as a final remark, adherents of collaborative power contend that it is feasible to change the economic system from within, efforts which can be seen to include far more proprietary rights than have been discussed in this chapter.

References

Allen, J. 2008. Pragmatism and power, or the power to make a difference in a radically contingent world. *Geoforum*, 39(4), 1613–24.

Asheim, B.T. 2011. Learning innovation and participation: Nordic experiences in a global context with a focus on innovation systems and work organization, in *Learning Regional Innovation: Scandinavian Models*, (eds.) M. Ekman, B. Gustavsen, B.T. Asheim, and Ø. Pålshaugen. Basingstoke: Palgrave Macmillan, 15–49.

Bohman, J. 1999. Democracy as inquiry, inquiry as democratic: Pragmatism, social science, and the cognitive division of labor. *American Journal of Political Science*, 43(2), 590–607.

Boje, D.M. and Rosile, G.A. 2001. Where is the power in empowerment: Answers from Follett and Clegg. *Journal of Applied Behavioral Science*, 37(1), 90–116.

Broström, A. 1982. *MBLs gränser: den privata äganderätten*. Stockholm: Arbetslivscentrum.

Caspary, W. 2000. *Dewey on Democracy*. Ithaca, NY: Cornell University Press.

Clegg, S. 1989. *Frameworks of Power*. London: Sage.

Clegg, S. 2009a. Managing power in organizations: The hidden history of its constitution, in *The Sage Handbook of Power*, (ed.) S. Clegg and M. Haugaard. London: Sage, 310–31.

Clegg, S. 2009b. Foundations of Organization Power. *Journal of Power*, 2(1), 35–64.

Clegg, S., Courpasson, D. and Phillips, N. 2006. *Power in Organizations*. London: Sage.

Clegg, S. and Haugaard, M. (eds). 2009. *The Sage Handbook of Power*. London: Sage.

Dewey, J. 1916a. Force, violence and law, in *The Middle Works, 1899–1924, Volume 10: 1916–17*, (ed.) Boydston, J.A. Carbondale, IL: Southern Illinois University Press, 211–16.

Dewey, J. 1916b. Force and coercion, in *The Middle Works, 1899–1924, Volume 10: 1916–17*, edited Boydston, J.A. Carbondale, IL: Southern Illinois University Press, 244–51.

Dewey, J. 1927. *The Public and its Problems*. Athens: Swallow Press/Ohio University Press.

Dewey, J. 1935. *Liberalism and Social Action*. New York: Prometheus Books.

Dewey, J. 1937. Authority and social change, in *The Later Works, 1925–53, Volume 11*, (ed.) Boydson, J.A. Carbondale, IL: Southern Illinois University Press, 130–45.

Dewey, J. 1939a. *Logic: The Theory of Inquiry*. London: George Allen & Unwin Ltd.

Dewey, J. 1939b. Creative democracy: The task before us, in *The Later Works, 1925–53, Volume 14: 1939–41*, (ed.) Boydston, J.A. Carbondale, IL: Southern Illinois University Press, 224–31.

Dewey, J.1939c. The economic basis of the new society, in *The Later Works, 1925–53, Volume 13: 1938–39*, (ed.) Boydston, J.A. Carbondale, IL: Southern Illinois University Press, 309–22.

Dewey, J. 1946. *Problems of Men*. New York: Philosophical library.

Ekman, M., Gustavsen, B., Qvale, T. and Pålshaugen, Ø. (eds) 2011. *Learning Regional Innovation: Scandinavian Models*. Basingstoke: Palgrave Macmillan.

Eikeland, O. 2001. Action research as the hidden curriculum of the Western tradition, in *Handbook of Action Research: Participative Inquiry & Practice*, (ed.) P. Reason H. and Bradbury. London: Sage, 145–55.

Emery, F. and Thorsrud, E. 1976. *Democracy at Work*. Leiden: Nijhoff.

Engelstad, F. 2004. Democracy at work?, in *Power and Democracy: Critical Interventions*, (ed.) F. Engelstad and Ø. Østerud. Aldershot: Ashgate, 209–34.

Engelstad, F., Hagen, I.M. and Storvik, Å.E. and Svalund, J. (eds). 2009. Makt og demokrati i arbeidslivet. Oslo: Gyldendal Akademisk.

Ennals, R. and Gustavsen, B. 1999. *Work Organization and Europe as a Development Coalition*. Amsterdam/Philadelphia: John Benjamin.

Flyvbjerg, B. 1998. *Rationality and Power: Democracy in Practice*. Chicago, IL: University of Chicago Press.

Follett, M.P. 1918. *The New State: Group Organization, the Solution for Popular Government*. The University Park, PA: The Pennsylvania State University Press.

Follett, M.P. 1924. *Creative Experience*. London: Longmans, Green and Co.

Follett, M.P. 1949. *Freedom and Coordination: Lectures in Business Organization*. New York: Garland Publishing.

Follett, M.P. 1995. *Prophet of Management*. Boston, MA: HBS Press.

Foucault, M. 2000. *Power*, (ed.) J.D. Faubion, New York: The New York Press.

Fudge, S. and Williams, S. 2006. Beyond Left and Right: Can the Third Way Deliver a Reinvigorated Social Democracy? [Online]. Available at: http://est.sagepub.com/content/early [accessed: 9 January 2012].

Gaventa, J. and Cornwall, A. (2001). Power and knowledge, in *Handbook of Action Research: Participative Inquiry and Practice*, (ed.) P.Reason and H. Bradbury. London: Sage, 70–80.

Giddens, A. 2000. *The Third Way and its Critics*. Cambridge: Polity Press.

Gordon, R. 2009. Power and legitimacy: From Weber to contemporary theory, in *The Sage Handbook of Power*, (ed.) S. Clegg and M. Haugaard. London: Sage, 256–73.

Gran, T. 1978. *Samarbeidsforsøkene LO/NAF. En organisasjonsteoretisk analyse*. University of Bergen, Institute of Public Administration and Organisation Theory: University of Bergen. Papers.

Greenwood, D. 2002. Action Research: Unfulfilled Promises and Unmet Challenges. *Concepts and Transformation*, 7(2), 117–39.

Gustavsen, B. 1985. Workplace Reform and Democratic Dialogue. *Economic and Industrial Democracy*, 6(4), 461–79.

Gustavsen, B. 1988. *Creating Broad Change in Working Life: The LOM Programme*. Toronto: QWL Center, Ontario Ministry of Labor.

Gustavsen, B. 1991. The LOM Program: A network-based strategy for organization development in Sweden, in *Research in Organizational Change and Development*, (ed.) R.W. Woodman and W.A. Pasmore. London and Greenwich, CT: JAI Press, 285–331.

Gustavsen, B.1992. *Dialogue and Development: Theory of Communication, Action Research and the Restructuring of Working Life*. Assen and Maastricht: Van Gorcum.

Gustavsen, B.1996. Changes in Work Organization and Public Support: The Case of Swedish Work Life Fund. *Futures*, 28(2), 139–52.

Gustavsen, B. 1998a. From Experiments to Network Building: Trends in the Use of Research for Reconstructing Working Life. *Human Relations*, 51(3), 431–48.

Gustavsen, B. 1998b. European Development Coalitions: Workplace Democracy and Regional Development. *Wolfsburg* 3, 5.

Gustavsen, B. 2001a. Social partnership and workplace development, in *Creating Connectedness: The Role of Social Research in Innovation Policy*, (ed.) B. Gustavsen, H. Finne and B. Oscarsson. Amsterdam and Philadelphia, PA: John Benjamins, 73–83.

Gustavsen, B. 2001b. Research and the challenge of working life, in *Creating Connectedness: The Role of Social Research in Innovation Policy*, (ed.) B. Gustavsen, H. Finne and B. Oscarsson. Amsterdam and Philadelphia, PA: John Benjamins, 85–100.

Gustavsen, B. 2001c. The impact of ED 2000, in *Creating Connectedness: The Role of Social Research in Innovation Policy*, (ed.) B. Gustavsen, H. Finne and B. Oscarsson. Amsterdam and Philadelphia, PA: John Benjamins, 39–70.

Gustavsen, B. 2011. Promoting innovative organization, in *Learning Regional Innovation: Scandinavian Models*, (ed.) M. Ekman et al. Basingstoke: Palgrave Macmillan, 70–92.

Gustavsen, B, Finne, H. and Oscarsson, B. (eds) 2001. *Creating Connectedness: The Role of Social Research in Innovation Policy*. Amsterdam and Philadelphia, PA: John Benjamins.

Gustavsen, B., Hansson, A. and Qvale, T. 2008. Action research and the challenge of scope, in *The Sage Handbook of Action Research: Participative Inquiry and Practice*, (eds) P. Reason, and H. Bradbury. Sage: London, 63–77.

Gustavsen, B. and Hunnius, G. 1981. *New Patterns of Work Reform: The Case of Norway*. Oslo: Universitetsforlaget.

Habermas, J. 1984/1987. *The Theory of Communicative Action*, vols 1–2. London: Polity Press.

Hafting, T. 2004a. *Work Organisation, Competence Development, and Health*. Hedmark University College: Working paper no. 4–2004. Hedmark University College.

Hafting, T. 2004b. *The Parties of Working Life, Innovation and Regional Development*. Hedmark University College: Working Paper no. 1-2004. Hedmark University College.

Hafting, T. 2006. *The Researcher and the Enterprise. Dialogue and the Potential of Innovation*. Hedmark University College: Working paper no. 1-2006. Hedmark University College.

Hafting, T. and Lindhult, E. 2011. *American Pragmatism, Action Research and Power*. NEON Conference, 16–18 November, 2011, Oslo, Norway.

Hardy, C. and Phillips, N. 2004. Discourse and power, in *The Sage Handbook of Organizational Discourse*, (ed.) D. Grant, C. Hardy, C. Oswick and L. Putnam. London: Sage, 299–316.

Haugaard, M. 2003. Reflections on Seven Ways of Creating Power. [Online]. Available at: http://est.sagepub.com/content/abstract/6/1/87 [accessed: 26 November 2008].

Hildreth, R.W. 2009. Reconstructing Dewey on Power. *Political Theory*, 37(6), 780–807.

Joas, H. 1993. *Pragmatism and Social Theory*. Chicago, IL: The University of Chicago Press.

Joas, H. 1996. *The Creativity of Action*. Cambridge: Polity Press.

Johnsen, H.C.G and Normann, R. 2004. When Research and Practice Collide: The Role of Action Research when there is a Conflict of Interest with Stakeholders. *Systemic Practice and Action Research*, 17(3), 207–35.

Kadlec, A. 2007. *Dewey's Critical Pragmatism*. Lanham, MD: Lexington Books.

Leirvik, B. 2005. Dialogue and Power: The Use of Dialogue for Participatory Change. *AI & Society*, 19(4), 407–29.

Lindhult, E. 2005. Management by freedom. Essays in moving From Machiavellian to Rousseauian approaches to innovation and inquiry. Stockholm: Doctoral Thesis in Industrial economics and Management.

Lukes, S. 1974. *Power: A Radical View*. New York: Macmillan.

Lukes, S. 2005. *Power: A Radical View*, 2nd edn. Basingstoke: Palgrave Macmillian.

Lynch, R.A. 1998. Is Power All There Is? Michel Foucault and the 'Omnipresence' of Power Relations, *Philosophy Today*, 42(1), 65–70.

Machiavelli, N. 1532/2003. *The Prince*. Middlesex: Penguin Books.

Metcalf, H.C. and Urwick, L. 1941. *Dynamic Administration: Collected Papers of Mary Parker Follett*. London: Sir Isaac Pitman.

Midtgarden, T. 2012. Critical Pragmatism: Dewey's Social Philosophy Revisited. [Online]. Available at: http://est.sagepub.com/content/early [accessed: 14 April 2012].

Mills, C. Wright. 1964. *Sociology and Pragmatism*. New York: Oxford University Press.

Naschold, F. 1992. *Evaluation Report Commissioned by the Board of The LOM Programme*. Stockholm: Arbetsmiljöfonden.

Nohria, N. 1995. Mary Parker Follett's view on power, the giving of orders, and authority: An alternative to hierarchy or utopian ideology?, in *Mary Parker Follett: Prophet of Management*, (ed.) P. Graham. Boston, MA: HBS Press, 154–62.

O'Connor, E. 2000. Integrating Follett: History, Philosophy and Management. *Journal of Management History*, 6(4), 167–90.

Pratt, S.L. 2011. American Power: Mary Parker Follett and Michel Foucault. *Foucault Studies*, 11, 76–91.

Pålshaugen, Ø. 2002. Discourse Democracy at Work – On Public Spheres in Private Enterprises. *Concepts and Transformation*, 7(2), 141–92.

Qvale, T. 2000a. Innledning, i Forskning og Bedriftsutvikling – nye samarbeidsforsøk. Ø. Pålshaugen and T. Qvale (eds). Oslo: Arbeidsforskningsinstituttet, 1–28.

Qvale, T. 2000b. FNDP: Utviklingskoalisjon som metode for kunnskapsutvikling og spredning i ett grep, i Forskning og Bedriftsutvikling – nye samarbeidsforsøk. Ø. Pålshaugen and T. Qvale (red). Oslo: Arbeidsforskningsinstituttet, 149–94.

Qvale, T. 2007. IndustriClusteret Grenland – Nettverk, klynge og utviklingskoalisjon. Regionale Trender, Bind 2007, nr. 1. Norsk Institutt for By og regionforskning, 53–64.

Qvale, T. 2011. Participative democracy and the diffusion of organizational innovations: The long winding road from a plant level field experiment to regional economic development, in *Learning Regional Innovation: Scandinavian Models*, (ed.) M. Ekman et al. Basingstoke: Palgrave Macmillan, 187–206.

Reason, P. and Bradbury, H. (eds). 2008. *Handbook of Action Research: Participative Inquiry & Practice*, 2nd edn. London: Sage.

Rogers, M.L. 2009. Democracy, Elites and Power: John Dewey Reconsidered. *Contemporary Political Theory*, 8(1), 68–89.

Shields, P.M. 2003. The Community of Inquiry: Classical Pragmatism and Public Administration. Faculty Publications – Political Science, Paper 8. Texas: Texas State University.

Shotter, J. and Gustavsen, B. 1999. *The Role of Dialogue Conferences in the Development of Learning Regions: Doing from within Our Lives Together What We Cannot Do Apart*. Stockholm: The Centre of Advanced Studies in Leadership. Stockholm School of Economics.

Urwick, L. (ed.). 1949. *Freedom & Coordination: Lectures in Business Organization by Mary Parker Follett*. London: Management Publications.

Weber, M. 1922. *Wirtschaft und Gesellschaft* / bearbeitet von Max Weber.

Weber, M. 1947. *The Theory of Social and Economic Organization*. New York: Oxford University Press.

Weber, M 1968. *Economy and Society: An Outline of Interpretive Sociology*, (ed.) G. Roth and C. Wittisch. Berkeley: University of California Press.

Westbrook, R. 1991. *John Dewey and American Democracy*. Ithaca: Cornell University Press.

White, S.K. 2004. The very idea of a critical social science: A pragmatist turn, in *The Cambridge Companion to Critical Theory*, (ed.) F. Rush, New York: Cambridge University Press, 310–35.

Wilkinson, A. and Dundon, T. 2010. Direct employee participation, in *The Oxford Handbook of Participation in Organizations*, (eds.) A. Wilkinson, P.J. Gollan, M. Marchington and D. Lewin. Oxford: Oxford University Press, 167–85.

Index

For Product Safety Concerns and Information please contact our
EU representative GPSR@taylorandfrancis.com Taylor & Francis
Verlag GmbH, Kaufingerstraße 24, 80331 München, Germany